# Three Hundred Years With the Pennsylvania Traveler

*By William H. Shank, P.E.*

Published By
American Canal and Transportation Center
809 Rathton Road
York, Pennsylvania 17403

First printing - July 4, 1976
Second printing - February 1, 2000

ISBN – 0-933788-00-2

# TABLE OF CONTENTS

# INTRODUCTION

The State of Pennsylvania, one of the original thirteen colonies, has been known, with good reason, as the "Keystone State" during the history of our nation's development. It is flanked by New York and New Jersey to the Northeast, Delaware (originally part of Pennsylvania) and Maryland to the South, and Ohio and West Virginia (originally Virginia) to the Southwest. It was the "bridge" state between North and South, during and since the time when the Thirteen Colonies declared their independence from Great Britain.

Pennsylvania's strategic importance was early recognized when the nation's *first* capital was founded here. It is one of the few states in the nation which has a major seaport, a major riverport and a major lakeport all within its boundaries. It has an unbelieveable variety of topography – ranging from coastal plain to inland lake shore, with mountains and plateau areas in between. It was Pennsylvania's location, at the hub of the original colonies, and its unusual topography, which made the development of transportation facilities here of particular historic interest.

The most formidable obstacle to travel across Pennsylvania has always been the multi-ridged Appalachian Mountain Range running in a broad band westward from the Pocono section, where the Delaware River pierces it, and swinging southward in central Pennsylvania, cut through only by the Susquehanna River above Harrisburg and in a few places (farther west) by the Juniata River.

Since 1960, it has been my pleasure to investigate the history of transportation in Pennsylvania, in depth, and I have found to my astonishment that there have been a number of engineering "firsts" in the State, about which very little has been written. For instance; the *first* covered wooden bridge in the United States was built in Philadelphia. The *first* tunnel in the United States was built near Auburn, Pa. The *first* hard-surface, long-distance highway in the United States was constructed between Philadelphia and Lancaster. The *first* steam boat in the United States was placed in the water in Philadelphia.

The *first*, pier type, metal suspension bridge in the United States (and possibly in the world) was constructed near Connellsville, Pa. The world's *longest* covered wooden bridge was built between Columbia and Wrightsville, Pa. The *first* wire cable in the United States was created at Saxonburg, Pa. The *first* oil well in the world was drilled at Titusville, Pa. The *first* coal railroad in the United States was built at Mauch Chunk, Pa. The *first*, limited access, high-speed highway in the United States was built between Middlesex and Irwin, Pa. . . . And many others!

Perhaps we Pennsylvanians have just taken all these things for granted, or perhaps we really didn't know about them. This Bicentennial Year seems to be a good time for Pennsylvanians to learn about past accomplishments in their native state. We have a tremendous heritage in Pennsylvania, and we should be proud of it!

It is in this spirit that "Three Hundred Years with the Pennsylvania Traveler" has been written. Pennsylvania, because of the unusual variety of its topography, has been a testing ground for new and previously untried ideas in the development of our cross-state and interstate transportation systems. It is about these many innovations that this book has been written; and it is to the engineering pioneers in Pennsylvania that this book is dedicated.

York, Pennsylvania                    William H. Shank, P.E.
July 4, 1976

AMERICAN CANAL &
TRANSPORTATION CENTER

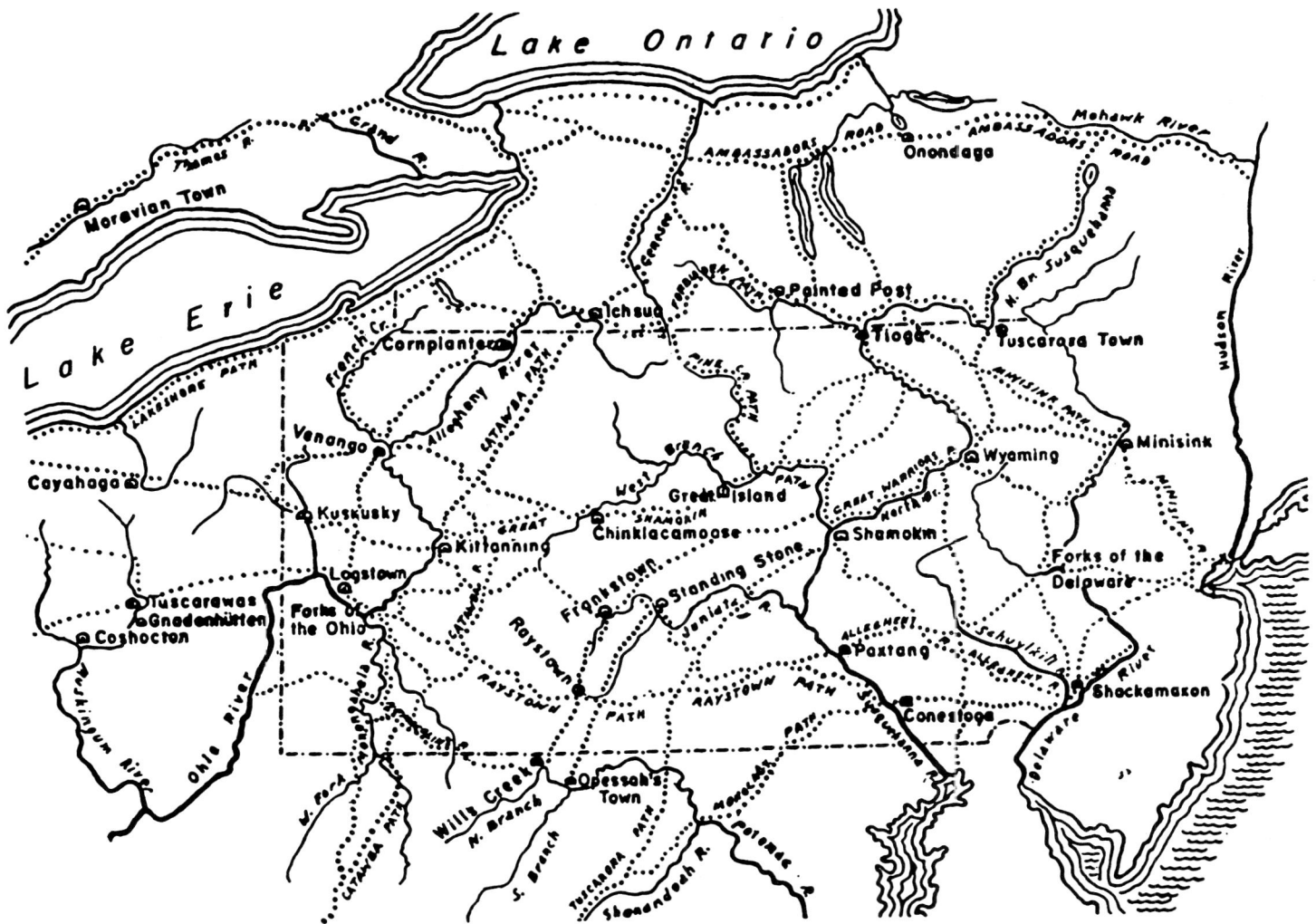

Main Indian paths through Pennsylvania, circa 1675 (Courtesy Pennsylvania Historical and Museum Commission.)

# Chapter I

# PENNSYLVANIA INDIAN TRAILS

Archeologists and students of world evolution are now agreed that the ancestors of the so-called American "Indians" came from Asia about 30,000 years ago, by way of the Bering Strait. During one of the ice ages, a lowering of the seas, through accumulated ice at the poles, permitted a dry-land crossing between Siberia and Alaska.

Over a period of thousands of years these Asiatic immigrants gradually moved southward and eastward from Alaska. The Eskimos represent the descendants of tribes who stayed in Alaska. Those tribes who found their way into Mexico and South America developed a high degree of civilization and culture, while many of our European ancestors were still living in caves and trees.

The ancestors of the Pennsylvania Indians, however, were a nomadic people who derived their existence by hunting with flint-tipped spears. They traveled on foot and were essentially still living in the stone age when they came here. They are thought to have arrived in Pennsylvania, from the West, about 12,000 to 18,000 years ago.

Settling here, these Indian tribes gradually developed an agricultural economy, raising corn and maize, which freed them from hunting as a sole source of food. They also built canoes from hollowed-out logs to travel the rivers, developed the bow and arrow, made good pottery, knew how to kindle fires, and banded together in villages, with primitive, but reasonably weather-proof houses. Before the coming

An Indian Village in Pennsylvania about 1500 A.D.

of the Europeans, the Pennsylvania Indians had no beasts of burden. Horses were unknown in both the Americas, although the Incas in South America had domesticated the Llamas and were using them to take the heavier loads off their own backs.

Pennsylvania Indians had no written language, although their spoken dialects were rich, soft and pleasing to the ear. Where else do we find preserved such melodious and delightful Indian names as: Towanda, Conemaugh, Tuscarora, Aliquippa, Tunkhannock, Lackawanna, Kiskiminetas, Quemahoning, Kittanning, Catasauqua, Tamaqua, Kittatinny, Catawissa, Mauch Chunk or Mahantango?

Some of the most important Indian peoples in Pennsylvania, when European infiltration began,

Indian woman making pottery.

were the Susquehannocks, inhabiting virtually all of the Susquehanna River Basin; the Lenni-Lenapes, later known as "Delawares", living in Eastern Pennsylvania near the Delaware River; and the Eriehronons or "Eries", living on the shores of Lake Erie. There was also a mysterious group of Indians living on the upper Ohio and its tributaries, the Allegheny and Monongahela rivers, who for want of a better name, are referred to as the "Monongahela People". This group of Indians vanished without a trace shortly after pressure from the whites caused the Delawares to migrate westward, into Monongahela territory.

Long before the coming of the white settlers from Europe, the Indians had developed an extensive network of foot-paths to connect their villages, some of them running over the mountains between Shackamaxen (the site of Philadelphia) and Shannopins (Pittsburgh). The white men soon found that these Indian trails offered the best means for traveling across the mountains to the western territories.

Today, it is almost impossible to find authentic Indian paths in Pennsylvania still in existence, even in areas where they have not been covered over by modern highways. We know they existed because of descriptions of them written by early European pioneers. Deeply indented in the ground by countless generations of moccasined feet, they measured about 18 inches wide by a foot deep and followed the higher ground and ridges, less subject to flooding or enemy attack. They crossed streams at the narrowest, most easily-forded spots.

Pennsylvania Indian Trails were developed over countless centuries with almost uncanny directness between the points they connected, as well as an amazing degree of dryness and levelness, except where they dipped down to cross a stream.

Early highway builders in Pennsylvania digressed from the Indian routes to their sorrow on numerous occasions. The Indians had an instinct for picking routes for their trails with excellent sub-soil conditions. Never were their trails undermined or washed out by hidden springs. Never did they pass through swampy ground. The Indians always managed to pick the sides of the hills best protected from the weather in winter and summer when a choice was available. Their highway engineering, whether instinctive, or the result of years of gradual improvement of location from generation to generation, was superb!

One of the most important Indian Trails in Pennsylvania was the Allegheny Path, running from Shackamaxen (Philadelphia) to Paxtang (Harrisburg), which there made a connection with the Raystown Path via the present towns of Carlisle and Bedford to Shannopins (Pittsburgh). This combination was a number of miles shorter than the present Pennsylvania Turnpike, which follows the same general route.

Another important cross-state Indian trail was the Great Shamokin Path, which ran from the Susquehanna River at Shamokin (Sunbury) via Muncy, Williamsport, Lock Haven, Snow Shoe, Clearfield and Punxsutawney to Kittanning on the Allegheny River.

Penn's treaty with the Delaware Indians in 1683 gave Pennsylvanians seventy years of peaceful co-existence. (Painting by Paul Domville.)

Pennsylvania Indians used "dug out" canoes, made by burning out and chipping out solid logs.

7

An Indian "Lean-To" for overnight stops along the trail.

Another famous east-west Indian trail, which closely approximated the route of the National Pike (now U.S. Route 40) was Nemacolin's Path running from Cumberland, Maryland, northwestward across Pennsylvania, via Uniontown, to Nemacolin's Village (Brownsville) where it joined the Mingo Path west to Ohio.

In the northeastern section of Pennsylvania was the Minisink Path, which centered around Minisink on the Delaware, a highly populated Indian settlement of the Lenni-Lanapes. Its eastern terminus was the New Jersey coast and it ran westward in Pennsylvania via Blooming Grove, Hamlin and Scranton to Wyoming, on the North Branch of the Susquehanna, making connection with the Great Warrior's Path northwest into New York.

Crossing eastern Pennsylvania from North to South was the Great Warriors Path, starting at Tioga and following the Susquehanna North Branch down to Shamokin (Sunbury) where it joined the Paxtang Path south to Conestoga, (Lancaster County) or southwest from Paxtang down the Cumberland Valley, past Chambersburg, and into Maryland, via the so-called "Virginia Road".

A major north-south Indian Trail in the western part of the State was the Catawba Path, sometimes referred to as the Iroquois Main Road, or the "Tennessee Road". This route began at Olean, New York and ran south via Tallyho, Highland Corners, Sigel, and Brookville to Indiana, making junction with the east-west trails there, and continuing out of the State by way of Palmertown, Ligonier, Connellsville and Uniontown to the Cheat River, and south.

Nearby, another north-south route, later made famous by George Washington's expedition to bargain with the French at Presqu' Isle, was the Venango Path, starting at Presqu' Isle (Erie) and extending south to Pittsburgh via Waterford, Meadville, Franklin, Harrisville, Prospect and Evansburg.

There were many more Indian Paths criss-crossing and interconnecting with those above, but space does not permit listing all of them.

Suffice it to say, the Indians in Pennsylvania had developed a highly sophisticated system of foot-roads, probably long before our northern European ancestors had anything comparable abroad. With the coming of the white man, and the retirement of the Indian westward, some of these old trails fell into disuse and Nature quickly obliterated them, but many were preserved by the white man to form the pattern for Pennsylvania's modern highway system.

# Chapter II

# EARLY ROAD DEVELOPMENT

The early history of European colonization of Pennsylvania is closely associated with the unusual personality of William Penn, born in 1644 in England, the talented son of Admiral Penn, a favorite of the reigning monarch of England, King Charles II.

Young William Penn did not endear himself to his father, or the king, when he espoused the cause of the persecuted and unpopular Quaker religious sect in England. For his ardent support of the Quakers, William was expelled from Oxford while still a student there, and was later imprisoned and tried by the courts for suspected treason.

In spite of this the outspoken William Penn was forgiven by his father, and ultimately became a powerful leader of the Quaker movement in England. Upon

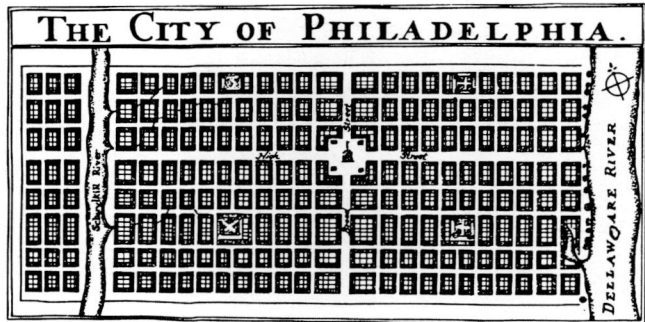

Advance planning map of the City of Philadelphia, showing the four public squares and the central square. Notice the "grid-iron" streets – new in America.

the death of the senior Penn, King Charles II settled a debt of 16,000 pounds which he owed Admiral Penn by granting to William, in 1681, a 50,000 square-mile tract in America.

This tract was named "Pennsylvania" in honor of William Penn's father, and as soon as the charter was signed by Charles II, Penn organized his fellow Quakers for a mass movement to Pennsylvania. While the King had granted to Penn unlimited personal powers of governing the new colony as he saw fit, Penn early gave his people in Pennsylvania the right to elect an assembly and make their own laws. Word of this democratic form of self government spread elsewhere in Europe and other oppressed peoples and religious sects also began moving to Pennsylvania, including many groups from Germany.

## Philadelphia Established – 1681

Philadelphia, whose site was picked by trusted subordinates of William Penn in 1681, a year or more before he was able to come to Pennsylvania personally, was referred to by Penn as his "Greene Country Towne". The site was carefully selected for access to the Delaware River and the Atlantic Ocean by ship, as well as for good high-level ground upon which to build a city.

So rapid was the movement of immigrants into Pennsylvania, that within a few short years Philadelphia had become a bustling city and one of the largest seaports in the New World. Penn's plans were not limited to the city alone.

As early as 1683 we find evidence that highways were being contemplated well beyond the city limits. In his 1682 "Frame of Government", Penn made the

William Penn (1644-1718), founder of Pennsylvania. His ideals of religious freedom and government by popular assembly brought a flood of settlers to his province from all parts of Europe. (Courtesy Hall of Fame, New York University.)

White "traders", bartering with the Pennsylvania Indians.

governor and provincial assembly responsible for "all necessary roads and highways in the province". A law dated March 10, 1683 provided for the building of bridges "over all the small creeks and rivers in the King's Highway from the Falls of Delaware to the southernmost parts of Sussex County and requiring the county court in every county in the seventh month to appoint three overseers, at least for the highways." The overseers were to summon "all the inhabitants of the respective limits, to come in and work at the making of all highways and bridges therein." In default of his duty, an inhabitant was compelled "to pay to the use of the public 20 shillings sterling."

The first record we find of a public road in the Colonial records is in the minutes of the Provincial Council of October 31, 1696. It gave the courses and distances of two roads in Oxford Township, Philadelphia County.

The Act of November 27, 1700, being the reenactment of a previous law, provided "that all the King's Highways or public roads within the province and territories, shall be laid out by orders from the Governor and Council for the time being, which roads shall be recorded in the Council Books with courses thereof as near as may be." The justices were authorized to appoint viewers for the laying out of roads

other than King's Highways and "to fix the width thereof provided that the width shall not exceed 50 feet and that the approval of the report of viewers be entered upon the record."

Descriptions giving courses and distance of King's Highways are to be found in the published volumes of Colonial Records. Also, a few such descriptions are to be found in the "Archives", extending from 1690 to 1790.

Among the earlier records (1711) is to be found a description of the roads leading from a point on the Delaware River opposite the landing of John Reading to Fourth and Vine Streets in Philadelphia, long known as the "York Road"; the Strasburg Road; the Lancaster-Philadelphia Road, running into the Philadelphia Road at John Spruces, near what is now Whitford, and many others.

Homesteaders and traders moved rapidly northward and westward, out of Philadelphia, establishing settlements and building primitive connecting roads behind them, while the Penns made treaties with the Indians to try to keep up with the white acquisition of land. Thus were established a number of towns and roads to Bethlehem, Lancaster, Reading, York, Harris Ferry, and Carlisle in the valleys southeast of the Allegheny Mountains.

## Pack Horse Trains

The first white men to cross the mountains into western Pennsylvania were the trappers and the traders, making use of the Indian trails. Some of them probably travelled on foot as did the Indians, but later they appear to have ridden horses and to have used pack horses for the transportation of their goods. The foot paths of the Indians could as a rule be traversed by small, sure-footed horses without great difficulty and such use doubtless widened and deepened them. Even after the navigable waters of the west were reached, the traders who were going further usually continued their journey by trail, as the overland routes were more direct than the streams and only a few of the traders had access to stables enroute where they could leave their horses. Pack horse transportation was used extensively by the British Army during the French and Indian War, and with the advent of settlers it developed into a business.

Pack horse trains were usually composed of twelve to fifteen horses, each horse tethered to the pack saddle of the horse ahead, with two men to attend them. The average load for a horse was about 200 lbs. One man led the train and the other brought up the rear, keeping an eye on the packs to see that they did not come loose.

The points at which the goods were trans-shipped from wagon to pack horses varied with the seasons but generally moved west as the roads were improved. Through south central Pennsylvania the transshipment point moved westward during the mid-1700's, from Lancaster, to York, to Harris Ferry, to Carlisle. Along the Maryland border, the "jumping off" point, east of the mountains, was successively Baltimore, Frederick, Hagerstown, Oldtown and finally Cumberland. The expense of this form of transportation added a high percentage to the cost of imports and exports in the "back country".

The era of the pack horse in western Pennsylvania approached its end in the 1790's as a result of the opening and improving of wider roads and increasing prosperity of the farmers, which enabled them to purchase wagons. The professional pack horsemen stubbornly resisted the transition, because their horses were too small to pull wagons and consequently it meant changing their whole method of operation to join the "wagoners".

## Wagon Roads

Nevertheless, wagons became increasingly plentiful and by the end of the Eighteenth Century they carried practically all the intersectional trade in Pennsylvania. Pack horses continued to be used, however, for internal transportation where roads were not available, and in some of the slow settling northern

A typical Pennsylvania pack horse train winding its way over a steep mountain trail.

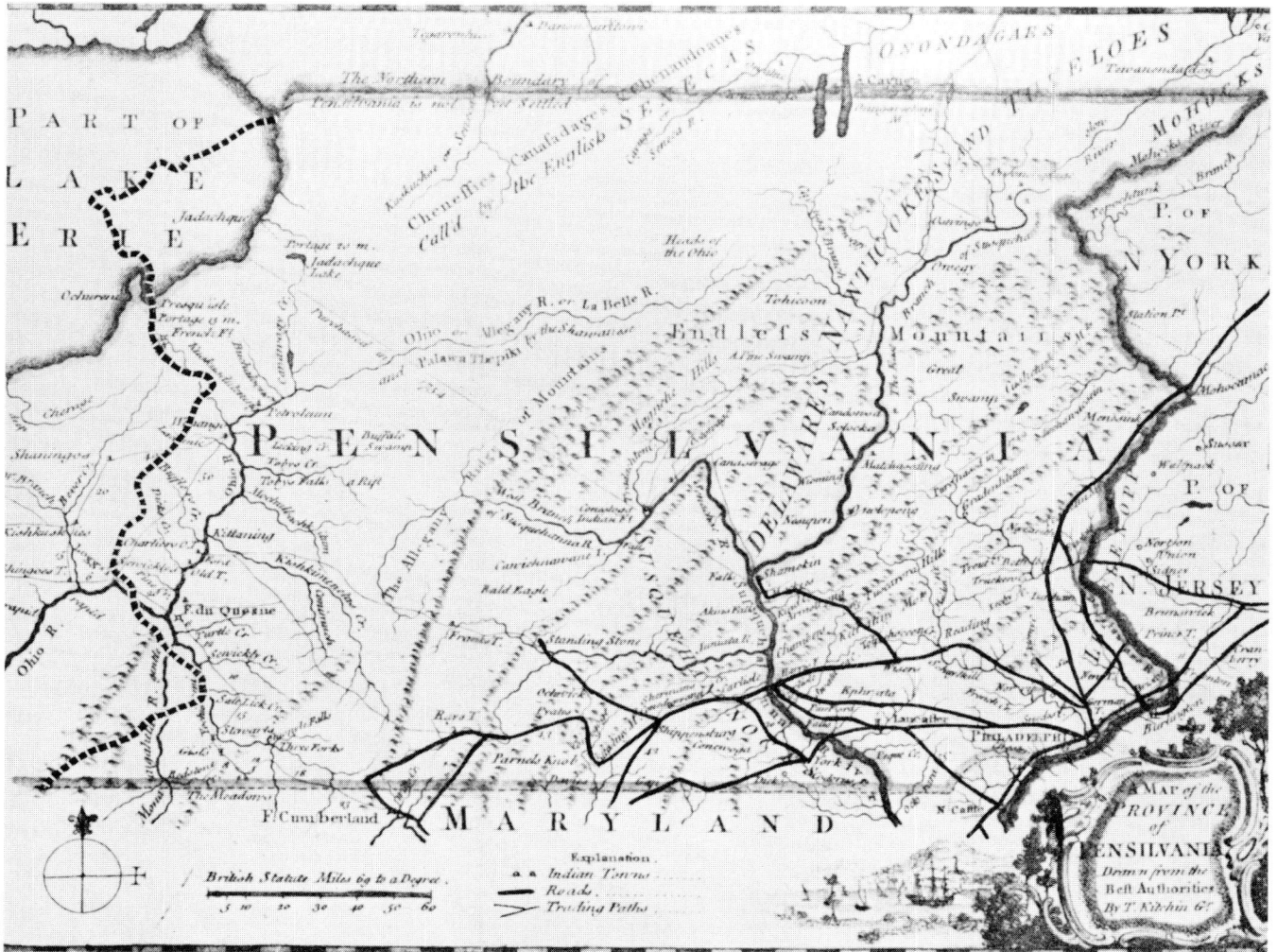

Pennsylvania roads and trading paths in 1756. Note the western provincial boundary, paralleling the Delaware River; also the northern boundary "not yet settled." (Courtesy Dr. Ernest Coleman.)

Pennsylvania counties, they could not be dispensed with for many years.

The first road opened into western Pennsylvania was that of the Ohio Company from the Potomac River at Wills Creek (Cumberland, Md.) to the Youghiogheny River in 1752, which was later improved and extended to Gist's Plantation, west of Chestnut Ridge, by George Washington in 1754, during the French-Indian War, when wagons and cannons were drawn over it.

## Washington's Mission

One of the earliest expeditions in connection with the French-Indian War was that of George Washington, who was sent in October of 1753 by the English Governor of Virginia when it was heard that the French were moving troops into the Ohio River Valley, then part of the Virginia colony, with a message to the French commander to "cease and desist".

Washington's difficult journey, under winter weather conditions, took him from Williamsburg, Virginia, first to Wills Creek (now Cumberland, Maryland) where he hired the famous Ohio territory guide, Christopher Gist, to help him cross the mountain wilderness to the forks of the Ohio (now Pittsburgh) which he described as an excellent site for a fort, and then on, via the Venango trail, to the headquarters of the French Commander, Legardeur de Saint Pierre, at Fort LeBoeuf, near the present town of Waterford in Erie County, Pa.

During Washington's difficult trip, by horse and canoe, over a three-month period, he was beset with bad weather, hostile Indians and uncooperative Frenchmen. Nevertheless, he delivered his message to Saint Pierre, was courteously received and entertained, but told firmly that the French had no intention of leaving the Ohio Valley. This incident set the stage for the 7-year French-Indian War.

Washington made many observations of French activities and west Pennsylvania terrain during this trip

which were of great value to the British during the course of the ensuing war. He subsequently led a force of Virginia militia, in 1754, into Western Pennsylvania which was forced to surrender when besieged by superior French forces.

## Braddock's Road

Washington was also an aide to British General Edward Braddock on the disastrous campaign of 1755 when Braddock, leading 2200 men, attempted to take the newly-built French Fort Duquesne, at the Forks of the Ohio. Benjamin Franklin was commissioned by Braddock to rent 150 wagons and horse teams in York and Lancaster to assist in transporting his supplies.

After assembling an amazing assortment of heavy artillery, equipment and supplies, Braddock planned his approach to Ft. Duquesne. His route through the wilderness began at Wills Creek (Cumberland, Maryland) and proceeded via Nemacolin's Path to the summit of Chestnut Ridge (a few miles southeast of Uniontown, Pa.) where it branched onto Catawba Path, then via Glades Path, to the Forks. The route also crossed eight major mountains. To provide a roadway for his heavy artillery – six pounders, twelve pounders, and howitzers – Braddock sent a detachment of several hundred men ahead of the main body to open a twelve-foot wide wagon and artillery road. These pioneers felled trees, bridged creeks and laid causeways across the swamps.

Braddock had undertaken an almost impossible task. The strain of hauling the heavy equipment over the rough roadway was too much for the horses, many of which sickened and died. The men assisted in pulling the wagons and guns out of the mud with block and tackle, and sometimes pure brute strength. Braddock was forced to change the route on several occasions to bypass the mountains. In spite of almost insurmountable difficulties, Braddock finally arrived, with much of his artillery, within a few miles of Ft. Duquesne, where he was engaged by a force of French and Indians.

After a disastrous defeat in which Braddock himself was killed, his forces, abandoning their artillery, beat a hasty retreat, back along the roadway they had built, to the safety of British territory once more. Washington, behaving with conspicuous gallantry and courage, assisted in bringing the survivors home.

After Braddock's defeat Indian raiding parties roamed almost at will along the frontier of Pennsylvania, killing the farmers and their families and occasionally attacking whole towns in force. The 1755 massacre at Penn's Grove near the present town of Selinsgrove awoke Pennsylvanians forcibly to the fact that William Penn's seventy-year peace pact with the Indians had reached a bloody conclusion. Even the Delawares, stirred up by the French, attacked the colonists of Pennsylvania, although many of the Indian tribes of the Six Nations espoused the British cause against the French. In fact, the Six Nations signed a treaty with the English in October of 1758 at Easton and forced the Delawares to join them in making peace. This treaty was a serious blow to French-Indian relations in the Ohio Valley. The stage was set for the successful campaign of British General John Forbes against the French at Fort Duquesne in late November of 1758.

Braddock's "tailor-made" route of 1755, through extremely difficult terrain.

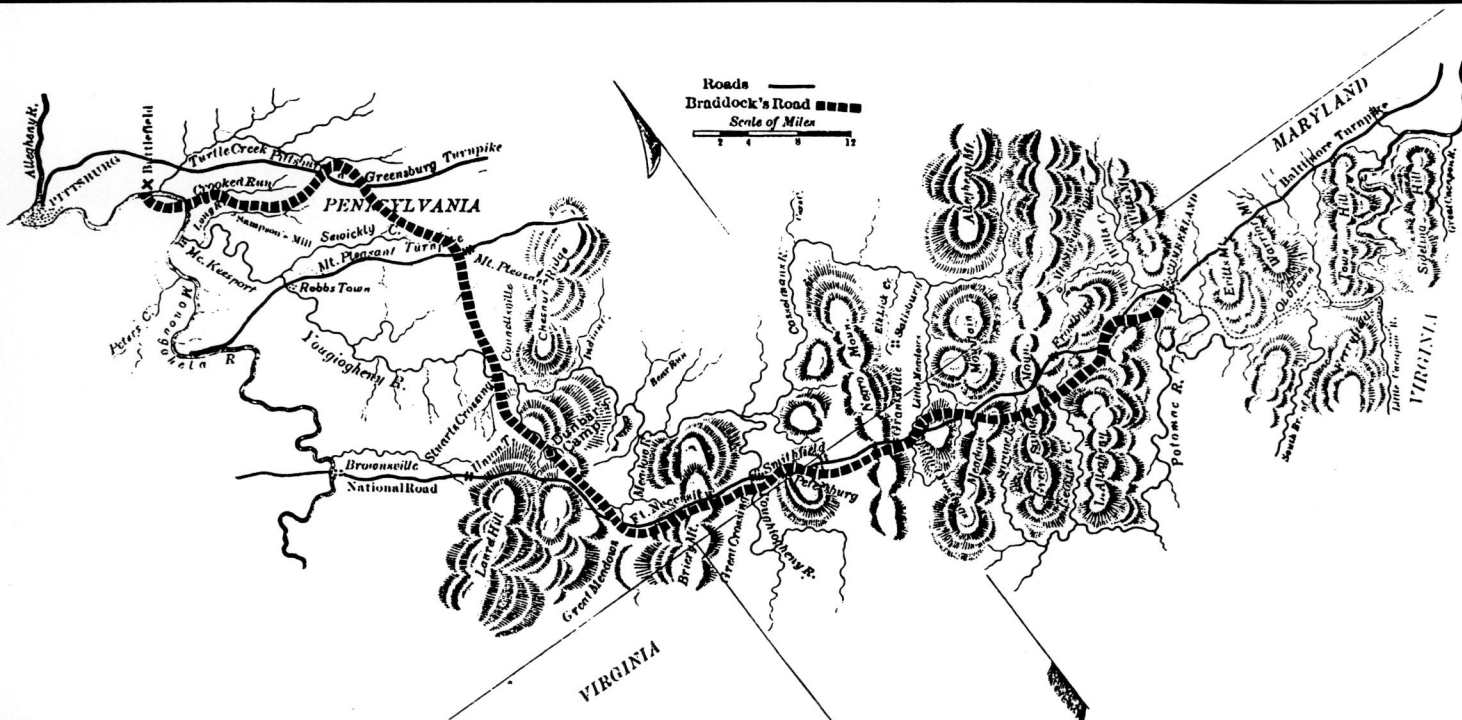

A stagecoach and Conestoga Wagon pass on an early Pennsylvania turnpike.

## Forbes Road

General Forbes' military road was constructed over a wagon-trail previously opened, in 1754, by James Burd from Shippensburg, through Bedford, to the top of Allegheny Ridge. Further west, the General built a new road over the Raystown Path to a point 10-miles west of Ligonier. From this point, his army traveled through the woods without stopping to make a road, hoping to surprise the French. However, French scouts evidently carried a warning back to Fort Duquesne in time for their hasty departure. Thus, when General Forbes arrived at Fort Duquesne, prepared for an all-out attack on that stronghold, he found that the French had burned the Fort and left the area the day before he arrived.

By this time, the French-English war, referred to in European history as the Seven Years' War, had turned in favor of the British and their allies, largely through the astute efforts of British Secretary of State William Pitt. In his honor, the English built a new fort at the Forks of the Ohio, named Fort Pitt, and in 1759 opened Forbes road through to the present site of Pittsburgh. Braddock Road was also re-opened, as well as a new road from Gist's plantation to Brownsville, with a water connection down the Monongahela to Fort Pitt. During the next five years, these roads were maintained by the British forces for military supplies to aid in the final defeat of the French in that area. When the British, under Sir William Johnson in 1759, captured Fort Niagara, the line of French communication from Canada to the Ohio was broken, and their ultimate defeat was assured.

After the French-Indian War, however, these military roads were allowed to deteriorate and it is doubtful if there was much wagon transportation over them during the Revolution.

## Other Early Pa. Roads

Hundreds of miles of additional inter-connecting roads in western Pennsylvania were opened in the next few years before interruption of domestic activities by the War of 1812.

Roads in the colonized sections of eastern Pennsylvania had historically begun developing much earlier than those of western Pennsylvania. By 1800 there were direct roads (many of them toll-roads) connecting Philadelphia with New Castle (Del.), Lancaster, Reading, Harrisburg, Bethlehem and Trenton (N.J.).

By this time, also, the U.S. coastal cities had a well-developed system of roads connecting them. One of the most famous of these was the Boston Post Road, originally developed by Benjamin Franklin in 1764 to carry mail between Boston and New York. A similar road was afterward extended to Philadelphia, Baltimore and South, approximating the present U.S. Route 1. Particularly during the War of 1812, this road became an important land artery and life-line between these American coastal cities, at the time of the British Blockade.

A square-ended, flat-bottom "Ark" for one-way travel on the Pennsylvania rivers, usually on the spring freshets.

# Chapter III

# EARLY RIVER TRAVEL IN PENNSYLVANIA

With major rivers and their tributaries extending into nearly every part of Pennsylvania, it appeared to the early European settlers that these rivers furnished the most practical avenues of transportation into the interior of the new colony. William Penn himself, envisioning a second city much further inland than Philadelphia, was quoted as follows;

"It is now my purpose to make another settlement upon the river Susquehanagh . . . and the most convenient place for communications with former plantations in the east . . . which will not be hard to do by water by benefit of the river Scoulkill, for a branch of that river (Tulpehocken Creek) lies near a branch that runs in the Susquehanagh River (Swatara Creek) and is the common course of the Indians with their skins and furrs into our parts . . . from the west and northwest parts of the continent."

However, water travel in Pennsylvania was not without its problems. Some of the streams and rivers, the Susquehanna in particular, were filled with large rocks and ledges which made navigation difficult and dangerous. About the only time of the year when good travel was possible was during the Spring freshets, and then only downstream.

15

Durham Boat, developed in 1750 by Robert Durham of Easton, Pa. for two-way travel on Pennsylvania rivers.

## Primitive Vessels

Early settlers in the interior of Pennsylvania developed various devices for river transportation. The simplest of these was the old "Dug-out" canoe, inherited from the Indians. A large log, hollowed out by fire or chisel, provided a satisfactory (but very heavy) vessel, which two men could paddle or pole.

"A "Pirogue", likewise of Indian origin, was a very large canoe, often forty to fifty feet long and six to eight feet wide, capable of carrying a family and several tons of household goods.

The "Skiff" was a wide, flat-bottomed boat, made of planks, with a flat bottom and square ends, with a very large edition called a "Bateau". The Bateau was clumsy, but had a very light draft, capable of maneuvering in shallow water. It was propelled by several long oars called "sweeps". A third sweep served as a rudder. Going upstream it was generally shoved along by poles to the river bottom. A bateau could carry an entire family and all its belongings.

The "Keel Boat", a more sophisticated development, took the shape of a more modern boat, with a heavy, 4-inch square keel running the full length of the bottom, to take the shock of collision with submerged rocks. Stout planks were used in the hull, and it sported a mast and sails. It was generally 40 to 75 feet long, and seven to nine feet wide. One steersman and two crewmen at the sweeps could handle the boat downstream; upstream travel was augmented not only by the sail, but by poling, and often by a towing rope approximately 1000 feet long called a "cordell", powered by a husky team of men on shore.

A specialized version of the keel boat was the "Durham Boat" developed by Robert Durham of Easton, Pa. in 1750, which became quite popular on the Delaware and Susquehanna Rivers. Durham boats were 60 feet long, eight feet wide, two feet deep, and when loaded with 15 tons of goods drew 20 inches of water. The stern and bow were sharp, with small decks both ends, and a cleated walkway extending the full length of the boat on each side, on which the "polers" would walk (or sometimes crawl) toward the stern pushing a long pole, two to a side, during upstream navigation. A fifth crewmember acted as steersman. The Durham boatmen were a hardy lot!

In the early 1800's a one-way flat-bottom vessel was developed in Pennsylvania primarily to ride the Spring freshets, known as the "Ark". It was 60 to 100 feet long, 15 to 20 feet wide, and 3 to 5 feet deep, drawing about two feet of water when carrying a load of fifty tons or more. Bow and stern were usually tapered to a broad point. So huge and unwieldy was the vessel that it was at the mercy of the current, and only general guidance could be provided by the broad, side sweeps and the powerful men who manned them. The boat (which was actually more like a large floating box) had no rudder. It bounced and tumbled over falls and rapids, but its heavy construction generally kept it from coming to pieces until it had reached its destination, where it was unloaded, and promptly torn apart and sold for the lumber it contained.

A log raft passes under the bridge at Warren, headed down the Allegheny River for Pittsburgh, circa 1875. (Courtesy George Wills.)

## Lumbering Rafts

As the lumbering industry became important in northern Pennsylvania and southern New York State, huge lumber rafts made their appearance in Springtime on the upper Delaware, Susquehanna and Allegheny Rivers. The logs were laid side by side, generally parallel to the current, and lashed together with sapling poles. The rafts were sufficiently flexible that they could flow over rapids, rocks and even low dams without coming apart. Huge sweeps fore and aft were used to guide them downstream to their destinations – Philadelphia, Baltimore or Pittsburgh. A tally made by one interested citizen on the Susquehanna at York Haven in the year 1817, counted 342 arks and 989 rafts passing down river between April 1 to July 5 that year.

There was acute rivalry between the ports of Baltimore and Philadelphia for trade with the great "hinterland" of central Pennsylvania served by the Susquehanna North and West Branches and Juniata Rivers in the late 1700's and early 1800's. Philadelphia lobbyists in the State legislature would not permit improvement of navigation on the Susquehanna below Columbia (where the Columbia-Philadelphia Turnpike and Railroad terminated), until 1840. In spite of this, much downstream trade found its way to Baltimore by ark and raft from as far north as Binghamton, New York.

A hewed timber raft of the kind that once crowded the Susquehanna and Allegheny rivers. This model, made for the Carnegie Museum by H.B. Rhines of Oil City, is 30 inches long and 10 inches wide. The scale is roughly 1 to 24. (Courtesy Walter Leuba.)

17

The Penrose Rope Ferry across the Schuylkill River at Philadelphia in 1776. Samuel Penrose, the owner, propelled his barge by pulling on ropes, stretched from bank to bank. (Courtesy of George Wills.)

## Ferries in Pennsylvania

Before the year 1800, bridges across the major streams and rivers in Pennsylvania were non-existent. Small streams were usually "forded" at the shallowest places. Ferries were the answer on larger streams. In Colonial times, ferries across major streams far removed from white settlements were frequently operated by the Indians using their canoes or "Dug-outs". The unlucky traveler who arrived on the wrong side of a river and could not make his voice heard above the rushing of the water to the far side (or if the operator had wandered away) simply had to wait until a traveler came the other way and brought the boat over.

Wagons and horses, as well as herds of animals, were transported across the deeper streams on rafts or flat-bottomed barges. Such conveyances were usually poled across the stream. Where the current was sufficiently strong, a rope was stretched from bank to bank and anchored at a height above the water if possible. The ferry was then hooked to a pulley wheel (or wheels) on the rope, and the barge was turned at an angle to the current. Thus, the force of the water was used to propell the craft to the opposite bank.

In 1810 an interesting "Team-Boat Ferry" operated between Philadelphia and Camden across the Delaware River. Tethered horses were arranged in a circle on a large tread-wheel which was, in turn, geared to the boat paddle-wheels. When the horses walked, the wheel turned and the paddle-wheels pushed the boat along at a good pace. A number of these "Team-Boats" were in operation at wide river crossings throughout the State.

Throughout the State, circa 1795, major river crossing points were often identified by the ferry-boat owner's name. Gray's Ferry and Penrose Ferry in Philadelphia; Wright's Ferry at Columbia (from which Wrightsville on the west bank of the Susquehanna took its name); Harris-Ferry (now Harrisburg); Clarks-Ferry (where the Clarks Ferry Bridge now stands); Dingman's Ferry and Well's Ferry on the Delaware; Fallston Ferry on the Beaver River, and so on. There were also heavy-duty, endless rope ferries at points where canal boats crossed the rivers.

18

Each time a major bridge was built it usually put some ferry-boatman out of business. Some of them hung on, at reduced rates, to compete with the tolls usually collected by the bridge companies, but most sued the bridge owners for damages and suspended operations.

However, some of the old ferries survived. A survey conducted in 1966 by the Pennsylvania Department of Transportation indicated the following ferry companies still doing business that year in various parts of the State:

Arensburg Ferry Company – between Arensburg, Fayette County and Crucible, Greene County

Elco Ferry Company – between Elco, Washington County and Newell, Fayette County

Fredericktown Ferry Company – between Fredericktown, Washington County and point opposite thereto in Fayette County

Hunter & Radel Ferry Company – over Susquehanna River at Millersburg

J. A. Jacobs Estate Ferry – between Allenport, Washington County and Fayette City, Fayette County

Kenshaw Ferry Corporation – from eastern terminus of State Highway No. 112 in Greene County to western terminus of State Highway No. 112 on the opposite side of the Monongahela River in Fayette County

J. W. Nolan – between the Public Dock at the foot of State Street in the City of Erie and Water Works Park on Presque Isle Peninsula, Erie County

Old Glassworks Ferry Company – across the Monongahela River between a landing in Greene County about one mile north of the Borough of Greensboro, and a landing on the opposite side of said river in Fayette County

Renner Ferry Company – between Suterville Borough, Westmoreland County and Elizabeth Township, Allegheny County

Columbia-Wrightsville steam tug, which carried passengers and also towed canal boats across the lower Susquehanna between the "Main Line" and Susquehanna and Tidewater Canals.

Shippingport Ferry Company – over the Ohio River between Cooks Ferry Station, Industry Township and Shippingport, Beaver County

Robert L. Simpson – between Coal Center and Newell

Since the ferry-boat operators were literally working at "cross-purposes" with the raftsmen, Durham boatmen and ark-boatmen, there were frequent clashes between the travelers on the river and the river-crossers. Many a ferry boatman found his cross-river rope or cable cut the morning after a Durham boat had tangled with it during the night.

River crossing by ferry was particularly hazardous during high water, and many a ferry boat was washed downstream, frequently with loss of life, when an ambitious operator overloaded his barge with too many wagons or passengers.

Millersburg Ferry, oldest surviving ferry across the Susquehanna River. Started in 1825; poled till 1873, when first paddle-wheeler was acquired. (Photo by Harold H. Huber, P.E.)

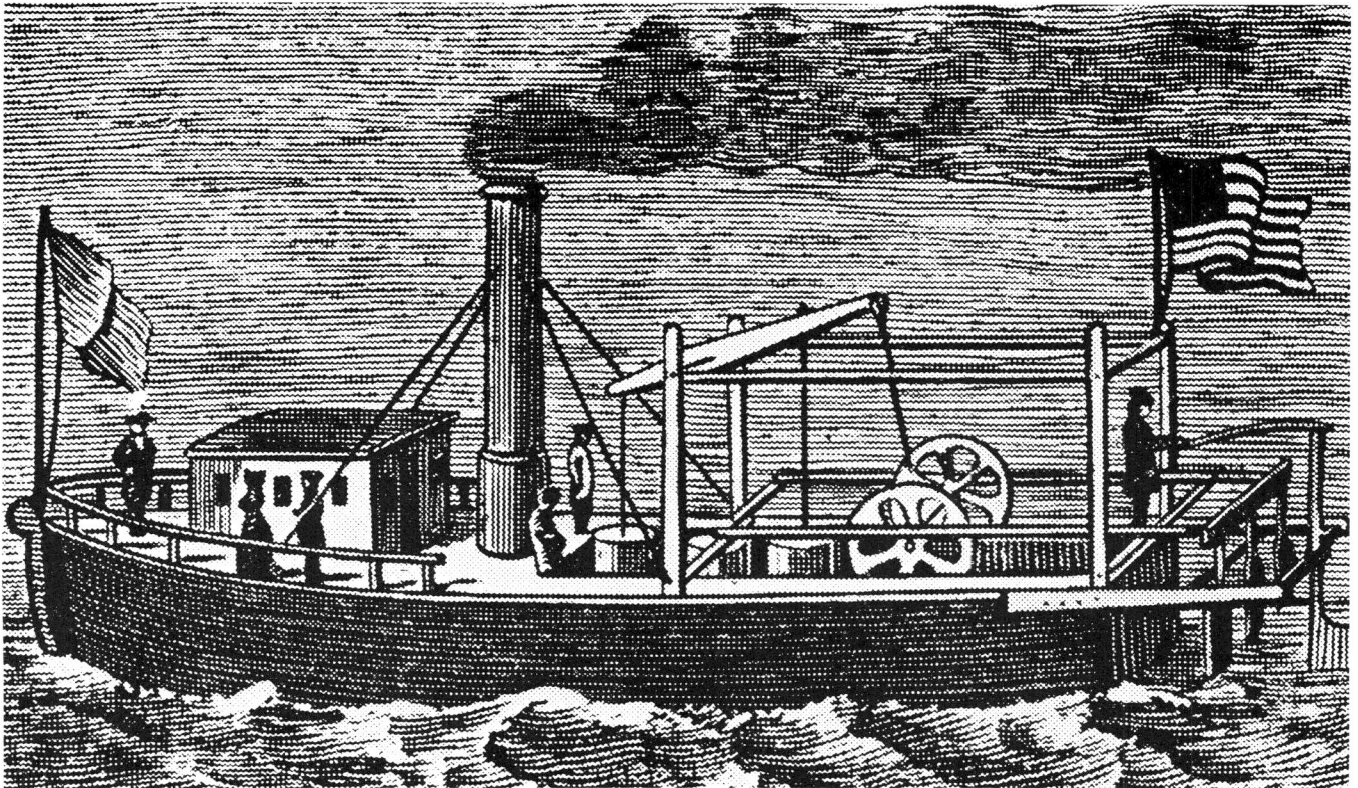

John Fitch is credited with the invention of the first steamboat in America, which he operated on the Delaware River at Philadelphia in 1786. He provided regular packet service in 1790.

# Early Steam Boats

While James Rumsey of Maryland is credited with having demonstrated the first hydraulic jet-propelled steamboat in America on the Potomac River in December of 1787, a Philadelphian – John Fitch – is generally considered the inventor of the first commercially successful steamboat. Fitch had been working on the idea of propelling a boat with a steam engine as early as 1785 and made his first model in August of that year. With the help of an ingenious watch-maker of Philadelphia named Henry Voight, he built a small skiff and an engine with a three-inch cylinder which operated a chain of paddles on either side of the boat. In July of 1786 he ran this boat successfully on the Delaware River, the first steam boat in America! Oddly enough, Fitch's remarkable achievement was not taken seriously by the public and was given very little publicity.

John Fitch became a sort of "prophet without honor" in his own community, where he was generally considered a "crack-pot". However, he persevered against competition with James Rumsey (who claimed prior patent rights) and developed various other steam-boat models, with the most successful (his third) being put into regular service carrying passengers in the summer and fall of 1790 between Philadelphia and Trenton and other ports on the Delaware River. Another boat, which Fitch was building for exclusive use in Virginia, was destroyed in a violent storm, and this disaster caused Fitch's financial backers to withdraw their support. Fitch had no personal capital at his disposal and his steam boat company collapsed. All he had was an idea, and a short-lived demonstration of its practicality, but the public was not ready for Fitch's almost fanatical attempts to convince them that he was right. His success on the Delaware was soon forgotten. He travelled throughout eastern United States and parts of Europe, trying unsuccessfully to sell the steam-boat principle. In frustration he moved to the Kentucky wilderness, where in 1798, the embittered inventor took poison and died.

In 1804, Oliver Evans of Philadelphia invented an amphibious, steam driven contraption, which steamed up the Delaware River, and traveled on wheels west on Market Street, Philadelphia, and down the Schuylkill to its starting point. No one took this amazing invention seriously either.

# Robert Fulton

It remained for Robert Fulton, a native of Lancaster County, Pennsylvania, to obtain the backing of wealthy friends and develop the highly successful side-wheeler steamer "Clermont", which on August 7, 1807 left New York City for Albany and made the trip up the Hudson in 32 hours. The event was given full publicity and within a few years powerful steamers were operating along the Atlantic seaboard and the rivers and lakes in the East, many of them built by Fulton and his associates. Fulton's success, where Fitch had failed, can be attributed both to the time and place of their demonstrations and the outgoing personality of Fulton, as opposed to the rather tactless approach of Fitch to those he was trying to "sell". Fulton also had the advantage of friends in high places, primarily in England, where he spent much time and where he made the personal acquaintance of James Watt, inventor of the steam engine. Watt's engine was fully perfected by the year 1800 and Fulton, a keen engineer, was quick to pick up its working details and used a Watt engine in the Clermont.

Prior to returning to the United States to build the "Clermont", Fulton had entered into partnership with Robert R. "Chancellor" Livingston, then in the diplomatic service in England, who had done some experimentation with primitive steamboats himself in New York. Livingston had petitioned the State of New York for exclusive steam-navigation rights in State waters, in 1798, which rights were extended until he and Fulton got the Clermont into successful operation in 1807.

# Ohio – Mississippi Steamers

After thus establishing a successful monopoly of steam-boat service in New York, the Livingston-Fulton combine turned their attention to Pittsburgh, Pennsylvania – at the head of the Ohio-Mississippi navigation, with the idea of developing a steam-boat monopoly along the entire route to New Orleans, if possible. It was an ambitious undertaking, later realized in part, but to demonstrate their capabilities in the so-called "western waters" they needed at least one good steam boat which could make the run between Pittsburgh and New Orleans.

To this end, in 1811, they sent Nicholas Roosevelt to Pittsburgh to build the first steam boat to navigate any stream in the interior of the United States. It was named the "New Orleans" and was a small boat of one hundred-ton capacity, with stern paddle wheel and two masts. The boat set out from Pittsburgh in October of 1811, with the Nicholas Roosevelt family on board, plus pilot, six crew members and servants. Passage

down the Ohio to Louisville was extremely rapid, and crowds of spectators gathered at every port of call along the way to gaze upon this new, fast mode of travel in sheer amazement. Her powerful steam whistle never failed to bring an entire town down to the docks, even in the dead of night! It was a six hundred-mile tour of triumph!

Shallow water below Louisville delayed passage of the "New Orleans" for several weeks and in the meantime she demonstrated her two-way capabilities by making several round-trips between Cincinnati and Louisville. Her southward voyage resumed in November. In January of 1812 she arrived in the city whose name she bore, being accorded a tremendous reception by the local populace. Fulton and Livingston had consumated an agreement with Governor Claiborne of Louisiana for exclusive navigation privileges in that State, so the "New Orleans" never returned to home base, but began serving at once on regular runs between New Orleans and Natchez, until she was wrecked on a snag in 1814.

Additional steam boats out of western Pennsylvania followed in fairly rapid sucession. Next was the "Comet", built by Daniel French of Brownsville in 1813. French had obtained a patent in 1809. The "Comet" went all the way to New Orleans the following year, and, with royalties to Fulton, served for several runs to Natchez, before being dismantled. Her engine was set up in a cotton factory.

Next came Fulton-Livingston's "Vesuvius", built at Pittsburgh in 1814, which made it to New Orleans after a five-month delay on a sandbar. She served the Natchez-New Orleans run till 1819.

Number four was the "Enterprise" built by French at Brownsville in 1814. After two trips to Louisville and return she went down to New Orleans and in the

**"New Orleans"**, first steamer to navigate the entire route of the Ohio and Mississippi – Pittsburgh to New Orleans.

The "Codorus", built at York, Pa. in 1825, was the first iron steamboat in the United States. It proved the impracticality of two-way steam navigation on the Susquehanna.

spring of 1815 returned to Louisville again – the first boat to travel the full distance upstream between New Orleans and Pittsburgh by steam power. A large and powerful steam boat, the "Washington", built at Wheeling in 1816 by Henry Shreve, dispelled all doubt that two-way steam navigation on the Ohio and Mississippi was here to stay. In 1827, the steam boat "Albion" successfully navigated the Allegheny River from Pittsburgh as far north as Kittanning. Its crew indicated they could have easily made it to Franklin had they had passengers bound for that town.

## First Iron Steamboat

What of navigation in central Pennsylvania while all these innovations were taking place on the Delaware, Hudson, Allegheny and Ohio? As we have stated previously, navigation on the rivers in central Pennsylvania was a most difficult operation except for downstream travel during Spring freshets.

In 1825, York, Pennsylvania became the birthplace of the first iron steamboat to be built in the United States. She was named the "Codorus" and was designed by John Elgar of York at the instigation of various Baltimore merchants, who felt that a power-boat on the Susquehanna River would increase many-fold the commerce and trade they would enjoy with river towns in central Pennsylvania. Elgar built his 60-foot long steam boat of riveted sheet iron, with nearly flat bottom and side-wheel drive to navigate the shallow and treacherous channels of the Susquehanna River. When completed the boat was transported on two wagons from York to Keesey's Ferry (now Accomac) on the Susquehanna where it was launched November 22, 1825 and fitted out with steam engine and machinery. The "Codorus" was the first vessel of any sort to use anthracite coal as fuel, although dry pitch pine also proved satisfactory. She had the distinction also of being the only steamboat, before or since, to ever ascend the Susquehanna – some 300 miles – into New York State. Remarkable though her maiden voyage to Binghamton was (not to mention the tremendous reception that the boat and her captain, John Elgar, received at each "port of call" along the way) her slow and painful three-month voyage proved that up-stream, steam navigation of the Susquehanna was completely impractical. She returned to York Haven July 17, 1826. When last heard from, the Baltimore owners were using the "Codorus" for passenger and freight service along the inland waterway in North Carolina.

Thus died the one and only attempt at early steamboat navigation of the Susquehanna River. It was not until the canal boat era began, a decade later, that more rapid, two-way water travel in central Pennsylvania became a practical reality.

A typical Pennsylvania "Corduroy Road" of the early 1800's, to keep the wagons out of the mud.

# Chapter IV
# LAND VEHICLES AND ROAD CONDITIONS
# EARLY 1800's

Up to this point we have said little about the *type* of roads which existed in Pennsylvania at the time of the War of 1812, or the conveyances used in traveling them.

In most cases it is not accurate to say that "a road was built" between two settlements, but rather that "a road was opened." By today's road-building standards, most of the early road-construction operations consisted of what we would consider simply right-of-way clearance – that is, the cutting of the trees and bushes and grubbing out the stumps, wide enough to permit the passage of a wagon or coach, with occasional "turnouts" for passing. A little digging was done on the sides of the hills and crude wooden bridges were constructed over the smaller streams. Paving materials, such as we know them today, were non-existent. Little effort appears to have been made to avoid steep inclines, and culverts were practically unknown.

## "Corduroy Roads"

Road maintenance generally consisted of dumping dirt into the deeper holes and removing fallen trees from across the road. In low, constantly boggy sections, logs were thrown into the mire at right angles to the line of travel with a little dirt on top. From the latter practice developed the so-called "corduroy roads," which, if traveled upon for any great distance, threatened to jolt even the sturdiest wagons or coaches to pieces, not to mention the passengers themselves. Even so, this was probably better than the alternative of sinking axle-deep in the mud.

## Stagecoaches

Travel over the roads to and in western Pennsylvania, in the early part of the period under consideration, was usually on foot or on horseback. As early as 1784, however, a passenger stage line began operations from Philadelphia to Lancaster and by 1796 it had been extended through York and Carlisle to Shippensburg, which remained its terminus until 1804. In the summer of that year, the first stage service across the Appalachian Mountains was established, with Pittsburgh as its objective. The line, which was made possible by a subsidy in the form of contract for carrying the U.S. mail, extended from Philadelphia through Lancaster, Harrisburg, Carlisle and Chambersburg to Bedford, and then followed the "Glade Road" to Somerset and Greensburg. At first the stage ran once a week but the service was increased to twice a week in December 1804. The trip was made in 6 to 7 days and the rate was $20.00 per passenger and 20-lbs. of baggage, with a charge of $12.00 per hundred weight for additional baggage.

A stage passenger line from Baltimore to connect with the above line at Chambersburg was also started in 1804. In November, 1804, the Post Master General wrote the citizens of Cannonsburg that he was "fully disposed to give every reasonable aid to the extension of the lines of stages beyond Pittsburgh." In 1805, a line was in operation through Cannonsburg and Washington to Wheeling. An attempt was made in 1805 and 1806 to continue the service through Chilicothe, Ohio to Lexington and Frankfort, Kentucky and stages were run over this route somewhat irregularly

Pennsylvania Stagecoach — early Eighteenth Century design.

in 1807, but it was not until 1808 that the line was in successful operation. No other stage lines to or in western Pennsylvania appear to have been established until after the War of 1812.

The vehicles used for stage service at this time are not comparable to the "stages" of later date, but were ordinary wagons with four hard, wooden seats, or benches, arranged crosswise, each of which would accommodate three passengers. The wagon was covered with a flat top, with curtains of canvas or leather which could be raised or lowered. These stage wagons were usually drawn by four horses, and "relays" were kept at various taverns along the route so that the horses could be changed frequently. These early wagons had no springs at all, but later, refinements were made, including hanging the body of the coach

on leather straps, which improved the riding qualities somewhat. The vehicles were called "stagecoaches" because the journey was made in stages, from place to place, between horse changes.

## Road Conditions

Travel over early Pennsylvania roads at most seasons of the year was often an extremely difficult and hazardous experience. Most travelers going any great distance by existing wagon or coach lines usually put their personal affairs in good order before leaving, often up-dating their wills.

Contemporary comments by travelers of the period indicate some of the hazards encountered. There was

"Luxury" Stagecoach of the Nineteenth Century.

always the danger of overturned coaches if a wheel hit a tree stump; or upset ferries at the river crossings if the load was too great or the current too swift.

In the wet season, parts of the main road appeared to be bottomless, and it is recorded that wagoners often spent three successive nights at the same tavern while working their wagon through a boggy section.

Christian Shultz, who traveled on horseback over the Portage Road from Erie to Waterford in August, 1807, reported that the route was the worst he had encountered: "What think you of starting at sunrise at this season of the year when the days are longest and making it dark night before you could whip and spur through fourteen miles of mud and mire, a great part of which is up to your knees, while sitting in the saddle?"

The wagon on which his trunk was shipped did not arrive "until the next day, when it made its appearance attached to a yoke of oxen. The decrepit condition of the wagon convinced me that it had seen hard times and upon inquiry I found the whole wagon and cargo, by one wheel running over the stump of a tree, had been upset in a deep mudhole."

As late as 1817, Henry Curran reported that near Bedford, "nothing could exceed the badness of the roads, yet the understanding between the driver and the horses was so perfect that we proceeded, although with almost broken bones, from the action of the mechanism. A London coachman under similar circumstances would in half an hour have dashed the strongest English stage to pieces and probably broken the legs of his passengers." Travelers frequently found it more comfortable to walk than to ride over the rough roads and sometimes they were required to walk uphill in order to lighten the load.

Sunday was not counted in the 6-days required by the mail contract to make the trip between Philadelphia and Pittsburgh, but short distances were usually driven on that day in order to ease the strain on the other days. Generally, travel on Sundays was frowned upon by the early settlers as a breach of the Sabbath.

The combination of steep mountain grades, bad roads and bad taverns made the western half of the trip a harrowing experience for most travelers, but fortunately the drivers were generally skillful and surprisingly few road casualties occurred.

Apparently human nature was much the same then as now. A Pittsburgh paper in 1806 published the following wagish "rules for coach travel": "Let every man get in first with all his baggage and take the best seat and at every town let every man light his cigar and continue smoking in the face of his fellow travelers." Despite the difficulties – the more philosophical travelers appeared to enjoy coach travel. Food and liquor were plentiful and cheap. Conversation among the passengers was free and easy and the experiences of the road left little opportunity for boredom.

## Taverns and Inns

An early development along well traveled roads was the "Stage Tavern" or "Inn". These establishments served as stopping, resting, eating and sleeping places for the many stage-coach travelers. Along the old Lancaster "King's Highway" it is said that inns or taverns averaged about one per mile. Greater intervals separated them in the western parts of the state. Some were rather primitive, some luxurious. All contained a bar, and usually a restaurant of sorts. All of them had some sort of sleeping accommodations, hopefully comfortable beds where the travelers slept, often "two to a bed and four to a room", and when these more comfortable quarters were filled, there was always a third-floor loft filled with mattresses, or even hay, for the overflow.

Philip Nicklin, a Philadelphia attorney, describing his trip between Bedford Springs and Pittsburgh by "Mail Coach" in 1835, writes of one overnight stop as follows:

"We reached the village of Somerset at half past seven, P.M. having been eight hours and a half in travelling thirty-eight miles from Bedford. The coach set us down at the Golden Swan, a very good house, where we found the rooms large and clean, the beds comfortable, and the table abundantly supplied with good things. In these far-away taverns, private tables and parlours, are neither thought of nor wanted. You eat at what would be called in Europe a Table d'Hote; not served indeed with so much ceremony, but furnished with more substantial fare. Here you meet a few quiet permanent boarders, young lawyers or merchants of the place; and the host and hostess, plain people, who bestir themselves to make you as comfortable as possible; and you can always get your meal in peace and plenty, unless some unhappy prejudice sticks in your throat, and impedes your deglutition: such as, that vegetables can only be eaten with a silver folk; or the horror of eating peas with a knife.

"There are generally, besides the dining room, one or two apartments furnished and used as parlours, but common to all the boarders, who use them as members of the same family. The hours of breakfast and dinner are six and twelve; rather early for our eastern habits, but if you will go to bed at eight, you will find breakfast welcome at six next morning.

"Several coaches pass here every day, both east and west; but none of them stay all night; so that travellers who have stopped here cannot be sure of a departure; we therefore retired with the intention, though not the certainty of getting into the coach for Pittsburgh, which passes at three A.M. It had been raining all day, which prevented us from perambulating the village.

"Sure enough, at 3½ A.M., the coach from the east, bound to Pittsburgh, came rattling up to the door of

Typical Inn and Tavern on a Pennsylvania highway in the early 1800's.

our Hotel in Somerset, and we were soon waked, washed, and willingly wending on our westward way.''

From a feminine viewpoint, overnight stops at these establishments were sometimes a bit harrowing. In 1800 a woman named Sarah Anderson, traveling through western and central Pennsylvania, writes of one experience at an unidentified Inn:

"When we arrived at the inn, and found it full of men of a savage appearance, in an outlandish dress, our short interval of Joy was succeeded by perplexity and Terror. However, there was no alternative and we entered the house . . . One large, unfinished and un-furnished Room with a kitchen of equal dimensions, composed the whole of the building. Both the apart-ments were enlivened by an exhilarating fire, round which sat upwards of 20 persons, engaged in different scenes of the most turbulent merriment. Our arrival produced a momentary calm; and the cheerful readi-ness with which they made way for us and procured us seats around the fire convinced us that they were not strangers to the dictates of Humanity.

"Our new companions were a set of hunters; from their conversation and Behavior, we were led to con-clude that Humanity was their cardinal virtue. The Innkeeper had no spiritous Liquors; and they were therefore forced to practice temperance. This exasper-ated them so highly that they swore they would extir-pate his Signpost. So, out they marched in Battle Array, with purpose as sanguinary, against the Sign-post, as was entertained by Columbia's Heavenborn Band when they marched over the Mountains some years since upon a similar expedition (against the Whiskey Rebellion) and this exploit was crowned with similar Success, for upon arriving at the place of Ac-tion, there was no signpost to be found . . .

"The landlady declared it out of her power to pre-pare us any supper; but proferred to supply us with every article necessary to prepare Victuals for our-selves . . .''

Daily stage coach travel generally began at three o'clock in the morning. At the better taverns, before departure, the ladies were fortified with strong coffee and the gentlemen with something even stronger. Stops were made at taverns for breakfast and dinner, and after covering a distance of 40 to 50 miles over an 18-hour period, the weary passengers were deposited at an inn where they might, or might not, find com-fortable accommodations.

## Winter Travel

In sub-freezing winter weather, with a foot or more of snow on the roads, travel conditions were considerably improved. Most farmers and other landowners of the period had well-built sleighs for winter travel and preferred to delay their trips for supplies or inter-community visits until the first snowfall.

Wagons engaged in the freighting business crossed the mountains by road, driven by their owners, or by hired men. Most of the "wagoners," at least in the early years, were German. The hired wagoners received wages from $8 to $10 per month. The wagon journey from Philadelphia to Pittsburgh, a distance of 297 miles, ordinarily required about three weeks and the charge for freight transportation during the first decade of the 19th Century was about $5.00 a hundred weight.

## The Conestoga Wagon

Perhaps no other vehicle ever developed in America has played such a vital part in the history of the country's growth as the Conestoga wagon, built in Lancaster County, Pa.

This vehicle was developed by German wagon makers in the Conestoga Valley of Lancaster County before the French and Indian War. Its chief characteristic was the peculiar shape of the bottom which was designed to prevent the displacement of the cargo on rough or sloping roads. The floor of the wagon sloped upward both front and rear and to a less extent on each side. The ends flared outward at a 45° angle.

A huge vehicle, approximately 26' long, 11' high and weighing 3000 to 3500 pounds, the Conestoga wagon needed a strong six-horse team to pull it over (or through), most of the existing dirt roads of its era.

For its intended use, the workmanship on the wagon was superb. Its graceful boat-shaped bed was usually fashioned out of white oak for the frame and poplar for the boards. Flooring and side boards were half-inch or five-eights of an inch thick. The end gates were held in position by a chain and staple that allowed the gate to be dropped for loading and unloading. Many parts of the wagon bed were braced with iron, and hand-made rivets secured the boards to the frame.

Arching over the wagon bed was a series of soaring wooden hoops securely stapled to the side boards. Depending upon the size of the wagon, these might number from six to thirteen. Over them was stretched the familiar white top of homespun or canvas. Roped to the side boards and drawn taut over the projecting end bows, the canopy stretched twenty-four feet or more, giving the impression of a great sheltering poke bonnet.

Axles and bolsters were made out of tough hickory wood, and the hubs from black or sour gum, a fibrous wood with high splitting resistance. The rough roads traveled by the wagons made it essential that axles, hubs, wheel spokes and felloes be sturdily built. For getting out of miry places and crossing streams the iron tire rim had to have a broad surface. Experience proved a four-inch rim most satisfactory, but widths varied from two to ten inches.

Iron tires were usually made of two pieces of iron a half inch thick, bent to the exact size of the wheel and welded at both joints. A fire was built around the iron

**The Conestoga Wagon, which transported millions of Americans for well over a century.**

rim and when sufficiently hot it was lifted off by means of tongs, placed around the wooden wheel and hammered into place. Cold water was then poured over the hot iron to shrink it to a tight fit. The front wheels of the wagon, as a freighter, stood about 3 feet 6 inches high, and the rear wheels might vary from 4 feet, to 4 feet 6 inches.

The Conestoga Wagoner, unlike the driver of the later prairie schooner, did not ride inside his wagon but either walked beside his team, rode the wheelhorse – the rearmost horse on the left – or perched precariously on the "lazy board." This last was a stout oak board that pulled out from beneath the wagon bed immediately in front of the left rear wheel. From this position the driver had a good view of the road ahead and from it he or his assistant operated the brake. Driving from the left side of the Conestoga, when all other vehicles were driven from the right, is believed to have established the present practice of driving American vehicles from the left.

A completed wagon, capable of holding five hogsheads or thirty barrels of flour, cost about $250. The six powerful Conestoga horses that pulled the wagon were valued in the vicinity of a thousand or twelve hundred dollars.

Each horse carried a set of bells attached to a special yoke on its collar. The bells varied in size for each horse. Thus, riding behind a six-horse Bell Team on a Conestoga wagon, customarily painted red, white and blue, was a cheerful and melodious experience. Tradition indicated that the bells were surrendered, when the rig was stuck in the mud, to any helpful fellow-traveler who pulled it out.

Ordinarily, however, this sturdy land-ship with its powerful six-horse team found few obstacles that it could not surmount, on even the worst roads.

The first Conestoga wagons were built about 1750 and by the end of the century they were a common sight on Pennsylvania roads wherever heavy freight or farm produce was transported.

After 1812, when the great westward push began, thousands upon thousands of these wagons were built in Lancaster County for pioneers headed into the new western territories. The familiar silhouette of this wagon became almost synonomous with the Great Western Movement, which carried the White Man through to the Pacific Ocean, and completed the displacement of the American Indians from their former homelands.

A luxurious "Coach and Four" of the mid-nineteenth century. (Courtesy of Wm. L. Seigford.)

Cross section of an early macadamized road in England, as designed by John McAdam. (Courtesy, The Asphalt Institute.)

# Chapter V

# THE FIRST STONE-SURFACED ROADS

The idea of building roads with stone is not a modern concept. The Romans had developed a network of excellent stone roads throughout the countries which they conquered two thousand years ago. The Roman roads had a massive foundation of two courses of cut block, a layer of coarse aggregate and mortar, a layer of fine aggregate with mortar and a final layer of carefully fitted stone paving blocks, mortared in place with a crown at the center and curbs on each side.

Portions of these roads can still be found, even as far north as England, a testimonial to the advanced highway engineering ability of the Romans.

Unfortunately, during the "dark ages" following the fall of the Roman Empire, these magnificent highways were abandoned, buried or allowed to deteriorate to the point that they were useless for travel.

It was not until the 18th Century that attention turned to the improvement of inland travel in Europe. Among the new breed of highway pioneers at that time was Pierre Marie Jerome Tresaguet, Inspector General of Roads & Bridges in France in 1775; England's John Metcalf, a blind engineer, who reached the peak of his activities in England about 1780; Scotland's Thomas Telford (1757-1843) founder of the Institute of Civil Engineers; and John Loudon McAdam (1756-1836), also a Scotsman.

Each of these men developed a highway construction method using various types and sizes of stone, with attention to proper drainage, as well as economy of construction. Tresaguet, Metcalf and Telford all insisted upon a very heavy stone foundation with varying degrees of smaller size stones for the upper layers of road surface. McAdam, on the other hand, developed a less expensive 10"-deep (maximum) road cross-section which involved clean, broken stones of uniform size throughout, all "passing a 2-inch ring" in size, and none exceeding six ounces each, in weight.

## John McAdam

McAdam's theory was that a heavy stone foundation was not needed, but that the ground surface under the road would support the stone surface and traffic, provided that the ground was kept dry by a raised road center, impervious construction, and generous run-off gutters at each side, in addition to proper road maintenance. Also McAdam felt that the road need not be laid as thick for light traffic as for heavy. "Do not make the traffic to suit the roads; make the roads to suit the traffic," he argued. Further, he theorized that the more traffic the road received, the more compact and impervious to moisture the road mass would become.

All of these stone road building methods were, of course, a great improvement over the old dirt roads previously in use, but it was McAdam's flexible base design which proved the best and most economical in the long run. Without doubt John Loudon McAdam, more than any other early road designer, can be called the "father of modern roads." Even his name has become part of the English language. The "macadamized" roads we know today now have a protective asphalt covering, but their sub-surface construction, with some modifications, it still almost identical to that prescribed by John McAdam.

As a young man, John McAdam lived with his uncle in New York City, while experimenting with model road cross sections, as a hobby. When the Revolution broke out, he sided with the Crown, and as a Tory, fled Manhattan in 1783 to return to his native Scotland. He held various government posts while investigating the unspeakably bad roads of Great Britain, at his own expense. Improvement of British roads to meet the needs of the dawning Industrial Revolution became an obsession with McAdam, and he traveled throughout Scotland and England preaching that Britain could only prosper and grow in stature by building and maintaining adequate roads. In 1816, he had his chance as General Surveyor of the Bristol (England) Municipality to prove his point. He was in direct charge of 146 miles of stage and wagon roads in and around Bristol. Immediately, he set to work to apply his theories to these roads. So successful was his work, not to mention his reorganization of the inefficient political system of road maintenance, that his roads were soon declared the best in Britain and visitors traveled from far and wide to see how he had done it.

In America, where road engineers were keeping a watchful eye open for new highway developments, John McAdam's work in Great Britain was soon common knowledge. Some stone roads had already been built in this country, but most of these were now torn up and rebuilt using the McAdam method. The "Age of Good Roads" at last appeared to be at hand.

John Loudon McAdam (1756-1836), father of the flexible-foundation stone road in Great Britain and United States. (Courtesy the American Trucking Association and the Asphalt Institute.)

## The Philadelphia-Lancaster Turnpike

The first road between Philadelphia and Lancaster (early known as Philadelphia's "Bread-basket") was called the "King's Highway". It was built in 1733 and it followed, in part, the old Allegheny Indian Path, and was financed by the colonial government. The word "highway" is really a misnomer, as it was simply a dirt road, which at times of rain and snow became an almost impassable morass. Agitation for a better connection between the two cities caused the creation of a special commission in 1786, which resulted in the chartering of the Philadelphia and Lancaster Turnpike April 7, 1792, to build the first long-distance, hard-surface road in the Country. The charter indicated that the new road was to be built "from the west side of the Schuylkill River opposite the city of Philadelphia, so as to pass over the bridge on Brandywine Creek, near Downingtown, from thence to Witmer's Bridge on the Conestoga Creek, and thence to the east end of King street, where the buildings cease, in the borough of Lancaster."

The road was to be fifty feet wide; twenty-four feet to be "an artificial road, bedded with wood, stone or gravel, and any other hard substance, well compacted together, a sufficient depth to secure a solid foundation of the same . . . faced with gravel, or stone pounded, or other small, hard substance, in such manner as to secure a firm, and as much as the materials will admit, an even surface, rising toward the middle by a gradual arch." Maximum grade on the route was to be 7%.

The money was raised by stock companies and the State is said to have subscribed for part of the Stock. Stock in the road was advertised at $300 per share. Each share was a sheepskin document; as many sheepskins were used as there were shares. At the top was a picture of the road, with a Conestoga wagon approaching a tollgate.

Of the building of the turnpike road one historian has written:

"There was between Philadelphia and Lancaster no town but merely a settlement, and thus the little army of road builders cut their way through what was pretty nearly a wilderness, sleeping sometimes in little

shacks that they built by the way. Their work must have been arduous. Often they would interrupt it to replenish their larder with bear meat and with fish. Often, too, they would be in terror of the Indians, for braves in war paint ran silently in single file through the great forest, busy with some little internecine war, and sometimes white men were taken unawares, bound and tortured terribly by the savages.''

The new road was constructed of broken limestone and gravel of many different sizes with no particular attempt at creating a heavy stone foundation. It was officially opened in December of 1795. The traffic passing over it compacted it and made it firmer. It was a good road and attracted wide attention. After McAdam's success in Bristol, England, the road was dug up and re-laid with crushed stone, all passing a two-inch ring.

The original construction cost of the project was $464,142.31. A three-arched stone bridge across Brandywine Creek, costing $12,000 was part of the project. The average cost for each of the seventy miles was

Milestone on the Philadelphia-Lancaster Turnpike, indicating mileage to both extremities of the road.

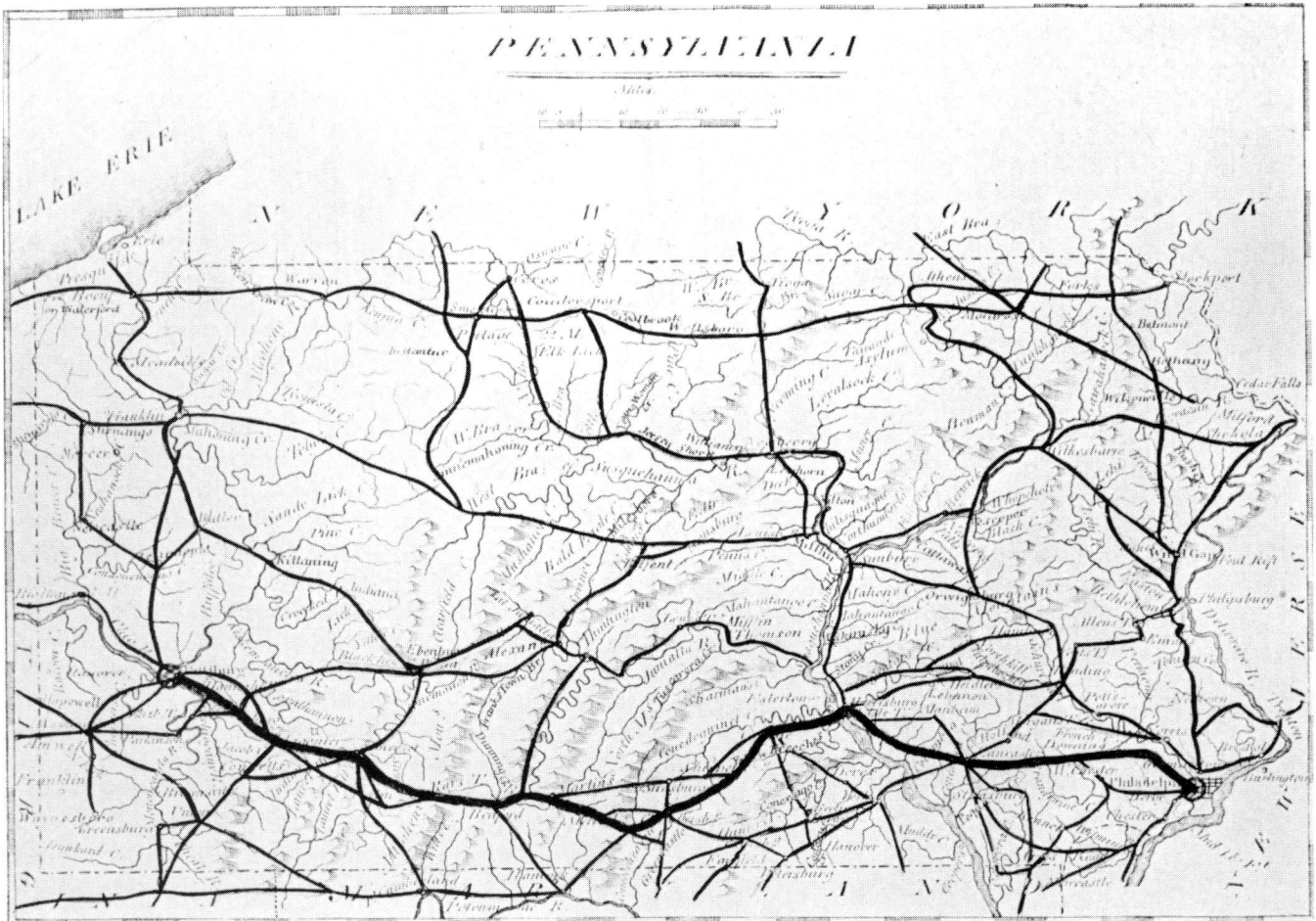

Road development in Pennsylvania, circa 1812. Most of the routes shown were still dirt roads. The Pennsylvania road (heavy line) was stone-surfaced its full length, Philadelphia to Pittsburgh, by 1820.

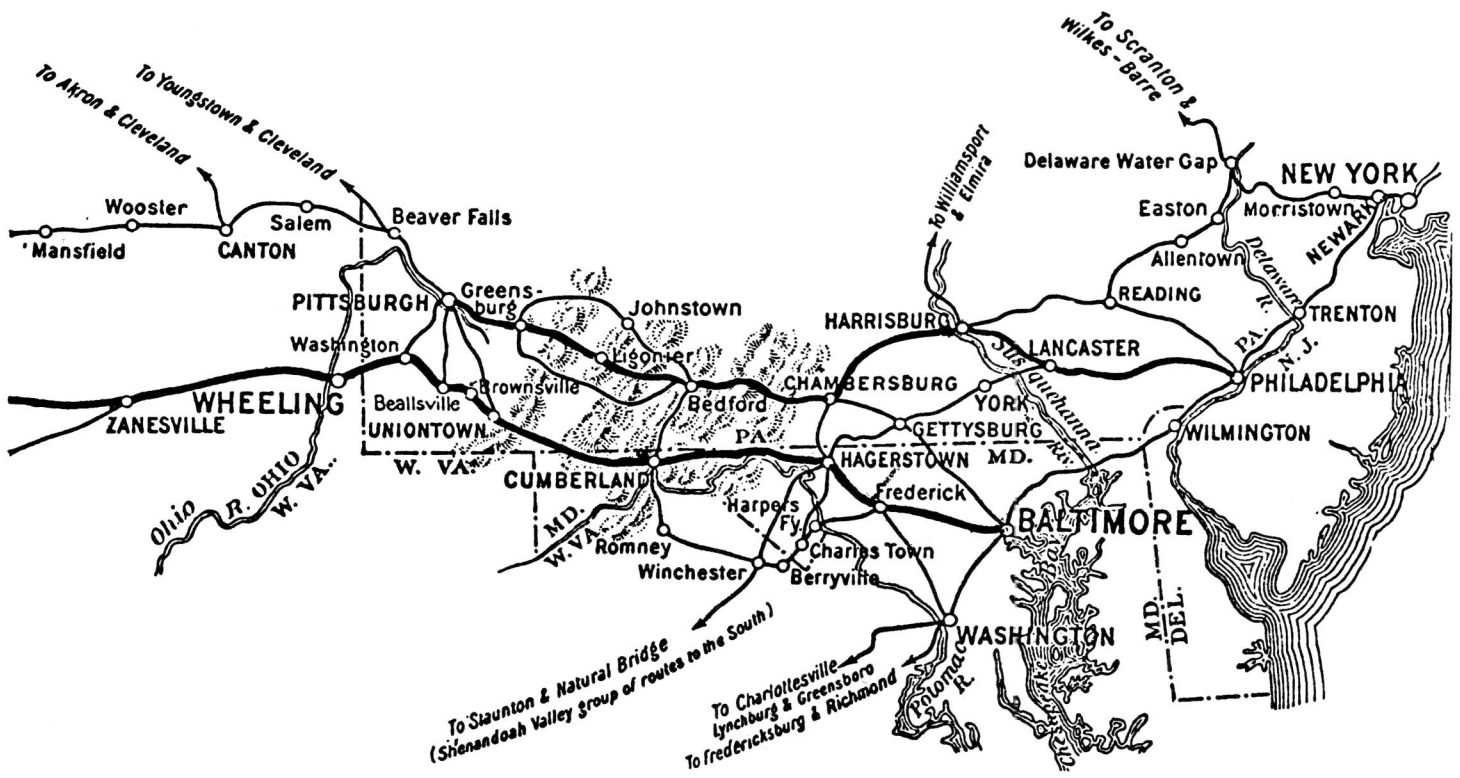

The two major roads to the west in the early 1800's – the National Road, opened to traffic in 1818, and the Pennsylvania Road, in prior use, but not completely macadamized until 1820.

$6,629. Those who advanced the money looked forward to returns through the funds collected at the nine toll gates. Four of these were on the first twenty miles out of Philadelphia, while the last of the nine was at Witmer's Bridge, Lancaster. The rate charged, for a horse and rider, or for a led horse, for each ten miles, was one-sixteenth of a dollar, while a two-wheeled sulky was charged twice as much. A coach, chariot, stage wagon, phaeton, with two horses and four wheels, paid a quarter of a dollar for ten miles, but if such a vehicle was drawn by four horses, the charge was fifty per cent greater.

The number of toll gates was later increased to thirteen to prevent evasion of tolls by "shun-piking," or by-passing the gates.

With the increase in commerce to the west by way of York County, the Lancaster Turnpike was extended to Columbia, and Wrights Ferry, in 1806, where the first Columbia-Wrightsville Bridge, built in 1812, ultimately carried traffic through to York and Chambersburg.

The Philadelphia and Lancaster Turnpike Company, whose charter was not officially dissolved until February 25th, 1902, thus introduced a period of good road building in America, at least until the canal and railroad era. Pennsylvania took the lead in building privately-financed turnpikes, most of them stone surfaced. By 1828, there were 3110 miles of chartered turnpike roads in Pennsylvania, costing over $8,000,000.

## The Pennsylvania Road

The "Pennsylvania Road" of the early 1800's leading from Philadelphia to Pittsburgh, was actually developed over a period of nearly 70 years. The old Allegheny Indian Path, the Raystown Path, the Philadelphia-Lancaster Turnpike, James Burd's Road and Forbes Road, all played a part in the evolution of this great highway to the West.

The first State-sponsored action for such a road began after the Revolution, when Hugh Henry Brackenridge spear-headed a movement to obtain State aid for improvement of East-West transportation in Pennsylvania. As a result of his efforts the Pennsylvania Legislation in the Spring of 1784, authorized a lottery to raise $42,000 for the purpose. In September 1785, another act of the Legislature provided for the appointment of three commissioners to lay out a highway from the western part of Cumberland County to Pittsburgh and appropriated £2000, (about $5,333) for the expense of the commissioners and to assist townships containing difficult mountains or other broken ground in opening and building the highway. The Commissioners made their first report in November 1787 and the route was confirmed as far west as Bedford.

The Pennsylvania Assembly was not satisfied with the work west of that point, however, and new surveys were ordered which were not completed until

1790. In the meantime, however, work was underway on the section east of Bedford, but the money appropriated was found to be insufficient for making the road 60-feet wide as the law directed and in January 1788, the State ordered that the road from the east side of Sideling Hill to the west side of Ray's Hill "be cleared and made good and sufficient by 12-feet on the side of the hills, or among the rocks and room to be made for not less than three wagons to draw off the one side of the narrow places at a convenient distance for others to pass by."

In 1791, the Assembly included £500 for the road from Bedford to Pittsburgh in an Omnibus Act for Internal Improvements, and additional sums were appropriated in 1792 and 1793.

Thus was created the great Pennsylvania Road from Philadelphia to Pittsburgh, via Lancaster, Harrisburg, Shippensburg and Bedford, following the main line of the old Forbes Road across the mountains to Ligonier and then taking a course a few miles south of that road through Greensburg to Pittsburgh, approximately the route of the modern Lincoln Highway. This became one of the main routes by which settlers and travelers by the thousands, arriving in the Port of Philadelphia, migrated to the new Western Territories.

The term "Pennsylvania Road" was first applied to the route by Continental Congress at the beginning of the Revolutionary War. During its early years of operation most of it was dirt road, subject to the usual mud holes in wet weather. However, the completion of the new Philadelphia-Lancaster Turnpike in 1795 was the first in a series of steps to "turnpike", or stone-surface, the entire route to Pittsburgh. This was accomplished, stage by stage, over the ensuing years and by 1820 it was stone-surfaced all the way.

## The National Road

The National Road, variously referred to as the "Cumberland Road," the "National Pike," the "United States," or the "Old Pike," was envisioned by George Washington as a means of connecting the coastal States with the new northern territories developing west of the Alleghenies. The need for strong political ties with the hardy pioneering settlements in the territories of Ohio, Indiana, and Illinois was readily apparent. Because of extreme communication difficulties east and west over the Alleghenies these western settlers did much of their trading "down

The Somerfield Bridge, sometimes called the "Great Crossing Bridge", where the National Road crossed the Youghiogheny River, now under water from a flood-control reservoir. (Photo by the Pennsylvania Historical and Museum Commission.)

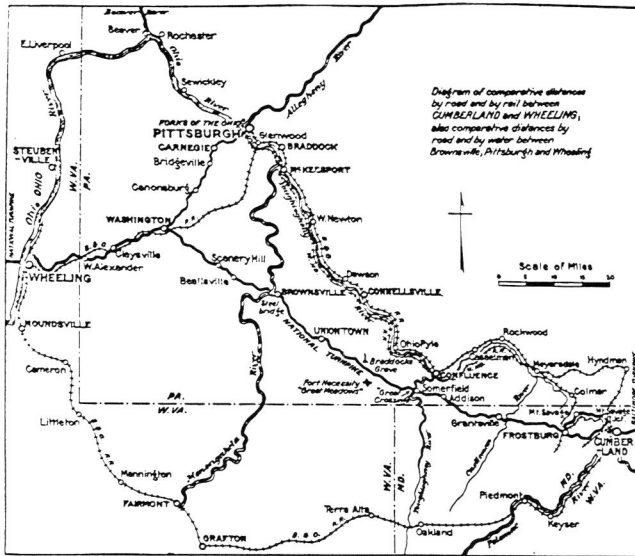

Route of the National Road through Southwestern Pennsylvania. (From "The National Road" by Robert Bruce.)

George Washington did not live to see it, but the first step toward the building of the National Road occurred when Congress on April 30, 1802, passed an Act to enable the people of Ohio to form a State government and obtain admission to the Union. One of the provisions of this Act read as follows:

"One-twentieth of the net proceeds of the lands lying within said State (Ohio) sold by Congress shall be applied to the laying out and making public roads leading from the navigable waters emptying into the Atlantic, to the Ohio, to the said State and through the same, such roads to be laid out under the authority of Congress, with the consent of the several States through which the roads shall pass."

The wording and the implications of this Act were the subject of considerable controversy before and after its passage. Prior to this all roads in the country had been conceived, chartered and financed (either publicly or privately) by the various States themselves. The States-Rightists argued that the federal government did not have the constitutional right to take upon itself a transportation function previously handled by the States.

The advocates of the National Road numbered in their ranks such influential personages as Albert Gallatin, Henry Clay, Thomas Jefferson, and James Madison – who pointed out that the need was so great that united and immediate action was necessary by the U.S. Congress. They temporarily satisfied the States Rights members of Congress by inserting the phrase "with the consent of the several States" through which the road would pass, and arranging the financing (at least initially) by means of revenue collected from the State of Ohio – the chief beneficiary of the Road.

The spectre of unconstitutionality hung over the

river" on the Ohio and Mississippi to New Orleans, and some even across the border into Canada. The French and British influence, consequently, in the territories west of the Alleghenies was very strong. As George Washington put it, "The Western States hang upon a pivot. The touch of a feather will turn them any way." Diplomatic pressure from foreign powers might have easily made them forget their loyalty to the remote thirteen states "back East." A strong life-line was needed to bind these new territories to the Union.

Searights Tollhouse, standing since 1835, on the National Road (U. S. Route 40) several miles northwest of Uniontown, Pa. A toll-gate across the old road at the left prevented traffic from passing until toll had been paid. (Photo by the author.)

34

One of the Bicentennial Wagon Trains passes through York, Pa., enroute to Valley Forge for July 4, 1976 ceremonies. Scenes like this were common on the National Road when it first opened in 1818! (Photo by the author.)

National Road throughout its entire history – each new administration re-examining the issue, as new appropriations were required for the Road's extension and maintenance. During their administrations, Presidents Monroe and Jackson both argued that the federal government had no authority to maintain the National Road, with the result that, in 1834, it reverted to the states. Had the National Road been ruled constitutional, it is possible that the railroads of the United States might later have been built and financed by the federal government, rather than private enterprise.

Despite opposition, however, President Jefferson in 1805 appointed a committee to investigate various routes into Ohio from east-coast seaports or riverports, including Philadelphia, Baltimore, Washington and Richmond. It was the committee's recommendation that a good road be built from Cumberland, Maryland, on the Potomac, in a northwesterly direction, across Pennsylvania and Virginia (now West Virginia) to connect with the Ohio River at Wheeling.

Cumberland, like Carlisle in Pennsylvania, had been for many years the "jumping off point" for individual horse travelers or pack-horse trains across the Alleghenies. Cumberland was connected with Washington and Baltimore by a road which Maryland was in the process of improving.

## Construction Begins

On March 29, 1806, an Act was signed into law by President Thomas Jefferson "to regulate the laying out and making a road from Cumberland, in the State of Maryland, to the State of Ohio," and three commissioners were appointed to get things started. $30,000 was appropriated by the Act and some guidelines were laid down for the construction of the road as follows:

"All parts of the road which the President shall direct to be made, in case the trees are standing, shall be cleared the whole width of four rods and the road shall be raised in the middle of the carriageway with stone, earth or gravel or sand, or a combination of some or all of them, leaving or making, as the case may be, a ditch or water course on each side and contiguous to said carriage-way, and in no instance shall there be an elevation in said road, when finished, greater than an angle of five degrees with the horizon. But the manner of making such road in every other particular, is left to the direction of the President." The National Road was built by the U.S. Government under the supervision of the War Department.

Permission to build the road was gained from each of the States through which it passed, Pennsylvania

A typical toll-house on an early Pennsylvania turnpike. The name "turnpike" derives from the gate (or pike) which prevented wagons or carriages from proceeding until they had paid their toll. The gate had to be turned aside, or raised, to let them pass. The gate-keeper generally lived on the premises, and was on call day and night. (Sketch by Philip Hoffmann.)

making the condition that the road should pass through Uniontown and Washington (Pa.).

Delayed by the War of 1812, construction progressed very slowly. The first ten-mile contract out of Cumberland, Maryland, was let in 1811, and by 1817 the road had crawled over the Alleghenies by way of Nemocolin's Path, over Negro mountain at an elevation of 2325 feet, down the Youghiogheny River, along Braddock Road, through the Laurel Hill Range to Brownsville (within reach of Pittsburgh) then to Washington, and finally to Wheeling on the Ohio River.

Officially opened in 1818, the hard-surfaced National Road immediately proved its worth. Although many pioneers coming from New England, New Jersey and Pennsylvania found the partially-paved Pennsylvania Road more direct, heavy traffic began at once on the National Road, out of Baltimore and points south. Conestoga Wagons, stagecoaches, mail carriers, traders, freight wagons, not to mention Ohio farmers and settlers coming east with produce and returning with much needed supplies – all added to the traffic.

So heavily traveled was this section that within a few years the Road was badly in need of repairs – the stone fill having been used sparingly and not too scientifically in the original construction.

Under considerable pressure by the friends of the National Road, State-Rightist President Monroe in 1824 finally signed a bill providing additional funds for its maintenance and extension. Part of the pavement of the old road was dug up, the foundation raked smooth and a course of uniform stone 30-feet wide was laid, using the McAdam system. The side ditches were deepened and culverts cleared. Depth of the stone varied from 3" to 9" depending upon local conditions.

The National Road was originally planned to run on to the Mississippi River and agreements similar to the one with Ohio were made by the federal government with Indiana, in 1816, and Illinois in 1818 as these States joined the Union. The Road's most vital function was to provide a route to supplement the heavily traveled Pennsylvania Road across the Alleghenies, which function it performed admirably in the critical early decades of the 19th century.

Its extension west of Wheeling was a slow and painful process, requiring new appropriations from Congress with each addition.

In 1825, appropriations were made to continue the Road to Zanesville, a project not completed till 1833. The next extension was to Springfield, Ohio, in 1838. Indianapolis, Indiana was the center of the next major operation on the Road, with sections being built both east and west from that city, but finished by the Wayne County Turnpike Company in 1850 after the federal government had turned the Road back to the States. The old National Road construction finally ground to a stop at Vandalia, Illinois after federal funds totaling $6,759,257 had been spent on it. The last few sections were still unmacadamized, and due to the pressure of competition with canals and railroads, little further was done to improve the road in Illinois. The States of Maryland, Pennsylvania, Ohio and Virginia accepted completed portions of the National Road from the federal government between 1831 and 1834, and immediately set up legislation to permit the erection of toll gates to provide revenue for its maintenance. In Pennsylvania, these gates were located near Petersburg, Mt. Washington, Searights, Beallsville, Washington and West Alexander.

The Pennsylvania Road, with its hard surface paving (completed in 1820) continued to share a heavy portion of the east-west traffic to the new western states and territories with the National Road, until the advent of the canals and railroads.

Badly damaged by a flood and ice jam in the winter of 1902, Theodore Burr's famous "Camelback Bridge" at Harrisburg was removed after more than eighty years of service. (East section shown.)

# Chapter VI

# PENNSYLVANIA'S PIONEER BRIDGE BUILDERS

As the pattern of Pennsylvania's highway system began to unfold in the early nineteenth century, it was obvious that the ferries which first handled all major river crossings were incapable of keeping up with the volume of traffic which was developing. Long delays at ferry crossings, when wagons and horses sometimes lined up for miles, and the dangers of river crossings in high water, forced turnpike companies and other agencies to investigate the design and construction of permanent river crossings at many points in the State. At major river crossings, private bridge companies were formed, with the blessing of the State legislature, to raise money, hire experienced designers, and construct bridges, which were then amortized and maintained by the tolls charged for their use.

In the year 1800, few experienced bridge designers were to be found in Pennsylvania. Those available were either inventors of untried structures, looking for a chance to put their theories into practice, or designers who had received prior training on bridges already built in New England.

Pennsylvania, therefore, became a testing ground for many new and unusual bridge structures, some of which were duplicated nowhere else in this country or abroad. The men who designed and built these bridges were a new breed of engineers, whose personalities and surprising ingenuity form the substance of this chapter, not to mention the illustrations of the amazing structures which they erected – some of which lasted a few years – others for many decades.

Sketch of one span of James Finley's patented chain bridge of 1801. The similarity between his design and the modern cable suspension bridge is strikingly apparent. (Sketch by the author.)

## James Finley

One of the "unsung heroes" among early American bridge pioneers was James Finley, a native of Fayette County, Pennsylvania. Little has been recorded of the life of this western Pennsylvanian, perhaps because his patented "chain bridge" was too far ahead of its time. Indeed, except for his use of chains rather than the then unknown wire cable, his basic bridge design was virtually identical to that of the Delaware River Bridge at Philadelphia, George Washington Bridge at New York, or the Golden Gate Bridge at San Francisco.

Believed to be the son of a Reverend James Finley, who migrated to western Pennsylvania before 1770, young "James Finley, Esquire" became, in the late 1700's, a political figure in Fayette County, serving at various times as Justice of the Peace, County Commissioner, State Representative and one of the Judges of the Court of Common Pleas of Fayette County. His term as judge began sometime before 1795, as we find a record of a case pleaded before Judge Finley on May 5, 1795.

A thoroughly successful lawyer and highly respected member of his community, Judge Finley in later life also demonstrated his ability as an inventor and engineer by developing a chain suspension bridge which was without doubt the first pier-type metal suspension bridge in the World. In previous rope-type suspension bridges, the floor had been laid directly on the catenary, whereas Finley's bridge had a level floor suspended from a looped span with catenary sagging one-seventh of the width of the major spans.

After experimenting with models and applying for patents, Finley built his first bridge over Jacobs Creek in 1801 on the principal turnpike between Connellsville and Mount Pleasant. A contemporary described the bridge as follows: "The bridge which Judge Finley has undertaken to erect at the expense ($600) of Fayette and Westmoreland Counties is now complete. Its construction is on principles entirely new and is perhaps the only one of its kind in the world. It is solely supported on two iron chains extending over four piers, 14 feet higher than the bridge, fastened in the ground at the ends, describing a curved line, touching the level of the bridge on the center. The bridge is of 70 foot span and 13 feet wide; the chains are of inch square bars in links from five to ten feet long; but so that there is a joist where each pendant must bear."

Although Finley's first bridge was built in 1801, he did not receive patent title until 1808.

Writing with great confidence of his invention in a paper published in June 1810, James Finley said, "There are eight of these bridges erected now, the largest of which is that at the Falls of the Schuylkill (Philadelphia) 306 feet span, aided by an intermediate pier, the passage eighteen feet wide, supported by two chains of inch and a half square bar . . . There are two erected near Brownsville, in Fayette County, the spans 120 and 112 feet, inch and a quarter iron, breadth 18 and 15 feet. There was one built last season over the Neshamany in Buck's County, near 200 feet span, one pier . . . Another incorporated company at Pawling's Ford, on Schuylkill, are taking measures to erect one this summer, at that place, near 200 feet span without any pier." He also referred to bridges out of the State which he had designed.

Subsequent records indicate that Finley also designed two bridges across the Lehigh River, one 475 feet long at Northampton, Pa., in 1811, and a second at Allentown, with two spans of 230 feet each, in 1815.

A number of other Finley bridges were constructed in the next few years, in Pennsylvania and surrounding states, mainly built by others on Finley's patents.

Finley's first bridge at Jacobs Creek survived until

1825 when it broke under a six-horse team, but it was repaired and put in service again. His largest bridge, at Schuylkill Falls, Philadelphia, broke down when crossed by herd of cattle in 1811. The owners sold their rights to Josiah White and Erskine Hazard, later renowned as builders of the Lehigh Canal. After a repair job and second collapse in 1816 under weight of ice and snow, White and Hazard replaced the old bridge with a small suspension bridge for pedestrian travel, only, using as the suspending medium, wire from their nearby rolling mill and wire plant. Thus to White and Erskine goes credit for having built the first wire suspension bridge in the world. About Finley's bridges, it can be said that his suspension principle was correct, but the material he used couldn't survive the continued stress and vibration of heavy loading. He was about a half century ahead of his time.

## Timothy Palmer

Timothy Palmer, a native of Newburyport, Massachusetts, was one of the most ingenious of the pioneer bridge builders. Completely self-taught and a self-styled "master carpenter and bridge architect," he patented his original bridge design in 1797. His reputation was made in building roofless combination arch and truss-type, long-span wooden bridges over the Merrimack, Kennebee and Connecticut Rivers in New England, not to mention his arched span across the Potomac River at Georgetown, Md.

Thus, when the directors of the Schuylkill Permanent Bridge Company of Philadelphia elected in 1801 to build a wooden structure across the Schuylkill instead of the stone arch bridge originally planned, they called on Timothy Palmer as the best-known "wood bridge" man in this country, to complete the job.

The "Permanent Bridge," located where Market Street now crosses the Schuylkill at Philadelphia, became Timothy Palmer's best-known work. During the Revolution, while the British were in possession of Philadelphia, there was a pontoon bridge at this point and later a plankfloor bridge on floating logs. The Permanent Bridge was needed as the final link in the Lancaster-Philadelphia Turnpike. Palmer and his workmen completed the structure on two piers built earlier, between 1801 and 1805, at a cost of $300,000. The Permanent Bridge had an over-all length, including abutments and wing walls, of 1300 feet. The center span was 195 feet long with a 12 foot rise, and the two side spans were 150 feet each.

The trusswork was sufficiently completed on January 1, 1805 to permit the bridge to be opened to traffic. Palmer would have let the structure open, but Judge Richard Peters, president of the bridge company, had other ideas. He asked Palmer if the bridge would not last longer, if protected from the wind and rain by a weather-proof covering. Palmer admitted that the life span of the bridge might be increased from the normal 10 to 12 years to 30 to 40 years by doing this and a roof and sidewalls were added. Thus was created the *first covered bridge in America*. As Palmer had predicted, the bridge stood with little attention until 1850, when a fire gutted it and it was rebuilt and widened for an additional car track.

Palmer's second and last covered bridge was erected to cross the Delaware River between Easton, Pennsylvania and Philipsburg, New Jersey. Built in 1805, this two-span, covered structure weathered storm and flood for 91 years, being replaced by a steel bridge in 1896.

After completion of the Easton Bridge, Timothy Palmer spent his last years in semi-retirement at his Massachusetts home. He lived long enough to see the principle of the covered bridge applied to countless wooden structures in Pennsylvania and other eastern states.

39

**Timothy Palmer's "Permanent Bridge" across the Schuylkill at Philadelphia – America's first covered bridge. (Sketch by the author.)**

The first Columbia-Wrightsville Bridge, built by Jonathan Walcott in 1812 – world's longest covered wooden bridge. (Courtesy Historical Society of York County.)

## Jonathan Walcott

The challenge of erecting bigger and better bridges in Pennsylvania attracted another of New England's self-taught bridge designers – Jonathan Walcott of Windham, Connecticut, who had established a reputation as the builder of three sizable, uncovered arch bridges over the lower Connecticut River. Walcott was only 36 years old when in 1812 he approached the managers of a newly formed bridge company in Columbia, Pa. who were desirous of spanning the Susquehanna River to extend the Columbia-Philadelphia Turnpike into York County, without resorting to the Wrights Ferry crossing. Walcott had keen competition in bidding for the bridge construction, against three other Connecticut bridge builders, and two more from Pennsylvania. He elected to team up with two local mason-carpenters, Henry and Samuel Slaymaker, who collectively offered to build the bridge for $150,000 – and got the contract!

While none of them realized it at the time, the trio succeeded in building the world's longest covered wooden bridge of all time – over a mile long, (5,690

feet) carried on a total of twenty-eight piers, an unbelievable accomplishment, with only manpower and horsepower available to help them do the work. The bridge was Walcott's masterpiece, and he retired to Connecticut, worn out and ill from his exertions, to die a few years later.

## Louis Wernwag

Born in Würtemberg, Germany, Louis Wernwag migrated to Philadelphia as a young man of 18 years, where he started building mills, mill wheels and machinery to make whetstones and nails. His first attempt at bridge building was made in 1810-11 when he successfully built two light wooden bridges to take the Post Road from Philadelphia to New York over Neshaminy and Frankford Creeks north of Philadelphia. Both these ingenious bridges contained draw spans to permit the passage of masted vessels.

When Philadelphians organized a company to bridge the Schuylkill River at a site known as "Upper Ferry" in 1812, they selected Wernwag as the de-

signer, because of his local reputation as a long-time master-mechanic as well as the builder of the first draw bridges in the area.

The Upper Ferry Bridge was Wernwag's ultimate masterpiece. In its day it was the longest single arch wooden bridge in America, with a clear span of 340 feet from bank to bank, unimpeded by central piers. With a rock foundation for the eastern end and 499 piles to provide a firm foundation for the western abutment, it carried the road-way 38 feet above its end foundations at the mid-stream over a graceful arch, heavily supported by truss work tied to an overhead arch which also included a roof and sidewalls. It was almost immediately dubbed "The Colossus" by the local citizenry. Ornate entrances were constructed at each end and it became one of Philadelphia's "show-places."

His reputation as a bridge builder firmly established, Louis Wernwag went on to build some 26 additional bridges in Pennsylvania, Maryland, Virginia, Ohio and Delaware. His Pennsylvania enterprises included bridges across the Delaware at New Hope, another Schuylkill Bridge at Reading, a bridge over the Susquehanna north branch at Wilkes Barre and, in Pittsburgh, some of that growing city's first bridges across the Allegheny and Monongahela.

During his bridge building career in Pennsylvania, he lived at Pawling's Ford where he established the Phoenix ironworks, consisting of shops and buildings, financed by Philadelphia capital (where he built still another Schuylkill River Bridge) – a settlement now known as Phoenixville, Pa. A decline in business after the War of 1812 caused the Phoenix Works to fail, and Wernwag transferred his activities to Conowingo, Maryland, and later, to Harper's Ferry, then in Virginia. A number of bridges, in and near these locations are Wernwag-designed.

Wernwag died at Harpers Ferry in 1843. His famous "Colossus" might easily have outlasted him but it was destroyed by fire in 1838, to be replaced by another history-making span, Col. Charles Ellet's suspension bridge.

**Louis Wernwag's famous "Colossus," crossing the Schuylkill at "Upper Ferry," Philadelphia. (Courtesy Pennsylvania Historical and Museum Commission.)**

Western Section of Theodore Burr's famous "Camelback" Bridge at Harrisburg. Note Cumberland Valley Railroad Bridge in background.

## Theodore Burr

No relation of Aaron Burr, Theodore Burr, born in Torrington, Connecticut in 1771, became equally well-known in his own right. After studying the arch-truss combinations of the contemporary wooden bridge builders, and, after considerable experimentation and the building of several models, Burr developed an arch-supported truss carrying a level roadway and patented in 1804. This became known as the "Burr Truss" and ultimately formed the basis for many of the covered bridges built in United States in the 1800's. Its distinguishing feature was a curved arch with ends firmly toed into the adjoining piers and supporting the upper and lower horizontal "chords" which formed the support for the bridge floor and roof. Multiple king posts between chords, each firmly pegged to the arch, completed the structure.

Burr's first important bridge, which some consider his masterpiece, was a four-span crossing at Troy, New York, the first over the Hudson River, with clear-spans varying from 154 to 180 feet in length.

In 1726, James Trent had been granted the right to operate a ferry at Trent's Town to provide a crossing of the Delaware River north of Philadelphia on the important Philadelphia-New York road. Following the Revolution, traffic increased so rapidly on this road that New Jersey officially recognized in 1798 the need for "a good and permanent bridge" across the Delaware at Trent's Town, a recommendation seconded by the Pennsylvania Assembly.

The Delaware River Bridge Company was formed, with General John Beatty as president, and Theodore Burr was commissioned to build the bridge. Burr completed his structure between 1804 and 1806, at a total cost of $180,000. The bridge had five spans varying from 161 to 203 feet in length and lasted for ninety years. During the War of 1812 the Trenton Bridge became of strategic importance on this inland turnpike when the British blockaded the American ports. His reputation as a bridge-builder thus established, Burr decided that Pennsylvania offered him his most challenging field of operation, particularly when the Pennsylvania legislature authorized four new bridge companies to build spans across the Susquehanna at Northumberland, Harrisburg, Columbia and McCall's Ferry. Burr, with supreme confidence, bid on all four and obtained contracts for all but the Columbia crossing.

He began work on the first of these three major bridges at Northumberland, a twin crossing of the North Branch between Northumberland and Sunbury, in 1812. He decided to handle all three jobs on a "mass production" basis, obtaining the tremendous quantities of lumber needed from a huge saw mill which he erected at Chenango Point (now Binghamton), New York, hiring raftsmen to float the lumber down the North Branch and main stem of the Susquehanna to his various sites.

Never one to do anything on a small scale, Burr also contracted for two more bridges along the way, one at Berwick (on the North Branch) and another for a toll bridge across the Susquehanna in Maryland.

Dismantling of the Western Section of the "Camelback" Bridge in 1902. The Burr arch and "X-truss" is clearly visible.

Interior of the Western Section of the "Camelback" – left side, first span of this two-way bridge.

Difficulties beset Burr on his Susquehanna projects almost from the outset, as he attempted to personally supervise the activities and pay the salaries of a veritable army of raftsmen, sawmill personnel, carpenters and masons scattered throughout three states.

Trading on his reputation and with a genial personality as one of his greatest assets, Theodore Burr kept his workers going, mainly on promises. Being constantly on the move, he was able to avoid most of his major creditors.

As advance payments were received from his client companies, he would distribute the money to the points where the financial pressure was greatest, until finally, and miraculously, all five bridges were completed. The last was his famous "Camelback" Bridge (another double-bridge crossing) at Harrisburg, opened to traffic in 1820. He also managed to sandwich into his busy schedule a three-span covered bridge at Bethlehem, Pa. (1816).

One of the most interesting Susquehanna structures created by Burr during this period was the bridge at McCall's Ferry, which, during its short life-span (1815-1818), boasted the longest single-span wooden arch in the world. The site of the bridge, now hidden beneath the water just above the present Holtwood Dam, was the narrowest part of the Susquehanna channel between Sunbury and the Chesapeake. At low water, it was only 348 feet wide, but with a swift current running in a channel approximately 100 feet deep.

Burr decided to span the gap with a huge 360 foot long wooden arch from the Lancaster County side to a pier on a shallow shelf on the York County side, with an additional 180-foot span from this pier to the York County shore line. Construction of the 360-foot sec-

tion was done on floats, lashed to the river bank until time to swing them into position. The swift current at this point, complicated by floods and storms, made the final erection of the huge span an almost impossible task. Seizing upon an early ice jam in the river and with the assistance of hundreds of farmers from both York and Lancaster Counties, Burr finally slid his tremendous arch into position over the ice and onto the piers before the ice moved out again. The entire positioning process took about two weeks.

Burr was an engineering genius, with luck on his side. His good fortune on the McCall's project did not last, however, for in March of 1818 an unprecedented ice jam carried the entire structure away. The McCalls Bridge Company never rebuilt, so the stock, with which Burr had been paid, was a total loss to him.

Burr's finances were by this time in extremely bad shape. His sawmill in New York State was sold for taxes at a mere fraction of its value. He made new promises, pleading with those who owed him money, stalling his creditors and snatching at every small bridge job he could get to try to recoup his losses. He was engaged in supervising the construction of one of these small bridges over the Swatara Creek at Middletown in 1822, when he suddenly, and mysteriously, died, with scarcely enough money for a decent burial. Thus one of the greatest Pennsylvania bridge builders lies in some unknown, unmarked grave somewhere in central Pennsylvania.

Some of his greatest bridges remained as a testimonial to his genius. The final section of his famous Camelback bridge at Harrisburg was removed (not destroyed) in 1902. His bridges at Berwick, Bethlehem and Trenton remained in service throughout most of the 18th century.

The second Columbia-Wrightsville Bridge, built by James Moore, was burned by Union militia June 28, 1863, to keep Confederate troops from invading Lancaster County. This dramatic contemporary sketch by A. Berghaus was published in Frank Leslie's "Illustrated Newspaper" (New York), looking west from the Columbia side.

## James Moore

The father of James Moore, James Moore, Sr., came from England before the Revolution and settled in Perth Amboy, New Jersey. Shortly afterward, he enlisted as an American soldier in the Revolutionary War. He was captured and taken away and his family never saw him again. Young James Moore, although born in New Jersey, always considered himself a Pennsylvanian as he was "bound out" after his father's disappearance to a German cabinet-maker at Northumberland at an early age. His formal education, such as it was, was given him by his "master" and he learned to read and write in German rather than English!

After his apprenticeship was complete, James Moore is said to have settled at Snydertown, east of Sunbury, and in his late twenties, shifted his attention from cabinet-making to bridge building. Moore became a devoted follower of the spectacular Theodore Burr, and even before Burr came to Northumberland in 1812, Moore had built his first small bridge over Buffalo Creek at Lewisburg.

Unlike Burr, however, Moore carried each bridge job to completion before starting the next.

From small bridges in his own area, he graduated to larger projects such as the Clarion River Bridge at Clarion, Pa., built in 1821 and a 1000-foot long bridge over Little Conestoga Creek near Lancaster, Pa.

In 1832, an ice jam and flood carried away the world's longest covered wooden bridge between Columbia and Wrightsville – Jonathan Wolcotts "masterpiece". James Moore went to Columbia to bid on the rebuilding. He was low bidder out of eleven competitors, and got the job for $123,247. Thus Moore had the distinction of re-building, in a slightly different location, the world's longest covered bridge, now reduced to 5620 feet in length.

It is said that James Moore was involved in the design of the Northern Central Railroad bridge at Dauphin, Pennsylvania although Gustavus Nagle is credited with the actual construction. A few of its weather-worn piers may still be seen in the Susquehanna River at that point.

James Moore, and his son, James Moore III, were quite active in the founding of Bucknell University at Lewisburg in 1846. James Moore, II died March 29, 1855, a highly respected member of his community.

44

## Capt. Richard Delafield

Capt. Richard Delafield, of the Army Engineer Corps, is given a place in our record of pioneer Pennsylvania bridgebuilders, since he was responsible for the design of the *first iron bridge in the United States*, at Brownsville, Pennsylvania.

Dunlap's Creek, at Brownsville, was originally spanned by one of James Finley's chain bridges, as part of the National Road. Finley's bridge collapsed in 1820, due to an unusually heavy snowfall which collected on it, plus a heavy wagon load of goods, exceeding its design capacity. It is thought to have been replaced by a wooden structure of questionable design. Capt. Delafield was placed in charge of the reconstruction of the National Road, in 1832 before it was to be turned over by the Federal government to the various states through which it ran. Delafield conceived the idea of rebuilding the Dunlap's Creek crossing with an iron bridge, because of the proximity of various iron foundries at Brownsville. A number of cast iron bridges had been built previously in Europe. Delafield's bridge had an eighty-foot span between high masonry abutments, with an eight-foot rise, consisting of various curved cast-iron sections bolted together, forming a horizontal floor for the roadway above. Construction of the bridge was completed by Capt. George Dutton, on July 4th, 1839, shortly after Capt. Delafield has been re-assigned to the Military Academy at West Point, as superintendent. Proof of the bridge's durability is the fact that it is still in use today, carrying heavy motor traffic never anticipated by the designer 140 years ago.

Col. Charles Ellet, Jr. (Circa 1850.)

## Col. Charles Ellet

A native Pennsylvanian, Col. Charles Ellet became the first of the great metal suspension bridge builders, using wire cable instead of chains. Born at Penn Manor, near Bristol, Pa., in 1810, Charles Ellet early evidenced unusual mathematical ability. As a young man he learned surveying and engineering on the

At Brownsville, where the National Road crossed Dunlap's Creek, still standing today, this bridge, the first iron bridge in the United States, was built in 1839. (Courtesy Dr. George Swetnam.)

Ellet's wire suspension bridge across the Schuylkill River, the first of its kind in the world. It replaced Wernwag's "Colossus", in 1842. Note Fairmount Waterworks to the left. (Courtesy of D.A. Sayenga.)

canals and earned enough money to complete his engineering education abroad.

At twenty-two, with a boldness and originality of thought which marked his entire career, he presented to Congress a proposal to build a 1000-foot suspension bridge over the Potomac at Washington! His design was so far ahead of its time that he received little encouragement from Congress. Undiscouraged, he continued to write articles promoting the use of the suspension type bridge. In 1841-42, he was commissioned to build his first wire suspension bridge across the Schuylkill at Philadelphia, to replace Wernwag's timber "Colossus." It had a span of 357 feet and was supported by wire cables, five to a side. This bridge was the first major bridge of its kind in America and was considered an engineering feat of the first magnitude. It remained in use until 1874.

His reputation made, Ellet proceeded to build additional, and larger, cable suspension bridges at Wheel-

ing on the Ohio in 1846-49, as well as the first railroad suspension bridge in 1848 over the Niagara River, and a basket ferry, the same year, over the Niagara Gorge.

Various other engineering projects occupied Ellet's attention until the outbreak of the Civil War. He perfected a plan for destroying warships by means of steam battering rams and was in command of a fleet of nine such rams during the Battle of Memphis, June 6, 1862.

Although the outcome of the battle was a Union victory, Col. Charles Ellet received a mortal wound and died several weeks later.

There were, of course, other bridge builders in Pennsylvania in the early 1800's, but those listed above designed some of the most unusual highway bridges in the days of heavy turnpike travel. Designers of canal aqueducts and railroad bridges in Pennsylvania are covered in later chapters.

A rare photograph of a Pennsylvania Canal Packet Boat passing under the Rockville Bridge of the Pennsylvania Railroad, north of Harrisburg. The date of the photo is established by the bridge, second built at this point, in 1877. Few packet boats were in operation after the Civil War, as most of the passenger business had been pulled away by the railroads. (Courtesy Dr. Ernest H. Coleman.)

# Chapter VII

# THE CANAL ERA

In the early 1820's, just as it appeared that the "good road" movement in Pennsylvania was well underway, the citizens of this State found themselves suffering from an ailment, best described as "Canal Fever", which set their highway building program back a hundred years. It all began with the building of the Erie Canal in New York State, a highly successful venture which ultimately put New York City in the Number One position as the country's leading seaport. "Canal Fever" in Pennsylvania lasted till about 1850. During this period, inter-city highways were almost forgotten. Everyone who lived anywhere near a source of water was planning and thinking about canals in their own backyard. Even the farmers were seriously talking of building boat "ditches" to the vast network of canals which began to take shape in this State.

The old Erie Canal, sometimes jokingly referred to as "Clinton's Ditch", was first proposed in 1810 to run from Albany on the Hudson to the nearest feasible point on Lake Ontario. The War of 1812 delayed construction and changed the planning. With Canada as a potential military antagonist, it was deemed more prudent to run the canal directly across upper New York State to Buffalo, a distance of 340 miles. No canal of such great length had ever been built before in America, and none of such magnitude even in Europe, where the canal building era had begun about fifty years earlier. New York Governor DeWitt Clinton, who actively promoted the canal, was considered a "crack-pot" even in his own state. Nevertheless, Clinton persevered, and construction of the canal with state funds began in 1817.

As mile after mile of the Erie Canal was opened and placed in operation, Pennsylvanians and Marylanders began to realize that their Pennsylvania Road and National Highway were going to provide very poor competition with the Erie Canal. On the canal, a packet boat with a team of two horses on the towpath could move a load of 50 to 80 passengers smoothly and quickly along the quiet waters between locks. A canal freight boat, loaded with possibly 100 tons of goods, could be towed along the canal with a team of three mules, and the trip from Albany to Buffalo could be

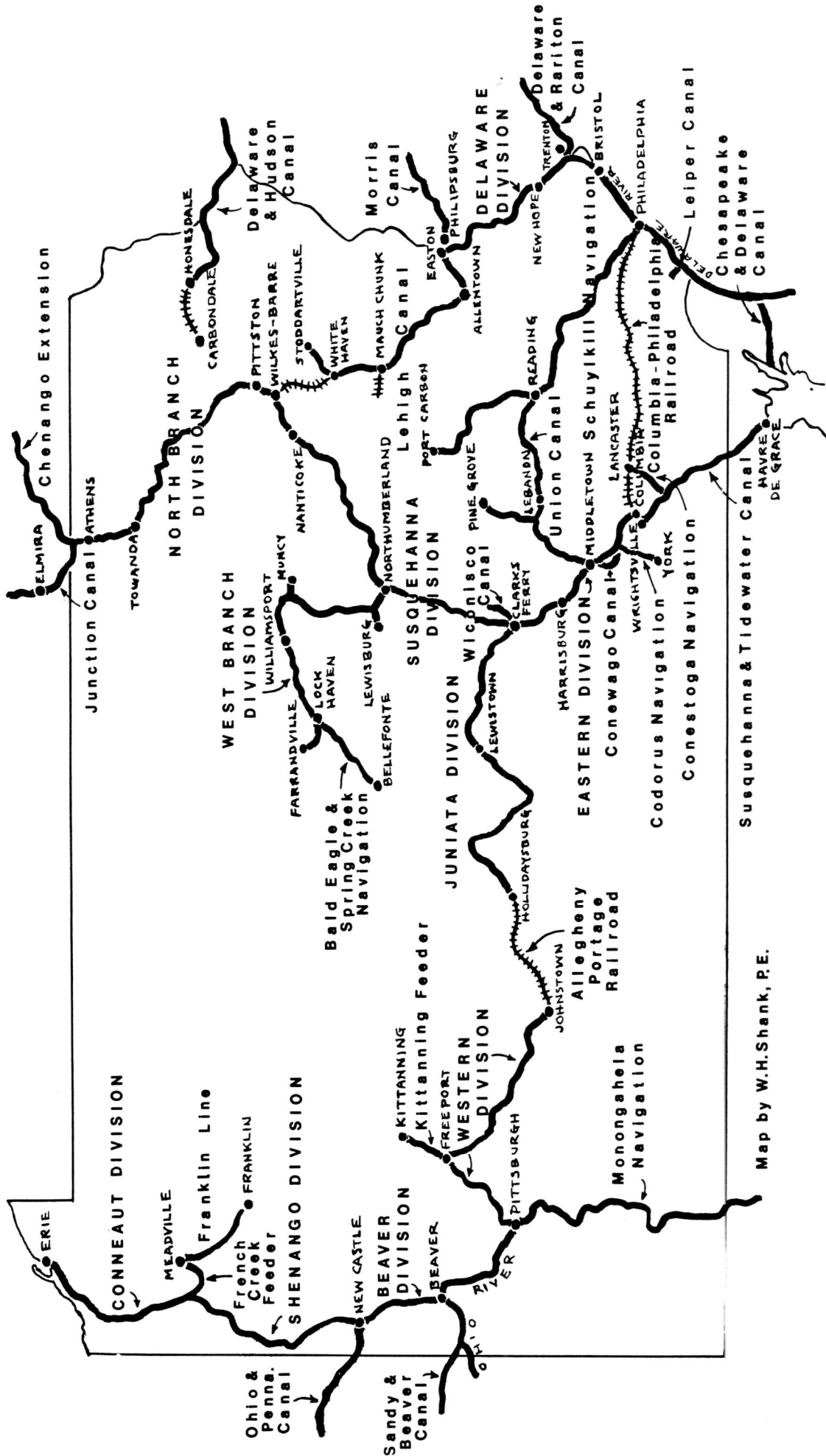

This map shows all the 1243 miles of state-owned, or privately owned canals operated within the boundaries of Pennsylvania over a period of nearly 135 years. Not all of these canals were in operation concurrently. Also indicated are the state-owned or privately owned railroads which formed an integral part of the canal system. Connecting canals or navigation systems to the six surrounding states are also shown.

Map by W. H. Shank, P.E.

48

made in about three days. As contrasted with a stage coach of six-passenger capacity, or a Conestoga wagon capable of hauling only several tons over the difficult mountain roads to the West, there was simply no comparison. From a cost-per-mile, or travel-time standpoint, it seemed obvious that canals were far superior to the existing highways.

As the Erie Canal neared completion (it was opened all the way in 1825) the citizens of both Pennsylvania and Maryland put great pressure on their legislatures to take active steps to combat this commercial menace to the North. Matters were brought to a head in Pennsylvania when the newly-formed Delaware and Hudson Canal Company (incorporated in New York in 1823) asked permission to extend its route into northeastern Pennsylvania.

Freight boat in "Benvenue Lock" on Duncan's Island. Freight boats were generally owned and operated by the family that lived on board.

## Canal Commissioners Appointed

A Canal Commission was appointed by Pennsylvania Governor J. Andrew Shulze in 1824 whose almost impossible assignment was to design a canal system to connect Philadelphia and Pittsburgh, with a line running from Pittsburgh to Lake Erie! Maryland reacted a year later by authorizing a canal to start at Georgetown, and to run, via Cumberland, across the Allegheny Mountains to Pittsburgh!

The intent of this chapter is to describe some of the major canals financed by the State of Pennsylvania, as well as the more important privately-financed canals connecting with the State system.

## Early Canal Surveys

The idea of canals in Pennsylvania was nothing new. In 1762 David Rittenhouse, the astronomer, and Dr. William Smith, provost of the University of Pennsylvania, had made surveys over a route originally proposed by William Penn, for a canal to connect Reading on the Schuylkill with Middletown on the Susquehanna. Middletown was selected as the western terminus for such a canal because it was the southernmost point of relatively easy down-stream navigation on the Susquehanna. Just below Middletown were the Conewago Falls, which made downstream travel, with existing vessels, extremely hazardous and upstream travel impossible. Hence Middletown became the most active southern port of the Susquehanna, in the late 1700's. Here many goods from up-state were unloaded and shipped overland, by very poor wagon roads, to Philadelphia.

Plans for a Middletown-Philadelphia canal were activated in 1792, when two companies were chartered by the state to begin construction of what later became the Union Canal and the Schuylkill Navigation. Work was actually begun at Lebanon shortly thereafter and was inspected several times by no less a personage than George Washington himself, who had been an active advocate of canals for years. Washington was himself president and chief engineer of a company formed to build a canal west from Alexandria along the Potomac.

## The Conewago Canal

Also in 1792 the State authorized the construction of a one-mile canal, four feet deep, with two brick locks, on the west bank of the Susquehanna at York Haven, to by-pass the treacherous Conewago Falls. Pennsylvania contributed $14,000 toward the cost of the project with the balance of the expense being borne by the newly-formed Schuylkill and Susquehanna Canal Company. The Conewago Canal was officially opened by Governor Mifflin November 22, 1797 with great ceremony. Thus was completed one of the first operating canals in northeastern United States. It was immediately declared "toll-free" to all river travelers bound upstream or down. The Pennsylvania governor pointedly avoided any reference to possible further improvement of the lower Susquehanna south of Columbia, because of efforts of Philadelphians to divert lower Susquehanna trade away from the rival port of Baltimore. Already some trade was taking place by overland wagon road from York Haven (opposite Middletown) to Baltimore.

The famous Union Canal Tunnel just west of Lebanon. 729 feet in length, it was cut through solid rock using hand pick and shovel and crude blasting methods. It pierced the watershed ridge on the summit level of the Union Canal between Reading and Middletown. Boats were poled through the tunnel, while the mules climbed over the hill. (Photo by the author.)

## The Union Canal and Schuylkill Navigation Companies

In 1792 the two companies chartered by the State of Pennsylvania were commissioned to build a navigable waterway between the Schuylkill and Susquehanna, improve the Schuylkill from Norristown to Reading, and build a canal from the Delaware River to Norristown. By 1794, the companies had completed 15 miles of work, including several locks, and had spent $440,000, which exhausted their funds, and the work ground to a stop – for the next twenty-seven years. The legislature granted the companies the right to raise another $400,000 by means of lotteries, but by

1811 the two companies, united under the name "Union Canal Company", had managed to raise only $60,000.

In 1815 by act of the Pennsylvania legislature a new enterprise, the "Schuylkill Navigation Company", was chartered to complete the work on the Schuylkill River. The portion of the Schuylkill which was made navigable extended from Port Carbon, just above Pottsville, to Philadelphia, a distance of 108 miles. Of this route, 62 miles were by canal, and 46 miles by so-called "slack water navigation pools" in the river itself, formed by a series of dams passed in each case by locks. Between Port Carbon and Philadelphia there were 92 lift locks to overcome a 588-foot difference in elevation. Locks on the Schuylkill Navigation system were 80 feet long by 17 feet wide. Much of the trade using the system consisted of arks, rafts and boats carrying anthracite from the coal region into Philadelphia.

## First Tunnel in the U.S.A.

An interesting side note on the construction of the Schuylkill system was a 450-foot-long tunnel, completed in 1821 near Auburn, Pennsylvania, through which the canal passed. The tunnel was constructed through a low hill, which might easily have been avoided by laying out the canal line about a hundred feet westward. However, the proprietors of the company wanted a tunnel, knowing that it would be the first one to be constructed in the United States. The tunnel grew to be a great curiosity and people came from as far as Philadelphia to see it. It was shortened from time to time until about the year 1857, when it was reduced

A winter scene on Canal Street in Schuylkill Haven, 1883. A Freighter of the type used on the Schuylkill Navigation awaits the spring thaw. (Courtesy Dean Aungst.)

to an open cutting. The Schuylkill Navigation Company continued to operate from 1825 until 1870 when it was sold to the Philadelphia and Reading Railroad Company, one of its largest competitors. Under the new management the system continued operations until 1931.

In the meantime the Union Canal Company, whose responsibility had now been narrowed to the water route between Reading and Middletown, was offered financial aid by the state of Pennsylvania due to the impending threat of New York State's partially completed Erie Canal. With this additional impetus the Union Canal was pushed through to completion between 1821 and 1828, to make a water link between Philadelphia and the Susquehanna.

The Union Canal, 4 feet deep, 36 feet wide at surface level and 24 feet wide at bottom, was a remarkable feat of engineering. In a distance of 81 miles (by canal) between Reading and Middletown it climbed 311 feet to the summit level of the canal at Lebanon and descended a total of 192 feet to the level of the Susquehanna River at the west end, using a total of 93 lift locks 75 feet long and 8½ feet wide. The summit level was approached by a consecutive series of 19 locks on the west side and 7 consecutive locks on the east side of Lebanon.

In addition, just west of Lebanon the canal ran through a 729 foot tunnel in the water shed ridge. Completed in 1826, it was the second tunnel in the country, and is today maintained by the Lebanon County Historical Society as the "oldest tunnel in the United States."

An additional 22-mile feeder, making connection west of Lebanon brought water from a large reservoir, created north of Blue Mountain, to supply the summit level of the Union Canal. (The Pine Grove Feeder.)

The Union Canal, costing a total of $6,000,000, was traversed in the spring of 1828 by its first boat, the "Fair Trader", which finished the trip from Philadelphia to Middletown in five days.

## "The Water Works"

Maintaining water in the summit level of the Union Canal was a tremendous problem. The limestone soil allowed rapid water leakage, which was subsequently offset somewhat by lining the canal walls with heavy planks at the bottom and sides. Inasmuch as the feeder canal was located some 85 feet below the summit level it was necessary to pump the water from the feeder canal junction (known as the "Water Works") using four huge pumping engines, rated at 120 H.P. apiece and two immense water wheels 40 feet high by 10 feet wide, to raise the water through a 3-foot-diameter wood pipe to the top of a 95-foot hill from which point the water flowed four miles through a round, brick pipe to the summit level of the canal.

A party of Pennsylvania Canal Society enthusiasts inspects the ruins of a tremendous flight of locks below Birdsboro, on the Schuylkill Navigation. (Photo by the author.)

The new Canal Commission, created at Harrisburg in 1824, to rush through plans for a canal route to compete with the Erie, had at first considered using the Schuylkill and Union Canals as the Eastern links in a cross-state canal system. However, the transportation situation west of Philadelphia had changed. Due to the construction of the Conewago Canal around the falls at Middletown, and the new Philadelphia-Lancaster Turnpike – Columbia had now succeeded Middletown as the important transfer point for Susquehanna River goods bound for Philadelphia.

Also, the Union Canal Company had unfortunately stuck with its original plans of using narrow locks, while the more recently designed canals were building locks twice as wide as those on the Union, permitting the use of much larger boats. Thus, the Union Canal to Middletown was ruled out as part of the State Canal system, and an overland railroad was planned from Philadelphia to Columbia instead.

Not until 1841, did the Union Canal Company correct its orginal error in building its locks too small. That year they widened both channel and locks, with the expenditure of an additional $6,000,000, and were then able to handle boats of from 75 to 80 tons capacity. However, the company never recovered from this expenditure and finally abandoned operations in 1885.

Canal basin at Columbia – terminus of the Columbia-Philadelphia Railroad, and eastern end of the "Main Line" Canal.

## The "Main Line" Canal System

With public pressure upon them, the Pennsylvania State legislature passed three canal acts between March 1824 and February 1826, empowering the governor to appoint canal commissioners and begin construction of the "Pennsylvania Canal" later referred to as the "Main Line." Ground was broken at Harrisburg by Governor John Andrew Shulze, with much ceremony, on July 4th, 1826, but with very little knowledge of the actual route to be followed across the State. The Commission had initially planned to use the Union and Schuylkill Canals and dig a four-mile canal tunnel to pierce Allegheny Mountain, making an all-water route between Philadelphia and Pittsburgh possible. However, the former part of the plan was abandoned for the reasons above, and a four-mile canal tunnel turned out to be almost an engineering impossibility.

Plans which finally emerged were as follows: A horse-powered railroad was built, approximately 82 miles long, to connect Philadelphia with Columbia. A canal was built from Columbia, through Middletown and Harrisburg, to Clark's Ferry, approximately 43 miles long, known as the Eastern Division Canal.

Connecting with this was the Juniata Division Canal, running 127 miles from the Juniata Aqueduct to Hollidaysburg.

To cross Allegheny Mountain a "Portage Railroad" was planned, about 39 miles in length, connecting Hollidaysburg with Johnstown. At Johnstown began the Western Division Canal, which ran along the Conemaugh, Kiskiminitas, and Allegheny Rivers into Pittsburgh, a distance of about 105 miles.

## Columbia and Philadelphia Railroad

In few sections of the state through which the Pennsylvania system of public works passed is the expression "Main Line" today more than just a memory. At the Philadelphia end, however, the term "Main Line" has stuck, and is used in referring to the various suburbs strung along the Lincoln Highway, immediately west of Philadelphia, although most of the inhabitants have forgotten the origin of the expression.

The state-owned Columbia and Philadelphia Railroad, extending 82 miles from Vine and Broad Streets in Philadelphia to the canal basin at Columbia, was started in 1828 and completed in 1834 – one of the

earliest railroads in America and the first in the world to be built by a government rather than private enterprise.

As previously mentioned, the Union Canal might have formed the eastern link in the Main Line from Philadelphia to Pittsburgh and did ultimately take some of the traffic between Philadelphia and the Susquehanna River.

In 1827 the Canal Board was authorized to make surveys and estimates for both canal and railroad routes between Philadelphia and the Susquehanna, through Chester and Lancaster Counties. It was quickly decided that a railroad would be more feasible, because the hilly country made a canal route difficult and expensive.

This railroad is described in Chapter X.

## Eastern Division

The Eastern Division of the Pennsylvania Canal was authorized by act of the state legislature February 25, 1826. While it was the first section to be started, it was the last of the three Main Line canal divisions to be completed. Originally this section was to connect with the Union Canal at Middletown and then run north, along the eastern bank of the Susquehanna, for 24 miles to Duncan's Island at the mouth of the Juniata River. However, the plans were changed in 1828, and the commissioners were authorized to extend the eastern division of the canal to a new terminus at Columbia, Pennsylvania, 19 miles further south, from which point a railroad connection with Philadelphia was planned. Thus the Eastern Division ultimately ran 43 miles from Columbia to Duncan's Island, with a

Penn Lock at Harrisburg, one block east of the present Penn Central Railroad terminal. Here, ground was broken by Governor Schulze for the Main Line Canal on July 4th, 1826.

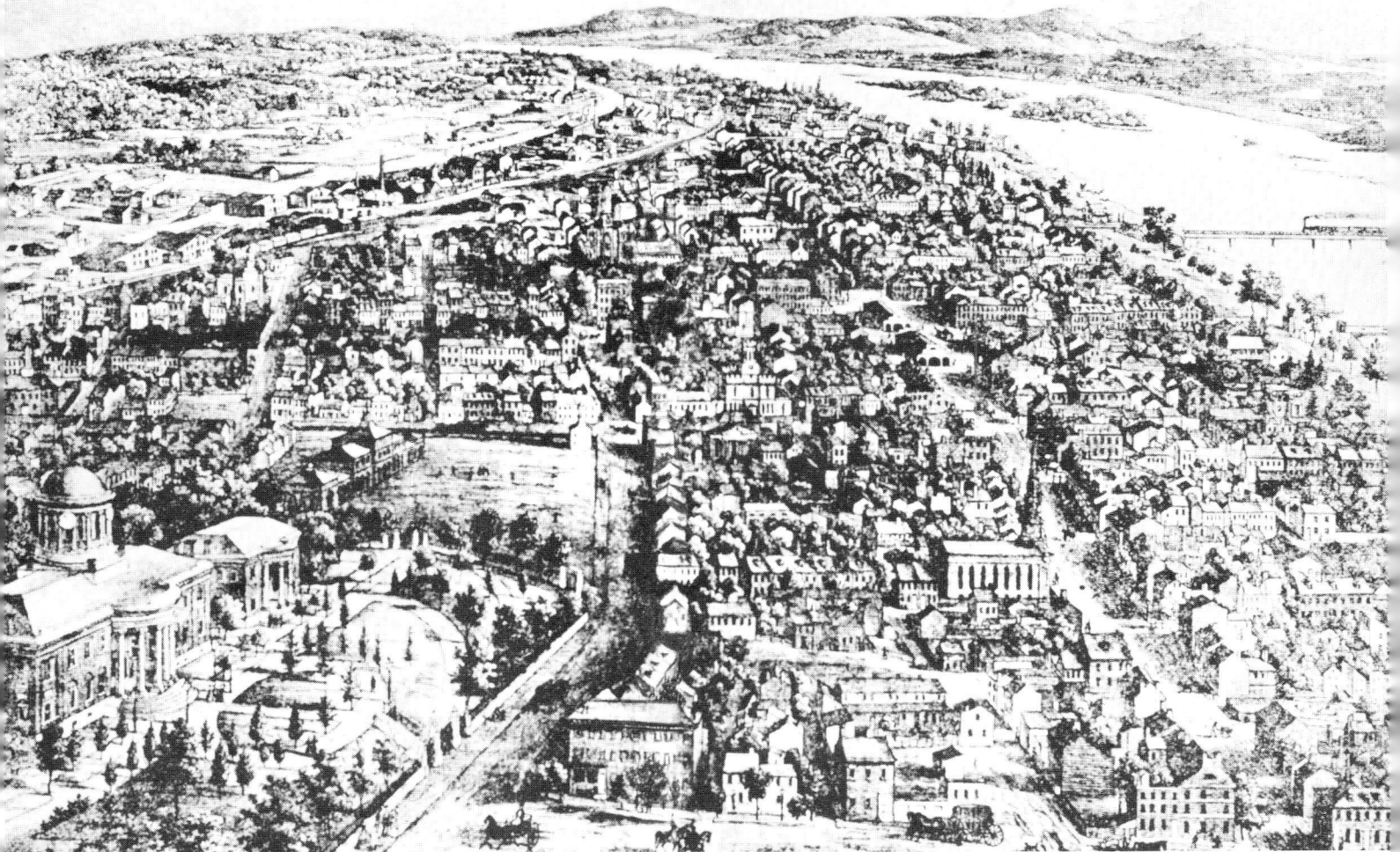

Harrisburg, in the mid-1800's. The Eastern Division of the Main Line Canal is the broad white band running across the upper left corner of this artist's view. The old capitol building is in the left foreground and the Cumberland Valley Railroad Bridge and "Camelback Bridge" to the right. (Courtesy Harrisburg Patriot News.)

total of 14 locks, including an outlet lock to permit access from the canal basin at Columbia to the Susquehanna River. The locks were constructed of cut stone masonry and were for the most part 90 feet in length by 17 feet wide, with an average lift of approximately 7½ feet.

When the Eastern Division Canal reached the junction of the Susquehanna and the Juniata 15 miles above Harrisburg, the engineers ran up against their first major problem. They had to get the canal across to the west bank of the Susquehanna to pick up the entrance to the Juniata Division Canal and also to make connection with the newly authorized branch running up the west bank of the river, known as the Susquehanna Division. It was decided to build a dam between the lower end of Duncan's Island and the east bank of the Susquehanna, at Peter's Mountain, to

form a deep and more or less placid pool across which canal boats could be drawn from a towing path bridge. Hence a dam 1998 feet long and 8½ feet high with a base 30 feet thick was built of strong timbers with an embankment of broken stone and gravel. A short distance above the dam the canal commissioners then built the first Clark's Ferry bridge, a covered wooden structure with a double-deck towpath down-stream. The pool formed by the dam also provided water for the entire Eastern Division of the canal.

Two additional liftlocks on Duncan's Island (first two locks on the Susquehanna Division) raised the boats from Clark's Ferry pool to a junction with the Juniata Division on Duncan's Island at a canal basin just south of the old Amity Hall Inn. The Eastern Division was put into operation early in 1833.

54

Clark's Ferry Bridge, where the "Main Line" crossed the Susquehanna River between Peter's Mountain and Duncan's Island. A group of picnickers on a freight boat are shown leaving the Duncan's Island lock. The "slack-water" dam is out of the photo to the right. (Courtesy James A. O'Boyle.)

## The Juniata Division

The Juniata Division of the Main Line Canal System began officially at the canal basin on the northwest corner of the triangle of ground where the Susquehanna and Juniata Rivers join, known as Duncan's Island. This old canal basin is still quite visible about 300 or 400 yards south of the Amity Hall Inn. Well preserved ruins of the No. 1 lift lock on the Juniata Division can still be found about 100 yards due west of this canal basin. Here the boats were elevated approximately 10 feet to the level of the 600-foot long Juniata aqueduct where the Main Line crossed the Juniata River. This wooden trough type aqueduct, with towpath on one side and a passenger path on the other, rested on five sturdy stone piers, three of which (as of this writing) are still standing, although the structure of the bridge has long since disappeared.

The Pennsylvania legislature authorized the first leg of the Juniata Division to be constructed in 1827. This was a 40-mile section, running from Duncan's Island to Lewistown, but before work on the line was much more than started subsequent acts of the legislature authorized an extension to Huntington and finally to Hollidaysburg, 127 miles up the Juniata from the Duncan's Island basin.

At North's Island, eighteen miles up the Juniata, the narrow water gap through Tuscarora Mountain made it necessary to swing the canal back to the north bank of the river. An eight-foot dam was constructed across the river at this point to provide a slack water pool across which the canal boats could be towed. An endless rope type ferry was employed for this purpose and the higher water level of the canal on the north side was used to actuate a water wheel, which worked the machinery for the ferry.

Passenger-carrying packet boat at the Thompsontown Lock. Well-preserved ruins of the lock still remain, also the house in the background. (Courtesy Dr. Ernest H. Coleman.)

The dimensions of the canal channel cross section on the Juniata Division were the same as on other portions of the Main Line. The standard lock on the Juniata was 90 feet long by 15 feet wide – two feet narrower than those on the Eastern Division. In general the locks on this division were not as well constructed as on the Eastern and Western Divisions; four were of solid cut-stone masonry; seven were of so-called rubble stone laid in mortar, and the remaining 77 locks on the division consisted of wooden frames, planked water tight with boards 4 inches thick, the sides being supported by walls of dry masonry with heavy puddling (a mixture of mud and clay) worked in at the ends to keep the water from escaping through the fill. Each lock had a flume or spillway along the inland side four feet wide and two feet deep with shut-off gates to regulate the water permitted to pass the locks.

The Juniata Division required 88 locks to overcome a change in elevation of 584 feet in the 127 miles between Duncan's Island and Hollidaysburg. There were 25 aqueducts to carry the canal over the larger tributaries, mainly wooden structures on stone piers.

It had originally been planned to end the Juniata Division at Frankstown, but due to the resistance of a farmer who owned the land at the point where the canal basin was originally planned, the canal was extended two miles further west to Hollidaysburg.

Extension of the terminus of the canal brought with it some additional problems in supplying the summit level of the canal with sufficient water. Reservoirs were ultimately constructed at three different points on various tributaries of the Juniata above Hollidays-

burg to keep the upper reach of the canal full of water.

The Juniata Division was officially opened to traffic with the passage of the packet boat "John Blair" between Huntington and Hollidaysburg on November 27, 1832. It was subsequently discovered that some of the workmanship along that section was faulty and certain locks and several of the aqueducts had to be rebuilt before full operation was possible the following year.

# The Allegheny Portage Railroad

From the days of the early planning of the Main Line, the plan for passing Allegheny Mountain had been somewhat nebulous. The original surveys indicated that there would be no great difficulty following the routes of the Susquehanna, Juniata, Conemaugh, Kiskiminetas and Allegheny Rivers with a canal, but the one big obstacle on this route had, from the first, been Allegheny Mountain between Hollidaysburg and Johnstown.

One plan originally considered was the running of the canal approach south of Hollidaysburg along a small tributary of the Juniata, virtually to the base of Allegheny Mountain, and a similar extension east of Johnstown along a tributary of the Conemaugh, which would have brought the ends of the Juniata and Western Divisions within approximately six miles of each other. A four mile canal tunnel through Allegheny Mountain was suggested as the final connecting link.

So anxious were the citizens of Pennsylvania and the legislature at Harrisburg to get something started that the canal bills authorizing the initial construction on the eastern and western divisions were rushed through before any serious thought was given to the tunnel.

As construction of the Main Line system moved rapidly up the waterways approaching Allegheny Mountain from both east and west, the canal commissioners realized that they had a much greater problem on their hands than they had anticipated.

First of all, the idea of a four-mile tunnel through Allegheny Mountain had the engineers of the day shaking their heads dubiously. At that time the only other tunnels in the United States were on the Schuylkill Navigation system, the Union Canal, and the Main Line itself. None of these tunnels measured more than 850 feet in length. Even today the digging of a four-mile tunnel would be a major undertaking. The prospect of such an enterprise in 1828 was overwhelming.

Even if the tunnel had been completed, its elevation would have been at such a height that the maintenance of proper water level in this section of the canal would have presented tremendous problems.

Therefore, the canal commissioners reluctantly abandoned the Allegheny Tunnel and turned their attention to other means of passing the mountain. A turnpike was considered, but due to the extreme steepness of the grade on the east side of the mountain the canal commissioners finally decided upon a Portage Railroad, and Sylvester Welch was selected as its Chief Engineer.

Thus came into being one of the most unusual means of overland transportation ever devised, before or since. The Allegheny Portage Railroad was authorized by an act of the Pennsylvania legislature and approved by the Governor on March 31, 1831. This amazing railroad is fully described in Chapter IX.

## The Western Division

The Western Division Canal was authorized to start at Pittsburgh and run upstream along the Allegheny River from Pittsburgh to a junction with the Kiskiminetas River at Freeport.

The same legislative act of February 25, 1826 which had started work on the Eastern Division empowered the commissioners to proceed immediately with construction east from Pittsburgh. However, work did not get underway quite as promptly at this end of the state because there was considerable debate about the selection of a suitable route. Surveys were run on both banks of the Allegheny. The citizens of Pittsburgh favored a south bank route, which would bring the canal into the heart of old Pittsburgh, but the terrain on that side of the river made a north bank route much more feasible. Citizens of the newly incorporated

Downtown Pittsburgh about 1840, showing the canal basin along Liberty Street and locking connections to both the Allegheny and Monongahela Rivers. (Courtesy Julius W. Murphy.)

850-foot tunnel, near Saltsburg on the Western Division Canal. This view shows a masonry aqueduct crossing the Conemaugh River at the west tunnel portal. (Courtesy Richard H. Steinmetz, Sr.)

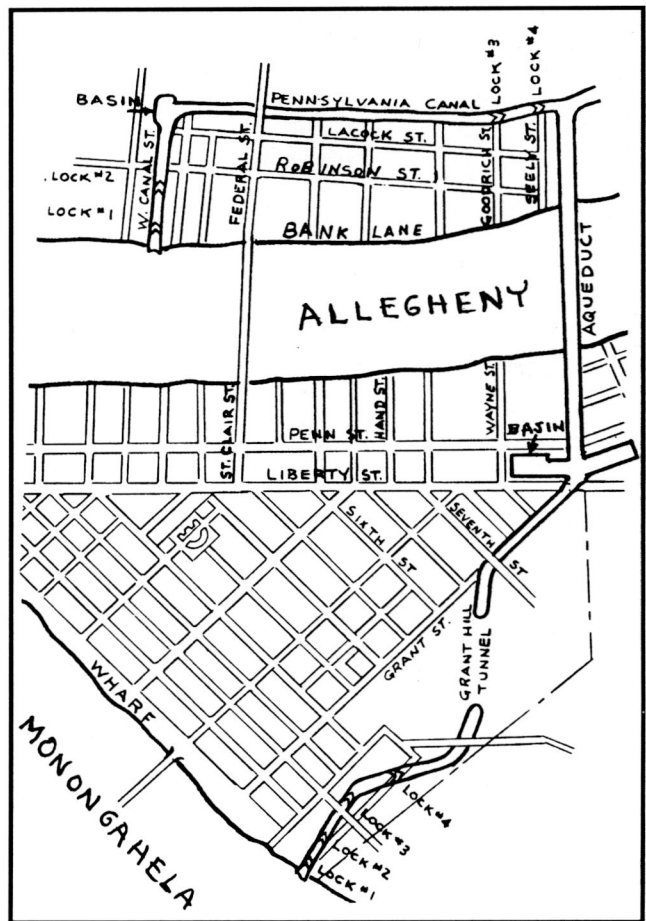

borough of Allegheny on the north side of the river directly opposite Pittsburgh were delighted at the prospect of a canal terminal in their community. However, Pittsburghers objected vehemently. They indicated that they had not agitated all these years for a canal, to have it terminate in a neighboring borough. A compromise was finally effected in the form of an aqueduct across the Allegheny River, entering Pittsburgh opposite the Grant-Liberty junction. This aqueduct was the longest and most troublesome on the entire Pennsylvania Main Line route.

Another point upon which Pittsburghers insisted was that the canal should be run south through Pittsburgh to connect with the Monongahela River at a point where the proposed Chesapeake and Ohio Canal was supposed to enter the city. This proved to be a most expensive and difficult engineering feat. An 810-foot canal tunnel had to be constructed under Grant's Hill and a series of four additional lift locks had to be built on the south side of the city to lower

A canal freight boat train stalled on a section of the Pennsylvania Canals, due to a water leak. The family on the near boat waits patiently for service to be restored.

the canal to the Monongahela River level. The main canal basin and unloading point for the terminus of the canal, however, was located on the north side of Pittsburgh. The "turning basin" ran east and west between Penn and Liberty Avenues, and the canal terminal depot was located on the east corner of Grant and Seventh.

The borough of Allegheny finally won the right to have its own branch and separate terminal facilities on the north side of the Allegheny River with a series of four additional locks west of the north end of the aqueduct, which permitted the canal boats to pass on down into the Allegheny River on that side. This connection proved quite valuable on the several occasions when the aqueduct collapsed.

After the foregoing details were settled, construction of the Western Division Canal proceeded along the northwest bank of the Allegheny to Freeport. Subsequently a 14-mile extension, known as the Kittanning Feeder, was built north along the Allegheny, terminating at Kittanning.

In 1827 the legislature authorized an additional 44 mile extension of the canal from the mouth of the Kiskiminetas up that stream and its major tributary, the Conemaugh River, as far as Blairsville. The following year a further extension was approved along the Conemaugh to Johnstown.

Construction on the Western Division followed the same pattern as the Eastern Division, with the canal channel measuring 40 feet at the top water line and 28 feet at the bottom, 4 feet minimum in depth. The locks, constructed of masonry as in the eastern division, were 90 feet long but only 15 feet wide. The total length of this section was 105 miles. Including the four lift locks between the Pittsburgh basin and the Monongahela River and the outlet locks in Allegheny Borough there were a total of 68 lift locks.

There were two canal tunnels on the route, one in downtown Pittsburgh as previously described, and the second along the Conemaugh east of Tunnelton. The latter, completed in 1830, was the third tunnel constructed in the United States. It was 850 feet in length and was built to avoid following the Conemaugh River on a long meandering loop. Exit from the west end of the tunnel was directly onto an aqueduct crossing the river.

Additional structures of the Western Division included 16 aqueducts, 10 river dams, 64 culverts, 39 waste weirs and 152 road bridges, passing over the canal channel.

Newspaper accounts in the Pittsburgh area indicate that some traffic began to move on the Western Division by autumn of 1830 but it was not until May of 1831 that the first fully loaded freight boat from Johnstown

arrived safely in Pittsburgh, carrying 7927 pounds of merchandise.

The Pittsburgh canal extension through Grant's Hill tunnel to the Monongahela River was not made operable until August of 1832. The Chesapeake and Ohio Canal never came closer to Pittsburgh than Cumberland, Maryland, so this extension and tunnel served mainly as a spillway to carry off excess water from the canal basin.

## Charles Dickens Rides the "Main Line"

One of the most famous, and prolific, writers who traveled the Pennsylvania Canal System was England's Charles Dickens. Read now excerpts from his description of the canal portions of the Main Line, during his trip from Harrisburg to Pittsburgh in 1842.

"It continued to rain heavily at Harrisburg, and when we went down to the Canal Boat (for that was the mode of conveyance by which we were to proceed) after dinner, the weather was as unpromising and obstinately wet as one would desire to see. Nor was the sight of this canal boat, in which we were to spend three or four days, by any means a cheerful one; as it involved some uneasy speculations concerning the disposal of the passengers at night, and opened a wide field of inquiry touching the other domestic arrangements of the establishment which was sufficiently disconcerting.

"However, there it was – a barge with a little house in it, viewed from the outside; and a caravan at a fair, viewed from within; the gentlemen being accommodated as the spectators usually are in one of those locomotive museums of penny wonders; and the ladies being partitioned off by a red curtain, after the manner of the dwarfs and giants in the same establishments, whose private lives are passed in rather close exclusiveness.

"We sat here, looking silently at the row of little tables which extended down both sides of the cabin, and listening to the rain until the arrival of the railway train, for whose final contribution to our stock of passengers our departure was alone deferred. Then a train of three horses was attached to the tow-rope, the boy upon the leader smacked his whip, the rudder creaked and groaned complainingly, and we had begun our journey.

"As it continued to rain most perseveringly, we all remained below; the damp gentlemen round the stove gradually becoming mildewed by the action of the fire; and the dry gentlemen lying at full length upon the seats, or slumbering uneasily with their faces on the tables. At about six o'clock all the small tables were put together to form one long table, and everybody sat down to tea, coffee, bread, butter, salmon, shad, liver,

A "swing bridge" designed by a Williamsport (Pa.) inventor. Forward movement of the canal boat opened it, and it returned to normal closed position automatically. (Courtesy Richard L. Mix.)

steak, potatoes, pickles, ham, chops, black puddings, and sausages.

"By the time the meal was over, the rain was nearly over, too; and it became feasible to go on deck; which was a great relief, notwithstanding its being a very small deck, and being rendered still smaller by the luggage. It was somewhat embarrassing at first, to have to duck nimbly every five minutes whenever the man at the helm cried, 'Bridge,' and sometimes, when the cry was 'Low Bridge,' to lie down nearly flat.

"As night came on, and we drew in sight of the first range of hills, which are the outposts of the Allegheny Mountains, the scenery, which had been uninteresting hitherto, became more bold and striking. The wet ground reeked and smoked after the heavy fall of rain; and the croaking of the frogs (whose noise in these parts is almost incredible) sounded as though a million of fairy teams with bells were travelling through the air and keeping pace with us. The night was cloudy yet, but moonlight, too; and when we crossed the Susquehanna River – over which there is an extraordinary wooden bridge with two galleries, one above the other, so that, even there, two boat-teams meeting may pass without confusion – it was wild and grand.

Susquehanna Division Canal Dock at Liverpool. Owens House, to the left, is still standing. State Routes 11-15 now travel the filled-in canal bed at this point. (Courtesy Dr. Ernest H. Coleman.)

"I have mentioned my having been in some uncertainty and doubt, at first, relative to the sleeping arrangements on board this boat. I remained in the same vague state of mind until ten o'clock or thereabouts, when, going below, I found suspended, on either side of the cabin, three long tiers of hanging bookshelves, designed apparently for volumes of the small octavo size. Looking with greater attention at these contrivances (wondering to find such literary preparations in such a place) I descried on each shelf a sort of microscopic sheet and blanket; then I began dimly to comprehend that the passengers were the library, and that they were to be arranged edgewise on these shelves till morning.

"As to the ladies, they were already abed, behind the red curtain, which was carefully drawn and pinned up in the center; though as every cough, or sneeze, or whisper, behind this curtain, was perfectly audible before it, we had still a lively consciousness of their society.

"My shelf being a bottom one, I finally determined on lying upon the floor, rolling gently in, stopping immediately I touched the mattress, and remaining for the night with that side uppermost, whatever it might be.

"Between five and six o'clock in the morning we got up, and some of us went on deck. The washing accommodations were primitive. There was a tin ladle chained to the deck, with which every gentleman who thought it necessary to cleanse himself (many were superior to this weakness) fished the dirty water out of the canal, and poured it into a tin basin, secured in like manner. There was also a jack-towel. And, hanging up before a little looking-glass in the bar, in the immediate vicinity of the bread and cheese and biscuits, were a public comb and hair-brush.

"At eight o'clock, the shelves being taken down and put away, and the tables joined together, everybody set down to the tea, coffee, bread, butter, salmon, shad, liver, steak, potatoes, pickles, ham, chops, black puddings, and sausages all over again. When everybody had done with everything, the fragments were cleared away, and one of the waiters, appearing in the character of a barber, shaved such of the company as desired to be shaved.

"I may go on to remark that breakfast was perhaps the least desirable meal of the day, as, in addition to the many savory odors arising from the eatables, already mentioned, there were whiffs of gin, whisky, brandy, and rum from the little bar hard by, and a decided seasoning of stale tobacco.

"And yet, despite these oddities – and even they had, for me at least, a humor of their own – there was much in this mode of travelling which I heartily enjoyed at this time, and look back upon with great pleasure. Even the running up, bare-necked, at five o'clock in the morning, from the tainted cabin to the dirty deck; scooping up the icy water, plunging one's head into it, and drawing it out all fresh and glowing with the cold; was a good thing. The fast, brisk walk upon the towing-path between that time and breakfast, when every vein and artery seemed to tingle with health; the exquisite beauty of the opening day, when light came gleaming off from everything; the lazy motion of the boat, when one lay idly on the deck, looking through, rather than at, the deep blue sky; the gliding

Canal boat-building yard and repair dock at Selinsgrove, on the Susquehanna Division Canal in 1882. There were a number of these "dry-docks" around the state.

on at night, so noiselessly, the shining out of the bright stars, undisturbed by noise of wheels or steam, or any other sound than the liquid rippling of the water as the boat went on; all these were pure delights . . .

"On Monday evening furnace fires and clanking hammers on the banks of the canal warned us that we approached the termination of this part of our journey. After going through another dreamy place – a long aqueduct across the Allegheny River, which was stranger than the bridge at Harrisburg, being a vast, low, wooden chamber full of water – we emerged upon that ugly confusion of backs of buildings and crazy galleries and stairs which always abuts on water, whether it be river, sea, canal, or ditch; and were at Pittsburgh."

While the "Main Line" was the principal system developed by the State for tying Pennsylvania together, east to west, there were also other State constructed and operated divisions to supplement the Main Line, connecting with it, either directly or indirectly.

## Susquehanna Division

The Susquehanna Division canal ran north from the outlet lock located just west of the Clark's Ferry Bridge, on Duncan's Island, along the west bank of the Susquehanna River for 41 miles to a point opposite Northumberland. Here the boats were towed to the east bank from a covered towpath bridge running into Northumberland. A slack water pool was created at this point by Shamokin Dam, which spanned the river below the junction of the north and west branches.

The engineers who designed and built the Susquehanna Division included: Simeon Guilford; Hother Hage, with canal office at Liverpool; Francis W. Rawle; and A. B. Waterford. Work began in 1827 and was completed in 1831. This division, with its 12 locks (90 feet x 17 feet) raising the canal boats 86 feet from the Clark's Ferry slack water pool to the Northumberland slack water pool, formed an important link with the Main Line and the canal divisions in the northern part of the state.

## North Branch Division

The North Branch of the Susquehanna Canal System commenced at the basin at Northumberland which united the Susquehanna, the North Branches and the West Branch. Including the outlet lock to the river at Northumberland, there were a total of nine locks on this section, of the standard 17 feet wide by 90 feet long type. The North Branch originally ran 55 miles to the feeder pool at Nanticoke Falls. Ground was broken at Berwick July 4, 1828 and the work on this section was completed in 1831. The important function of the North Branch was the supplying of coal to the entire Pennsylvania canal system south and west of Nanticoke, an important anthracite distribution point.

An 1834 project, known as The Wyoming Extension, carried the North Branch another 17 miles northeast, past Wilkes-Barre to Pittston. A further extension of the north branch division, from Pittston along the north branch of the Susquehanna River to Athens and the New York state line, was begun in 1836, and after several long interruptions, due to financial difficulties,

was finally placed in operation in 1856. This section went through a rather rugged portion of the state and over the entire route (169 miles) between Northumberland and the state line 43 locks were required to overcome 334 feet of elevation. Five river dams were built to provide stretches of slack water navigation, as well as water to feed the canal sections, 29 aqueducts were constructed, and 229 bridges were built to carry local roads over the canal.

Final connection to the Erie Canal was made through an 18 mile privately-built junction canal in New York state which linked the north branch extension with Elmira. From this point the Chemung Canal ran north along Seneca Lake to make connections with the Erie Canal.

## West Branch Division

The West Branch, also, had its southern terminus at the canal basin in Northumberland and from this point ran along the east bank of the West Branch of the Susquehanna River, north thru Muncy and west thru Williamsport, Jersey Shore and Lock Haven, to Far-

A "Flyer of the '80's" docked on the West Branch Division Canal at Williamsport. The Market Street "swing bridge" can be seen in the background.

Coal and freight boats near the outlet lock of the Delaware Division Canal at Bristol. From this point the boats travelled in the Delaware River itself, into Philadelphia.

randsville. The West Branch Canal, started in 1828 and completed in 1835, covered a total distance of 73 miles, with 19 locks overcoming 138½ feet of vertical lockage. The primary product transported was lumber from the vast forest areas in the section of the state north and west of Williamsport.

Local residents hoped that this branch might be extended to make connection with the Allegheny River to the northwest. However, the only subsequent additions were a 4 mile state-built section known as the "Bald Eagle Cut", west of Lock Haven along Bald Eagle Creek; which was later supplemented by a 22 mile privately financed addition called the Bald Eagle and Spring Creek Navigation, making connections into Bellefonte.

A short connection known as the "Lewisburg Cut", was built in 1833 across the Susquehanna by the State to tie Lewisburg directly into the West Branch Canal System. There was also a privately-built ¾-mile connection at Muncy, known as the "Muncy Cut."

## The Delaware Division

The Delaware Division of the Pennsylvania Canal was authorized by the state in 1827 and completed in 1832. It ran along the west bank of the Delaware River, from navigable water at Bristol, north to Easton, a distance of 60 miles, with 165 feet of vertical elevation being overcome by 23 lift-locks. It had no direct connection with the Main Line, serving principally as a connection between the Lehigh Canal terminus at Easton, and the Philadelphia market for the products of the Lehigh Coal and Navigation Company.

The line had nine aqueducts, 110 overhead bridges, a guard lock at Easton and a tide lock at Bristol. Water was supplied by a dam at the mouth of the Lehigh River at Easton. The sand and gravel channel of the Delaware Division leaked badly and additional water was provided to the lower section by a lifting wheel driven by a wing dam in the river at New Hope.

New York City connections with the Delaware Division were made via the Morris Canal at Phillipsburg, New Jersey, and the Delaware and Raritan Canal at Trenton, New Jersey, which reached tide water at New Brunswick.

The Delaware Division Canal is the only canal in Pennsylvania, with the possible exception of the Lehigh, which has been retained as a waterway until the present time, long after its demise as a commercial transport medium.

## Beaver and Erie Division

While the Main Line Systems and the Susquehanna Divisions were being planned, the people in Erie were also clamoring for the waterway connection to which the legislature had originally committed itself, which would tie in the city of Erie with the rest of the Pennsylvania Canal System. There was great disagreement about the route to be followed. Some people in the northwestern part of the state believed the water route should proceed from a point where the Western Division aqueduct crossed the Allegheny River at Freeport, northward along the Allegheny to Franklin, then up French Creek to Meadville and from there to Erie.

The people in Pittsburgh favored a route leaving the Ohio River downstream from Pittsburgh at Beaver and running through New Castle to Conneaut Lake and Erie, by way of the Beaver and Shenango Rivers. Pittsburghers felt that if the alternate route were chosen much of the Main Line traffic at Freeport would be directed to Erie without passing through Pittsburgh.

The State act of February 25, 1826 authorized the building of the French Creek feeder connecting Conneaut Lake, Meadville and Franklin. Work on this line was started before an ultimate decision was made regarding the main north-south connection to Erie.

Pittsburgh ultimately won out, and in 1831 a program of improvement was begun along the Beaver and Shenango Rivers as far north as Pulaski. This was known as the Beaver Division (31 miles).

In February of 1836 an extension from Pulaski northward to Conneaut Lake was approved, known as the Shenango Division, bringing the system 61 miles closer to Erie. In 1838 first contracts were awarded for the Conneaut Division to make final connection between Conneaut Lake and the city of Erie, an extension of 45 miles.

The state did not complete the Erie extension. In 1843, after spending more than $4,000,000 on construction, the state turned over the whole Erie and Beaver canal project to the Erie Canal Company, headed by R. S. Reed of Erie. After investment of another half million dollars the canal was finally opened to traffic in October of 1844.

The 136 mile route of the Beaver and Erie canal required 137 locks to overcome a total rise of 977 feet. Locks were 15 x 80 feet, smaller than the Main Line standard. There were also at one time 13 dams, 9 aqueducts, 30 basins and 221 crossing road-bridges. Slackwater sections accounted for 32 miles of the route.

The Ohio River itself formed the junction between the Beaver and Erie Canal and the Main Line at Pittsburgh. Packet steamers went back and forth on the Ohio, and canal freight boats were routed from one canal to another with little inconvenience.

The Pennsylvania and Ohio Canal made connection with the Beaver and Erie Canal at New Castle, running 85 miles west to Akron on the Ohio and Erie Canal in Ohio. This Ohio connection, known as the "Cross-Cut Canal," was completed in 1840 and the primary products transported were pig iron and iron ore, as well as passengers between Pittsburgh and Cleveland.

Another short-lived connection between Pennsylvania and Ohio was the Sandy and Beaver Canal, 76 miles long, connecting the Ohio and Erie Canal near Bolivar with the Ohio River in Pennsylvania, just east of the Pennsylvania-Ohio line.

## The Wiconisco Canal

A small, but important canal was the Wiconisco Line, running from the east end of the Clark's Ferry Bridge northward, on the east bank of the Susquehanna to Millersburg, a distance of 12 miles. It was begun by the state in 1838 but finished, and placed in operation, by a private concern.

This line furnished an essential outlet to the coal fields of Dauphin County, via the Lykens Valley Railroad junction at Millersburg. Much traffic moved over this connection to the Main Line system.

## Privately Owned Canals in Pennsylvania

We have already discussed the Union Canal and Schuylkill Navigation, both privately operated canals. The Union Canal, if not the most successful of the Pennsylvania Canals, at least resulted in wide publicity for the canal movement. Union Canal lottery tickets were sold throughout the entire eastern United States in the early 1800's, and it is said that millions of dollars were raised by this lottery, little of which actually found its way into the ultimate construction work.

## Delaware and Hudson Canal

One of the earliest out-of-state ventures, built by a New York concern to tap the rich coal region of northeastern Pennsylvania at Carbondale, was the Delaware and Hudson Canal, incorporated in 1823. Completed in 1829, it connected Eddyville, just off the Hudson River near Kingston, with Honesdale in Pennsylvania, a distance of 108 miles by canal. To reach Carbondale, a 16-mile gravity railroad was added, which is described in Chapter IX. The canal was 4 feet deep, from 32 to 36 feet in width and included 107 locks, 76 feet in length by 9½ feet wide, overcoming a total change of elevation of 950 feet on the uphill, downhill route. Some years after it began operation, the company replaced certain of its "at grade" river crossings with aqueducts, and hired John Roebling for much of the work. Of this, more later.

Delaware and Hudson Canal basin at Honesdale, about 1890. (Courtesy Richard H. Steinmetz, Sr.)

Canal basin of the Susquehanna and Tidewater Canal at Wrightsville. The extra large locks of the S. & T. could easily accommodate the huge tandem freight boats shown in the foreground. (Courtesy John G. Redmond.)

# The Lehigh Canal

The most successful of all Pennsylvania canals, the Lehigh Canal, was the brain-child of Josiah White, a Philadelphia entrepreneur who was one of the first men in the country to recognize the exceptional fuel properties of anthracite coal, and promoted its first use in Philadelphia. Failing to conclude workable coal transport arrangements with the owners of the Schuylkill Navigation Company, White transferred his activities to Bethlehem, Pa., where he formed several companies, later consolidated as the "Lehigh Coal and Navigation Company". He was one of the few individuals in history to obtain exclusive use of a river for his own purposes, when in 1818, the State Legislature authorized White and his partners "to build a slack water navigation by locks, dams or any other devices" which they might choose. When the downstream passage was complete they were permitted to charge toll. The State bill stipulated that one-way navigation must be finished by 1824 and two-way navigation by 1838. White completed his downstream facilities, including a device which he described as a "Bear Trap Lock", in 1823. By June of 1829 he had finished his two-way navigation lockage, with a combination of side canals and slack-water sections, from Mauch Chunk to Easton. He then waited impatiently for the State to complete its Delaware Division Canal (which it was supposed to have done in 1829, but failed to do until 1832) to get his canal boats down to Philadelphia.

Josiah White, a man of unusual talents and inventive ability, completed in April of 1827 the *first coal railroad in the country*, a gravity road 9 miles long, to carry coal from his mines at Summit Hill down to the canal boat loading chutes at Mauch Chunk. This unusual railroad, later re-built into what became known as the "Switch Back Railroad", is fully described in Chapter IX.

White also ran a canal further north, along some of the most rugged passages of the Lehigh River, to White Haven (named in his honor) and Stoddartville, with a connecting rail line across the mountains to Wilkes-Barre. One of the tremendous locks on this northern section of the canal had a lift of a full thirty feet! This extension of his facilities was completed about 1838. White also made arrangements for a rope ferry to carry his boats across the Delaware River at Easton to make connection with the new Morris Canal, running from Phillipsburg to Jersey City. The

Lock Twelve on the Susquehanna and Tidewater Canal, just north of the Norman Wood Bridge connecting southern York and Lancaster Counties. P.P. & L. has made a recreational park here. (Photo by G. Ross Bond.)

Lehigh Coal and Navigation Company acquired control of the Delaware Division Canal about 1860, and continued to carry on commercial operations on the Lehigh and Delaware Canals until 1931.

## The Susquehanna and Tidewater Canal

Ever since the late 1700's there had been a constant "tug of war" going on between the ports of Baltimore and Philadelphia, to obtain more direct lines of transportation into the rich Susquehanna Valley farm and forest lands of central and northern Pennsylvania.

Canal buffs may now ride this mule-drawn boat at New Hope on the Delaware Division Canal. (Photo by the author.)

Many Pennsylvania residents of the counties west of the Susquehanna, such as York, Adams, and Cumberland preferred to trade with Baltimore, because it was closer than Philadelphia, and was also the natural seaport connection at the mouth of the Susquehanna. Protected by the state line, however, powerful Philadelphia lobbyists were able to defeat almost every attempt in the Pennsylvania State legislature to pass transportation bills favorable to Baltimore. As a result, improvements to Susquehanna navigation below Columbia were delayed for decades, not to mention attempts to extend highways and railroads into central Maryland.

However, the Baltimorians were not easily discouraged, and with the support of Pennsylvanians west of the Susquehanna were able to introduce bill after bill into the Pennsylvania legislature for better highway and navigation facilities across the Mason-Dixon line. Some of them got through. A large amount of downstream Susquehanna River traffic eventually found its way to Baltimore, particularly after the one-way "Ark" had been perfected.

So confident were the Baltimorians that they would someday extend their inland water operations into Pennsylvania that in 1783 a Maryland company was chartered to build the "Susquehanna Canal" on the east bank of the river, from Port Deposit to Love Island, close to the Pennsylvania state line. This undertaking was the first of its kind in the United States. There were some forty men in the original organization, whose charter called for them to raise "twenty thousand pounds" and complete the canal by 1801. Work progressed slowly. The canal was 30 feet wide, 3 feet deep, and nine miles long. There were eight stone locks, 100 feet long by 12 feet wide, water being supplied from the river, with dams to permit crossings of the Conowingo and Octoraro Rivers.

Second highway and tow-path bridge between Columbia and Wrightsville, from the Wrightsville end. Note the double deck, canopy covered tow-path arrangement. This bridge was burned in 1863 to prevent a Confederate invasion of Philadelphia.

An official inspection of the completed canal was made in 1802 by the Governors of Pennsylvania and Maryland. However, with the lower portion of the Susquehanna in Pennsylvania still unimproved, little river traffic found its way through the narrow locks of the new canal. Arks and rafts simply bypassed it. It became a most unprofitable operation for the owners, who finally sold it at a great loss to another group, who ultimately abandoned it.

It was not till the "Main Line" canal system in Pennsylvania was completed that Baltimore again made a bid for a canal connection into Pennsylvania, this time on the west bank of the Susquehanna. In spite of violent opposition from Philadelphians in the Pennsylvania legislature, a bill was finally signed into law on April 15, 1835, permitting the "Susquehanna Canal Company" to build a canal from Wrightsville 26 miles south along the Susquehanna to the State line. In the meantime, the "Tidewater Canal Company" in Maryland had been authorized to build a nineteen-mile connecting canal northward from Havre de Grace. The two companies were later united under the name "Susquehanna and Tidewater Canal Company."

The Susquehanna and Tidewater Canal turned out to be a successful venture. Unlike its predecessor on the east bank, and the Union Canal to the north, its 28 locks were made large enough (17 feet wide by 170 feet in length) and its channel deep enough (50 feet wide by 6 feet deep) to accommodate almost any river traffic bound upstream or down, including log rafts. Part of its success was due to the Chesapeake and Delaware Canal, which had been opened in 1829 between upper Chesapeake Bay and the lower Delaware River. Philadelphians now grudgingly perceived that the latter canal, combined with the new S. & T. Canal, gave them an all-water route to the west, which, while longer than the Union Canal route, was able to accommodate much larger vessels. A connection, of course, was made across the Susquehanna River from Wrightsville to Columbia via slack-water behind a mile-wide dam, and a double-deck towpath on the downstream side of the "world's longest covered bridge". Large canal freight boats were now able to travel from anywhere in the Susquehanna canal complex to the ports of Baltimore, Philadelphia and even New York. Thousands of coal boats from the Nanticoke coal region now traveled this route to the country's three major seaports.

## The Conestoga Navigation Company

Lancaster had felt the urge to canalize the Conestoga Creek to the Susquehanna River as early as 1806, when the first company was chartered for this purpose. However, nothing was done until May of 1824, when the citizens of Lancaster held a mass meeting and sent a petition to the State legislature to take definite action. In March of 1825 the "Conestoga Navigation Company" was officially chartered. It began construction of a slack-water navigation, with nine dam-lock combinations between Lancaster and the Susquehanna at Safe Harbor. Locks were 22 feet wide by 100 feet in length and the pools between dams were maintained at a depth of about four feet. Construction of the Susquehanna and Tidewater in 1840 gave Lancastrians a direct water connection to Baltimore, with a dam across the Susquehanna and an outlet lock on the S. & T. at Lockport. The company also provided water power to mills located near each

One of the dam-lock combinations of the Conestoga Navigation system. There were nine such facilities to make the stream navigable from Lancaster to the Susquehanna.

Map of the Leiper Canal and Railroad System (Courtesy Herb O'Hanlon.)

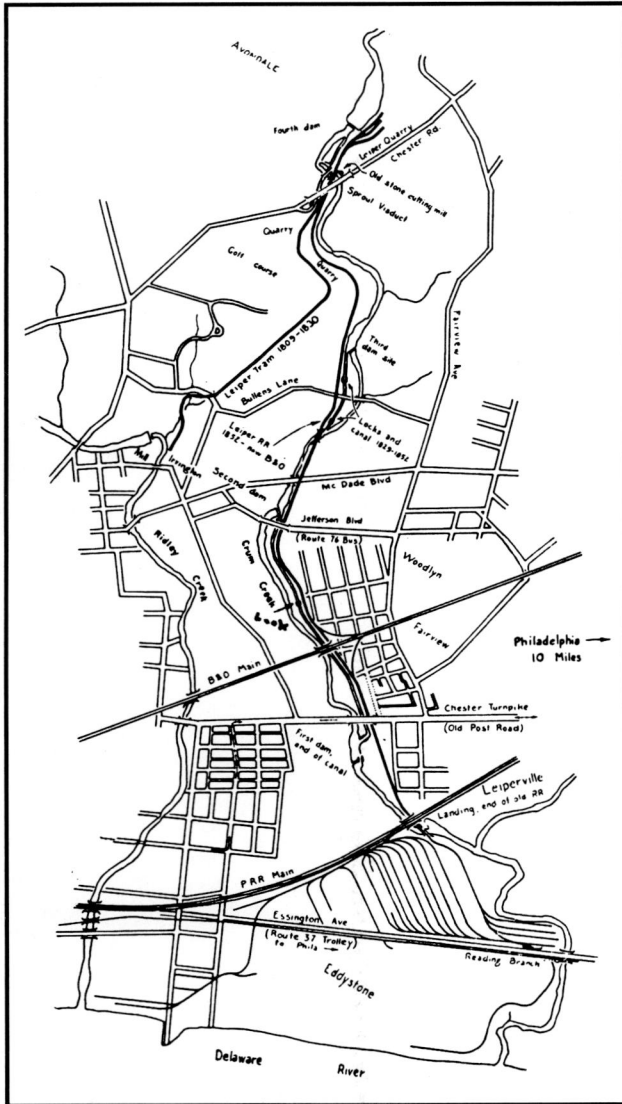

dam. However, financial difficulties beset the company from the start, not to mention numerous floods and "washouts", and the company went through several ownership changes before final abandonment.

## The Leiper Canal

From about 1829 to 1852 a several mile section of Crum Creek, near Chester, Pa., was canalized by George C. Leiper, who used this means of transporting stone from a quarry at Springfield to tidewater at Eddystone. The system included three locks, through which ran flat-bottom boats of eight tons capacity. The canal replaced an earlier tramway (or railroad) built in 1908, using wooden cars with flanged iron wheels powered by oxen – probably the first "railroad" in Pennsylvania.

## The Codorus Navigation Company

The canalization of the Codorus Creek from the city of York to the Susquehanna River, several miles below York Haven, resulted from a bitter political contest between York and Philadelphia concerning a railroad between Baltimore and York. The Baltimore and Susquehanna Railroad was chartered in Maryland in 1828 to build a line from Baltimore, through York, to York Haven, for a connection with river traffic above the still troublesome Conewago Falls. After securing approval in Maryland, the promoters of the railroad petitioned the Pennsylvania legislature for entry into this State. The petition was immediately defeated by

Philadelphia representatives at Harrisburg, much to the chagrin of the citizens of York county.

With the backing of York countians additional bills were introduced over the next few years, petitioning for the railroad, all of which were roundly defeated. Trying another tack, York then asked for permission to form the Codorus Navigation Company, which permission was granted in 1829. This would provide them with the northern connection needed to the Susquehanna. The next railroad bill was altered to terminate the Baltimore line at York. This would have made York the land-water transfer point instead of York Haven, a condition much desired by the local citizenry.

Stock in the new Codorus Navigation enterprise was offered for sale in York and enthusiastically purchased. Work commenced at once. Plans called for eight miles of slack-water and three miles of canals, from York to the Susquehanna, above Chestnut Ripples. Ten dams and thirteen locks were planned, including two guard locks. Locks were 95 feet in length, 18 feet wide, with an average lift of seven feet. Operations on the canal began in 1833, with the arrival in York of various boats and arks from northern Pennsylvania.

In the meantime, after lengthy controversy, a bill passed the Pennsylvania legislature in March of 1832, permitting the incorporation of the "York and Maryland Railroad", the last link in the new transportation system to Baltimore. However, with the opening of the Eastern Division Canal in 1833, and the State Railroad from Philadelphia to Columbia in 1834, – the entire situation had changed. Since the water-transfer point had now moved south from York Haven to Columbia, interest in the Codorus Navigation waned rapidly. Instead, the Baltimore promoters of the railroad now favored a rail connection to Columbia. In 1835 the York and Wrightsville Railroad Company was formed, with a connection across the bridge to Columbia. With the completion of the York-Baltimore line in August of 1838 and the York-Wrightsville railroad in May of 1840 – operations on the Codorus Navigation system very soon came to a halt.

# Railroads Versus Canals

Within the next ten years, the situation so apparent in York County became felt throughout the State. Railroads were being built everywhere and canals were on their way out. By the time of the Civil War, traffic on the canals had slowed considerably. Passengers now traveled by rail instead of packet boat. Freight boat traffic continued on the canals, on an ever decreasing scale, until about 1900, by which time most of the Pennsylvania canals had been abandoned.

"End of an Era". An abandoned canal boat rotting into the bank of the old Main Line Canal at Dauphin, Pa. The tow-path is already overgrown with weeds and has been turned into a wagon road (circa 1905.)

70

Interior of Aqueduct Number One on the Juniata Division of the Pennsylvania Main Line Canal. Here the canal channel ran across the Juniata River, a few hundred yards west of Amity Hall. The superstructure was all wood, with a channel roughly 17 feet wide and six feet deep. Piers of this old aqueduct can still be seen about a half mile north of the Route 11-15 crossing of the Juniata.

# Chapter VIII

# AQUEDUCTS AND CANAL ENGINEERING

The canal aqueduct was such an unusual structure, and there are so few of them left in the United States, that we feel they rate special attention. Visualize, if you will, what looks (from the side) like an ordinary bridge across a stream or river. Upon close inspection you find that, instead of a highway or rail track, there is a 17-feet wide, 5-feet deep channel of water running through it, high above the stream it crosses. Then you will have some idea of what an aqueduct was like. It was a water bridge for running one stream of water across another.

In early planning of canals in Pennsylvania, there was always a problem when the canal route had to cross another stream. If the elevation of the canal was not too far above the normal stream level, a dam was thrown across the stream below the crossing, to create a "slack-water" pool back of the dam and provide deep water for crossing. Generally this required guard locks on one or both sides of the crossing to maintain the proper level of water in the canal, unaffected by variations in the level of the stream. Still there were problems when the crossed stream was in flood, or

71

Artist Phil Hoffmann's conception of the east portal of the Freeport Aqueduct, where the Western Division of the Main Line Canal crossed the Allegheny River. This was a wooden structure, similar to the Juniata Aqueduct shown on the preceding page.

very dry. Canal engineers reasoned that if you could take a road across a stream, why not a canal? England, in the late 1700's was building canal aqueducts at great heights across entire valleys, many of which are still carrying canal traffic today. The St. Lawrence Seaway has a number of aqueducts, crossing highways as well as streams.

Canal aqueducts in Pennsylvania were variously built of wood, masonry or even metal, using the same type of suspension structures as other early bridges. However, because of the additional weight load of the flume of water they were carrying, their piers and suspension system had to be much sturdier than those of other bridges. Few remnants remain in Pennsylvania of the wide and heavy piers, and especially of the wood or metal structure of the flume itself, in these

Typical open aqueduct on the Pennsylvania Canal system. Surplus water from the canal was frequently allowed to spill over to the stream below. (Courtesy of Dr. Ernest H. Coleman.)

old aqueducts of the 1800's. Some of the drawings and photos included in this chapter will convey an idea of what they looked like and how they operated.

All this may give our readers the thought that there was some unusual engineering involved in building and operating canals. There was! Therefore, at this point we would like to introduce an engineer well known as the designer of the great Brooklyn Bridge, but who few Pennsylvanians realize got his start as an engineer on the Pennsylvania canals and aqueducts.

## John Augustus Roebling

The life of John Roebling reads like a Horatio Alger novel. Born in the town of Muhlhausen in Thuringen, Prussia, Roebling grew to young manhood in an atmosphere of military intrigue during and following the Napoleonic Wars.

John Roebling's father was a drab German merchant who ran a pipe shop. It was Roebling's mother who recognized her son's unusual talents and saw that he got the best education available, in the Royal

Ruins of the Mahantango Creek Aqueduct on the Susquehanna Division Canal a few miles south of Selinsgrove. Note the canal channel cross section. A well-preserved lock is hidden from the highway, just south of these ruins. (Photo by the author.)

Polytechnic School of Berlin, majoring in architecture and engineering.

After graduation, with the degree of civil engineer (1826), young Roebling built roads and bridges for the Prussian Government. The work was dull and routine and Roebling became restless. A friend, just returned from America, painted glowing pictures of the opportunities there, and John Roebling and his brother, Karl, quietly organized a small group in Muhlhausen to move to the New World and start a colony.

Political intrigue among the German states caused severe restrictions of freedom. It became illegal for a German technician to leave the country. This merely strengthened Roebling's determination to go to America. He continued plotting to take his followers out of the country, and was listed by the police as one of the most dangerous liberals in Muhlhausen.

In a real cloak-and-dagger type operation and aided by his mother, Roebling and his followers secretly and individually made their way to Bremen, where they chartered a boat and made their escape. After eleven weeks at sea, during which time they were blown off their course by heavy winds and chased by pirates, they landed at Philadelphia, in the summer of 1831.

Under the leadership of John Roebling, the group purchased seven thousand acres of land in Butler County, Pennsylvania (north of Pittsburgh) and set up a farm community, which they named Germania. The name was later changed to Saxonburg. The Roebling farming operation was not a great success, and in September of 1836, John Roebling had a chance at his first paid job in the United States, assisting with some part-time repair work on the Beaver Division of the State Canal System. His supervisor liked John's work, and he was called back again in June of 1838 as a "sub

John A. Roebling

Roebling's suspension aqueduct carrying the Delaware and Hudson Canal across the Delaware River at Lackawaxen. This structure was quite similar to his first aqueduct at Pittsburgh. So well constructed was this suspension system that it is still in use today as a highway crossing. It has been declared an historic landmark by the National Park Service and the American Society of Civil Engineers.

assistant engineer" and assigned to the Sinnemahoning Extension of the West Branch Susquehanna Canal. It was hoped that this extension would make a connection with the Allegheny River, but the entire project was shortly afterward abandoned.

Roebling was then re-assigned by the State to work with Engineer Charles L. Schlatter on the Kittanning Canal Feeder, which ran South along the Allegheny River to join the "Main Line" canal at Freeport. Schlatter soon recognized Roebling's exceptional technical ability, and made him his assistant on other parts of the canal system for which he had full responsibility, including the Western Division and the Beaver Division.

## Wire Cable for the Portage Railroad

Some of Roebling's assignments took him along the Allegheny Portage Railroad. Observing the operation of the steep planes, which carried the cars and boats upward or downward at the end of large hemp ropes, Roebling was shocked to witness the breaking of one of the ropes, causing a wreck in which two men were killed.

The accident set Roebling to thinking about an article he had read in a German paper concerning the manufacture of wire rope at Freiburg, Saxony. He began thinking of how a flexible wire rope could be made, which would not wear out as fast as the hemp, and would have far greater strength with considerably less cross-sectional area.

The Jackstown Aqueduct, on the Juniata Division Canal near Mt. Union. This was a tubular cast-iron structure with wrought-iron cross bracing. Some idea of its size may be obtained by noting that a man is standing just in front of the left entrance column.

Returning to his farm in Saxonburg, he bought a quantity of iron wire and after experimentation, and with the help of his neighbors, succeeded in twisting a series of individual wires into America's first twisted wire cable. The desirable qualities of this cable were surprising even to Roebling himself.

Roebling's wire cable was first substituted for a 600 feet length of rope for Thomas Young, on a boat-slip at Johnstown, in the Spring of 1842. It worked well, and Roebling was given permission to install his cable on the entire length of Plane Number Three on the Portage Railroad on an experimental basis that summer. The lasting qualities and safety of his cable were soon apparent and during the next few years he was commissioned by the State to install his cables at most of the other inclined planes throughout the "public works" system.

## The Pittsburgh Aqueduct

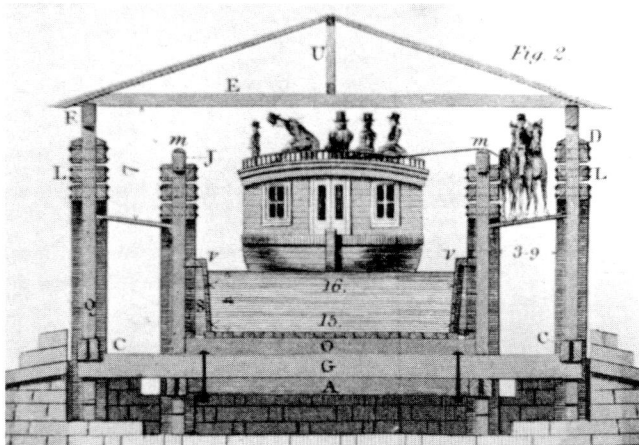

Patent drawing of the Allegheny River Aqueduct which brought the Main Line Canal from the borough of Allegheny into downtown Pittsburgh. (Built in 1829.)

Now that he had established a reputation as a manufacturer of wire cable, Roebling next turned his attention to the application of wire to the building of suspension bridges. In this area, Col. Charles Ellet had already done the pioneering, with his first successful wire cable suspension bridge of 1842 across the Schuylkill in Philadelphia. However, Roebling had some ideas of his own for improving on Ellet's design.

An open, wooden-arch aqueduct at Johnstown, circa 1862, where the Western Division Canal crossed the Conemaugh River, just west of the Johnstown Canal Basin. (Courtesy Ralph J. Michaels.)

Roebling had an opportunity in 1844 to put his own bridge theories into practice. That year the old 1092-foot long wooden aqueduct, which brought the Pennsylvania Canal into downtown Pittsburgh across the Allegheny River, was rated as unsafe by the Canal engineers. This aqueduct had been built in 1829 by a Mr. Lothrop of Pittsburgh, at a cost of $104,000. It had six piers and seven Burr-type arches of 150 feet span each. The overall width of the aqueduct, including pedestrian walk on one side and mule towpath on the other, was about 34 feet, with a water-channel (or "trunk") 16 feet wide at the top, 15 feet wide at the bottom, and 5 feet deep. Depth of water carried was generally about 4 feet, 3 inches. The arches (four to a span) were reinforced with a wooden truss, although most of the floor weight was supported directly on vertical 1-1/2" iron rods hanging from the arches.

The entire structure was surmounted by a peak-roof to protect the wooden arches from external weathering.

Difficulties were encountered with this aqueduct on several occasions. At one time a section of the channel bottom dropped out, draining water out of good portions of the canal system on both sides of the river. Flood damaged various individual spans. In 1845 a fire hastened the decision of the canal commissioners to build a new aqueduct at this point. John Roebling was contacted for advice.

Roebling felt the problem could be solved with a "bundled" wire cable suspension structure and laid his plans before the canal engineers. There was considerable opposition but Roebling was finally told to proceed. He rebuilt the seven-span structure with 162-foot slack spans of two 7-inch diameter bundles of 1900 wires each, laid parallel to each other, taking great care to insure equal tension in each wire. Each cable was protected and tightly bound together by an external wrapping of annealed wire. The slack spans of these cables supported the water flume.

Roebling's second achievement in the suspension bridge field was the 1847 Smithfield Street Bridge in Pittsburgh, replacing a burned-out wooden structure across the Monongahela. Note the Monongahela Inclined Plane in the background. (Courtesy Dr. George Swetnam.)

The success of Roebling's first structure in Pittsburgh led immediately to another – a suspension replacement to the Smithfield Street Bridge over the Monongahela in 1847, on the piers of the old wooden structure destroyed by the Great Fire of 1845. This unusual structure had eight suspension spans of 188 feet each, supported by two 4-1/2 inch diameter cables.

It had cast iron suspension towers 16 feet high and a 35 foot roadway which carried two lines of car tracks, pedestrian promenades on both sides, and the heaviest kind of street traffic, for the next 35 years.

Roebling's reputation as a bridge builder spread rapidly and he was petitioned by a number of canal companies both in and out of Pennsylvania to assist them with their canal aqueduct problems.

Method used by Roebling to anchor his early suspension structures. This photo was made recently on the Delaware crossing at Lackawaxen, originally an aqueduct on the Delaware and Hudson Canal, now a highway toll bridge – still in use!

# Aqueducts on the D. & H. Canal

Another of his aqueduct projects in Pennsylvania was the double-crossing of the Delaware and Hudson Canal over both the Lackawaxen and Delaware Rivers near their junction. Formerly a dam-created, slack-water crossing of the Delaware River only, the D. & H. had problems with the river raftsmen, who sued continually for damages incurred while crossing the D. & H. dam, and who were in constant conflict with the rope ferry crossing of D. & H. canal boats, at right angles to their line of travel.

The managers of the canal in 1846 elected to build two aqueducts at this point to correct their difficulties and called in John Roebling as one of two bidders on the job.

Roebling's competition proposed a five-pier covered bridge crossing the Delaware, contrasted to Roebling's three-pier cable-supported spans. After inspection of Roebling's aqueduct at Pittsburgh, the management awarded him the contract.

Roebling soon began work on this double-aqueduct crossing at a combined cost of $60,400. The two aqueducts were completed and opened in the Spring of 1849. The Lackawaxen aqueduct was a fairly easy two-span suspension crossing, whereas the Delaware aqueduct had four spans for a total length of 600 feet. The cable supports on the sides of the aqueduct contained 2150 wire strands each and were 8-1/2 inches in diameter. Width of the canal channel was 19 feet.

So well was the Delaware Aqueduct constructed that after the abandonment of the D. & H. canal (in 1899) it was converted into a highway crossing and is still in use today.

The management of the Delaware and Hudson Canal Company were so pleased with Roebling's work on the Lackawaxen and Delaware Aqueducts that he was commissioned to build two more sizable aqueducts, one crossing the Neversink River, and the other at the High Falls crossing of the Rondout Creek. These aqueducts, both in the New York section of the canal, were completed 1849 to 1851.

Another Roebling Aqueduct on the Delaware and Hudson Canal – a short one, where the Canal crossed the Lackawaxen River just above its confluence with the Delaware River. Note coal boat part way across. Roebling designed and built two more aqueducts for the D. & H. Canal Company, on the New York side of the river.

Hoffmann drawing of the west portal of the Freeport Aqueduct.

By the time John Roebling designed this interesting bridge for the Sixth Street crossing of the Allegheny River at Pittsburgh in 1860, he had acquired an eye for appearance as well as engineering utility. Replacing the old 1818 wooden structure across the Allegheny, it was hailed at the opening as the "finest and most beautiful bridge in the world".

# Other Roebling Structures

Another of Roebling's Pennsylvania suspension structures, built in 1860, replaced the 1818 wooden Sixth Street Bridge across the Allegheny River at Pittsburgh. This bridge was Roebling's fanciest, with ten 45-foot high cast-iron supporting towers, two 344-foot center spans and two 171-foot side spans for a total length of 1030 feet. The deck, 40 feet wide, including two 10-foot pedestrian promenades, was supported by four cables, two 7-inches and two 4-inches in diameter. (See photo.)

He also built major bridges in Ohio and across the Niagara River near the Falls.

John Augustus Roebling, engineering genius and adopted son of Pennsylvania, died July 22, 1869, of an injury received while running surveys for the Brooklyn Bridge. It remained for his son, Colonel Washington Roebling to complete, in 1883, Roebling's greatest triumph in America, which has set the pattern for tremendous river crossings throughout the world — the famous, still-standing Brooklyn Bridge.

Inclined Plane Number Six on the Allegheny Portage Railroad as depicted by artist George W. Storm. The "Lemon House", a travelers tavern, at this highest point on the Allegheny Mountain Crossing, is shown at the left. This was part of the "Main Line" system between Philadelphia and Pittsburgh in the 1830's.

# Chapter IX

# INCLINED PLANES AND GRAVITY RAILWAYS

Ever since 1781, the year when James Watt improved the old Newcomen steam pumping engine to the point where it could turn a wheel and do useful work, inventors everywhere had dreamed of applying the steam engine to vehicular travel. John Fitch proved, at Philadelphia in 1790, that the steam engine could be successfully used to propel a commercial water vessel. However, early steam engines, and their appurtenances, were extremely heavy and cumbersome. The problems of applying steam power to relatively small land vehicles seemed almost insurmountable, although many inventors, in Britain and America, were working to this end in the early days of the nineteenth century.

Long before a practical steam locomotive had been invented, crude "tramways" had been developed in the coal mines of England, with a sort of flat wood "track" to keep the loaded carts and wagons from sinking into the ground. Over the years, improvements were made to create wooden "rails" above ground level, and flanges on the cart wheels to keep them on the rails. The motive power was provided by mules, or other beasts of burden.

Silas Whitney is credited with the first "tramway" (1807) in America to transport gravel from the western slope of Beacon Hill to Charles Street in Boston, but in Pennsylvania, Thomas Leiper built a true "railroad" in 1809, to carry stone from his quarries at Springfield to tidewater at Ridley Creek, near Chester. It had timber rails mounted on "sleepers" with wooden cars and flanged iron wheels, pulled by oxen. Short wooden-rail lines were also built in Pennsylvania at Kiskiminetas Creek in 1816, and at Bear Creek in 1818, the latter to move iron made at a furnace.

double-inclined plane for raising canal boats from one level to another. There is also a reference to an inclined plane with wood rails constructed on Beacon Hill in Boston, circa 1795, to lower bricks from a kiln to a street below. The loaded cars came down the track and were hauled up by cable when emptied.

Several coal-mining operations in eastern Pennsylvania elected to use inclined planes as a source of power for their railroads, utilizing gravity to move the coal cars between planes. These were the Delaware and Hudson Canal Company, which began construction of their 17-mile "Gravity Railroad" in 1826 completing it in 1829; and The Lehigh Coal and Navigation Company, which began construction of what was later called the "Switchback Railroad" in January of 1827 and completed all nine miles in April of the same year. In both cases the terrain covered by these two railroads was admirably suited for the purpose.

The big advantage of the inclined plane, as opposed to the yet unperfected steam locomotive, was that the power plant was stationary and could be built as large and efficiently as necessary for the power requirements of the project. Cars were picked up by a towing device at the base of each plane, and after reaching the summit of the plane, were cut loose and allowed to coast (with suitable braking) to the base of the next inclined plane, where they were again boosted to a higher altitude. This process was repeated as many times as necessary to get them to their destination.

With the canal-building period well underway in Pennsylvania in the 1820's, the proponents of railways as a means of public transportation were generally ignored and discredited. Only in the anthracite coal fields, or in terrain where canals were impractical, were railroads even considered. Since the Stephensons of England did not come up with their first practical steam locomotive until 1829, any railroads developed prior to this date were limited for a source of locomotion to animal power, or the Inclined Plane.

Sources examined by your author do not indicate clearly whether the inclined plane, as we knew it here in Pennsylvania, was a British or American invention. Robert Fulton, while in England in 1794, patented a

Passenger car being shoved up Mount Jefferson on the "Switchback" by the Booster Car. Note gravity return line passing under the inclined plane.

With some modifications the same principle was applied to passenger and freight cars traveling the state-owned Allegheny Portage Railroad and portions of the Columbia-Philadelphia Railroad. Inclined planes remained popular in certain sections of Pennsylvania for many decades after the coming of the steam locomotive. The "Switchback Railroad" became one of the biggest tourist attractions in Eastern Pennsylvania in the late 1800's. Inclined planes still provide colorful transportation and wonderful views of the cities in Johnstown and Pittsburgh.

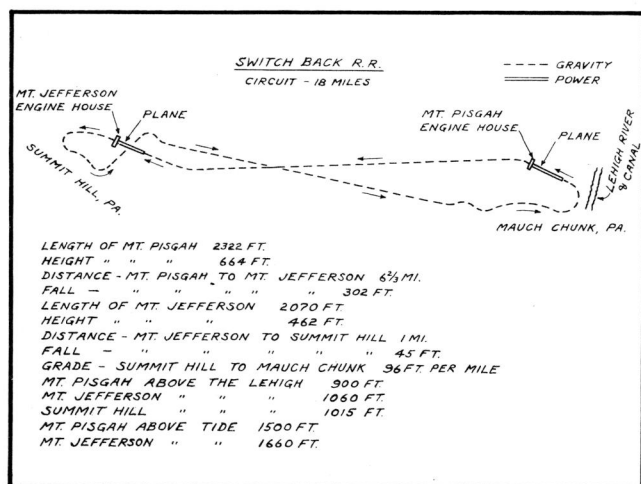

SWITCH BACK R.R.
CIRCUIT - 18 MILES

- - - - GRAVITY
===== POWER

MT. JEFFERSON
ENGINE HOUSE
PLANE

SUMMIT HILL, PA.

MT. PISGAH
ENGINE HOUSE
PLANE

LEHIGH RIVER & CANAL

MAUCH CHUNK, PA.

LENGTH OF MT. PISGAH 2322 FT.
HEIGHT " " " 664 FT.
DISTANCE - MT. PISGAH TO MT. JEFFERSON 6⅔ MI.
FALL - " " " " " 302 FT.
LENGTH OF MT. JEFFERSON 2070 FT.
HEIGHT " " " 462 FT.
DISTANCE - MT. JEFFERSON TO SUMMIT HILL 1 MI.
FALL - " " " " " 45 FT.
GRADE - SUMMIT HILL TO MAUCH CHUNK 96 FT. PER MILE
MT. PISGAH ABOVE THE LEHIGH 900 FT.
MT. JEFFERSON " " " 1060 FT.
SUMMIT HILL " " " 1015 FT.
MT. PISGAH ABOVE TIDE 1500 FT.
MT. JEFFERSON " " 1660 FT.

**Data on the "Switchback", supplied by G. Ross Bond.**

# Josiah White's Railroads

In the **book** on canals, we have told something of Josiah White's ingenuity as a builder of canals. He was equally talented in the field of railroad engineering. After completing his first navigation system to carry coal down the Lehigh River to Easton, he turned his attention to the problem of more rapid transportation of coal from his mines back in the hills to the river at Mauch Chunk. With true pioneer spirit, Josiah White elected to build a gravity railroad, the *first of its kind completed in the United States,* from Summit Hill to Mauch Chunk to replace a previous mule-cart dirt road. Ground was broken for the line January 1, 1827 and it was completed in April of the same year. The downhill trip with loaded coal cars, or "wagons," was made entirely by gravity. Each wagon carried a ton and a half of coal. A brake, attached to a cable, was the only control provided. One driver could manage a complete gang of wagons hitched together. The system worked beautifully and was soon dubbed the "Gravity Road." Mules were used to tow the empty cars up to the mine after each down-hill trip. Special "mule cars" were included in the down-hill

run to bring the animals back to Mauch Chunk. To save time, the mules were also fed during the ride down. The descending cars made the nine mile journey in 20 minutes, an unbelievable speed for the times!

Josiah White's next railroad project was a 25-mile portage railroad, which he named the "Lehigh and Susquehanna Railroad" designed to interchange freight from the northernmost extremity of his two-way navigation on the Lehigh River at White Haven, across the mountains to Wilkes-Barre on the Susquehanna North Branch Canal. This unusual rail line included an 1800-foot tunnel north of White Haven, and a three-stage, double-track series of inclined planes running down Solomon's gap to the town of Ashley near the North Branch of the Susquehanna. These planes, said to have the highest lift of any in the world, were placed in partial operation May 23, 1843, with one track operating "by horsepower", and full steam operation of the power house for both tracks by 1851.

Traffic became so heavy on the Lehigh and Susquehanna Railroad that the two tracks (operating in opposite directions) were taxed to capacity and in May of 1866, a "back-line" gravity track was opened down the mountain for passenger cars and empty freight cars. This freed the planes for up-hill travel exclusively.

Meanwhile, White's coal operation at Summit Hill had expanded into Panther Creek Valley to the north, and he developed a two-stage, four-track inclined plane railroad here to bring coal from Panther Creek to Summit Hill and from there to the Lehigh Canal at Mauch Chunk. These new planes were completed August 18, 1849, but a bottleneck developed in returning the empty cars to the mines at Panther Creek. Hence, an ingenious gravity "switch back" railroad was built to return the "empties" to the valley, passing through two tunnels, and with short up-grades to control the cars on the steep hillside. This was a true "switch-back" railroad, and the name was also later applied to White's rail-line from Summit Hill to Mauch Chunk.

**"Booster", or Safety Car, on the Switchback Railroad, as photographed by G. Ross Bond in 1920.**

Looking up Mount Jefferson Inclined Plane on the "Switchback", toward the Engine House. The Swedish iron bands show plainly on rollers on the right track; booster car cable, at the left. (Photo by G. Ross Bond, October 8, 1920.)

The latter railroad was rebuilt in 1846, to eliminate the mule-haul return line for "empties". It replaced the original "Gravity Railroad" and became the most famous of all White's lines.

This amazing system between Summit Hill and Mauch Chunk operated solely by gravity over 17 of its 18 miles of track. Like a "roller-coaster," the cars were given a boost in elevation at two points on the up-grade by means of a 2322 foot long by 664 foot high inclined plane up Mt. Pisgah, and a 2070 foot long by 462 foot high plane at Mt. Jefferson. At the foot of each of these planes, a "booster car," which Josiah White named his Safety Car, came out of a pit beneath the track and pushed the passenger or coal cars up the incline. The motive power for the booster was a stationary steam engine at the head of each plane driving a 28 foot diameter drum which reeled in two Swedish iron bands, each 7½ inches wide, to which the boosters were attached. At the head of each plane the cars were free to coast, with no control other than a brake on the wheels. By this means the cars attained an elevation of 1500 feet above sea level on top of Mt. Pisgah and 1660 feet at Mt. Jefferson. The down-hill ride between planes, and particularly on the 9-mile return descent from Summit Hill to Mauch Chunk, was quiet, as fast as the brakeman deemed

Photo made by G. Ross Bond October 8, 1920, from the front end of an ascending car on the Mount Pisgah Inclined Plane of the "Switchback". Note brake handwheel to the right.

safe, and altogether awe-inspiring and thrilling to the thousands of tourists who flocked to the Lehigh Valley each summer to ride the famous "Switch-Back," between loads of coal. This novel system continued operations until 1932.

Students of railroads contend that this best-known of all Josiah White's railroads was mis-named the "Switch-Back". However, there were three safety "turn-outs", or up-grades, on the gravity part of the system, which could not be by-passed until the down-hill cars had come to a complete stop and the operators had turned the switches to permit the cars to pass. If by any chance the cars were out of control at these three points, they would automatically take the up-hill route (since the switches were set that way) and would shortly come to a safe stop. These safety devices were probably responsible for the name "Switch-Back".

**Identification of this old photo simply reads "Mahanoy Plane". Believed to be one of the inclined planes on the Hazelton Railroad, opened in 1838, which made connection with the Lehigh and Mahanoy Railroad at Black Creek Junction. (Courtesy of George R. Wills.)**

# Delaware and Hudson Railroads

There were actually two inclined-plane railroads serving the Delaware and Hudson Canal system in northeastern Pennsylvania. One was the Delaware and Hudson Gravity Railroad, part of the original canal-rail system, to transport coal from the mines at Carbondale to the western terminus of the canal at Honesdale; and later, a separate enterprise known as the "Pennsylvania Coal Company Gravity Railroad," connecting the Susquehanna North Branch Canal near Pittston, with the Delaware and Hudson Canal at Hawley. The former was always part of the D. & H. Company; the latter a D. & H. supplier after 1850.

The Carbondale-Honesdale Gravity Road, completed in 1829, originally consisted of five inclined planes up the steep, west side of the Moosic Mountains to Rix's Gap and three more inclined planes down the Honesdale side. Planes were numbered "One to Eight" from the west end. A change of elevation of 950 feet was overcome on the west; 970 feet on the east. The rails were wooden, with iron-strap topping, and chains were initially used to raise and lower the cars on the planes. Since an up-bound train of cars was always balanced against a down-bound train on the planes,

A gravity passenger car loaded with picnickers, just starting to eat lunch. Exact date and location are unknown, but this car is believed to be somewhere on the D. & H. Gravity Railroad, about 1895. (Courtesy of Raymond H. LeCates, Jr.)

trackage was saved by using only one track on each plane, with a double-track "turnout" (with appropriate automatic switches) halfway up each plane for the cars to pass, in opposite directions. Power had to be applied by means of stationary steam power plants to Planes Number One to Five, as the heavy, loaded coal cars from the mines were boosted up the west side of the mountains, balanced against the "Empties" coming down. However, on the east side, with the loaded cars out-weighing the "empties" it was necessary only to supply braking power to the plane mechanism. This was handled by large "friction brakes upon the shaft of an upright fan-wheel!" No power plants were used initially on this side. Transportation of the cars on the relatively level stretches between planes was handled by horses.

During its nearly seventy years of operation, the D. & H. Gravity Railroad underwent many changes to improve its efficiency and extend its service, both as a coal and passenger line. First of all, the use of chains on the planes proved troublesome and dangerous. Hemp ropes were substituted, with better results, followed by Roebling type wire cables, as the ultimate solution.

As the coal business of the company increased in New York, the original Gravity Road became overloaded. Hence a completely separate empty-car return line was built over the Moosic 1844-56 like the "Switch-Back", with stationary power plants (some using water power, rather than steam) giving both loaded and empty cars a "boost" to higher elevation, and letting them coast downhill between planes.

84

When the Gravity was finally shut down, it had a total of twenty-eight water or steam powered planes operating from Olyphant (to which it had been extended) to Carbondale, to Honesdale.

Also, like Josiah White's "Switch-Back", it had become a tourist attraction, and many visitors came to the area just to ride its gravity-operated passenger cars. January 3, 1899 marks the last date that the railroad operated as a gravity line. Subsequently, portions of its trackage continued in use as a steam-locomotive route until 1931, when operations finally ceased, over 100 years since they began.

In 1847, the Delaware and Hudson Canal Company, contracted with the Wyoming Coal Association to form a separate company, which became known as the Pennsylvania Coal Company. The prime objective of the new firm was to transport coal from the Nanticoke area of the Susquehanna North Branch, and coal fields between, overland to Hawley on the D. & H. Canal. Here the coal was to be sold to the D. & H. Canal Company, and it was part of the original agreement that the new Pennsylvania Coal Company was also to be charged a special toll rate for use of the canal into New York. It was on the latter point that legal difficulties developed, and resulting strained relationship between the two companies led to early termination of the entire operation.

However, the Pennsylvania Coal Company did build a Gravity Railroad approximately forty miles long connecting Port Griffith on the Susquehanna, through Dunmore, to Hawley on the Lackawaxen River. It was quite similar in operation to the D. & H. (improved) Gravity Railroad, with a total of twenty-two inclined planes, most of them operated by steam, but four using water wheels as a power source. Like the D. & H. it had both a loaded-car line and an empty-car return line, each following quite different

This photo is identified as the interior of an "Engineer House", showing "Whiting Hoist, Mahanoy Plane". Probably the same engine house as that at the top of the plane on page 83. (Courtesy George R. Wills.)

routes to take advantage of the terrain for the best "coasting route" between planes. Completed in the Spring of 1850, it continued to do business with the D. & H. Canal until about 1860, when the company built its own locomotive line into Lackawaxen.

## Inclined Planes on the "Main Line"

Much better known to travelers through Pennsylvania in the 1830's and '40's were the inclined planes of the Pennsylvania "System of Public Works" connecting Philadelphia with Pittsburgh. The "Main Line" traveler immediately became aware of the Belmont Inclined Plane, after crossing the Columbia Bridge over the Schuylkill a few miles north of the city center. This plane, operated by a steam power plant at the top, climbed the west bank of the Schuylkill, overcoming an elevation of 187 feet, with an up-grade length of 2805 feet.

At the western extremity of the 82-mile Columbia-Philadelphia Railroad the traveler was dropped 90 feet into the town of Columbia, along an 1800-foot long inclined plane.

The Columbia and Philadelphia Railroad was officially opened in 1834. About four years later a sectional canal boat was developed, which permitted cross-state travelers to board their boat, deposit their belongings inside, and never leave it (if they so desired) until they arrived in Pittsburgh, some five or six days later.

Looking down the Belmont Plane on the Columbia-Philadelphia Railroad, toward Columbia Bridge over the Schuylkill River. (Drawing by Philip Hoffmann.)

Constructed as part of the Allegheny Portage Railroad in 1834, the Conemaugh Viaduct, when built, was one of the largest single stone-arch bridges in the country. Used by the Pennsylvania Railroad after 1857, it was destroyed by the Johnstown flood in 1889.

Transporting these sectional boats overland on the Columbia-Philadelphia Railroad, and the Allegheny Portage Railroad, created additional work for the operators of the planes on the two railroads. While somewhat impractical, it was a novelty enjoyed by a few of the more prosperous passengers who wished to travel in style.

The Allegheny Portage Railroad was the most widely publicized inclined plane railroad in Pennsylvania between the years of its opening in 1834 and its final abandonment in 1857. Travelers from Europe took the "Main Line" route to the west in preference to the Erie Canal, primarily to enjoy the splendid scenery and awe-inspiring heights to which they climbed on the Portage Railroad. As a prime tourist attraction of the mid-1800's, we feel it rates special attention.

The Allegheny Portage Railroad was authorized by an act of the Pennsylvania legislature and approved by

the Governor on March 31, 1831. The line was surveyed and located by Chief Engineer Sylvester Welch, working under the direction of the Canal Commissioners, who on May 25, 1831 let the contract for that part of the road between Johnstown and the summit of the mountain. Contracts for the work between the summit and Hollidaysburg were awarded on July 29 of the same year. The first track was completed on March 18, 1834. The route was open for traffic at that time and the second track was completed late in the spring of 1835.

Basically, this 37-mile railroad consisted of a series of ten inclined planes, five on one side of the mountain and five on the opposite side. Traffic, of course, moved both upward and downward on both series of planes. Each plane had two tracks with an endless hemp cable moving up one track and down the other,

to which the ascending or descending cars were attached. An attempt was usually made to balance the weight of the ascending cars against the descending cars at each plane. When the ascending weight was greater than the descending weight, stationary steam engines at the head of each plane were used to supply additional power. When the descending weight was greater, an ingenious water cylinder brake was used to control the speed of descent. In between the planes were stretches of track with a slight up-hill slope over which the cars were initially transported by horse or mule power, later by primitive steam locomotives. The planes were numbered from the Johnstown end of the route and varied in length from 1500 feet (plane No. 3) to 3100 feet (plane No. 8). The slope of the planes varied from a minimum of 6% (6 foot rise to 100 feet) on plane No. 9 to a maximum of 10% on plane No. 7. The highest point on the route was at the top of plane No. 6 on the Hollidaysburg side, 2334 feet above sea level, nearly 1400 feet above the level of the canal basin at Hollidaysburg and approximately 1150 feet above the Johnstown station at the west end of the route. The horizontal tracks were laid on two rows of stone "sleepers" with metal fasteners set into the rock. The tracks of the planes were iron straps nailed on wooden rails and held in place by wooden cross-ties.

This Storm drawing shows Plane Number Eight, longest on the Portage. The "hitching shed" at the bottom of the plane is shown at the right.

Travel along the Portage Railroad can perhaps be best described by means of excerpts from the writings of some of its passengers. One such literary traveler was a Philadelphia writer who used the pen name "Peregrin Prolix." This gentleman, whose real name was Philip Holbrook Nicklin, traveled the route from

Passengers boarding a car of the Allegheny Portage Railroad for transport between Hollidaysburg and Johnstown. When the road opened in 1834, horses were generally used between inclined planes. (Drawing by Philip J. Hoffmann.)

A mixture of freight cars, passenger cars and portable canal boat cars on the summit level of the Portage, near Cresson. (Drawing by Philip J. Hoffmann.)

Johnstown to Hollidaysburg August 20, 1835. Here is his description of the trip over the Portage Railroad:

"Yesterday at Johnstown we soon dispatched a good breakfast and at 6 a.m. were in motion on the first level, as it is called, of four miles length, leading to the foot of the first inclined plane. The level has an ascent of 101 feet and we passed over it in horse-drawn cars with a speed of six miles an hour. This is a very interesting part of the route, not only on account of the wildness and beauty of the scenery, but also because of the excitement mingled with vague apprehension which takes possession of everybody in approaching the great wonder of the internal improvements of Pennsylvania. In six hours the cars and passengers were to be raised 1172 feet of perpendicular height and be lowered 1400 feet of perpendicular descent by complicated, powerful and frangible machinery, and were to pass a mountain, to overcome which with a similar weight three years ago would have required the space of three days. As soon as we arrived at the foot of the Plane No. 1 the horses were unhitched and the cars were fastened to a rope which passes up the middle of one track and down the middle of the other. The stationary steam engine at the head of the plane was started and the cars moved majestically up the steep and long acclivity in four minutes, the length of the plane being 1608 feet, with perpendicular height of 150 feet.

"The cars were now attached to horses and drawn through a magnificent tunnel 900 feet long having two tracks and being cut through solid rock nearly the whole distance. (This was the first railroad tunnel built in America.) Now the train of cars were attached to a steam tug (locomotive) to pass a level of fourteen miles in length. This lengthy level is one of the most interesting portions of the Portage Railroad from the beauty of its location and the ingenuity of its construction. It ascends almost imperceptibly through its whole course, overcoming a perpendicular height of 190 feet.

Hoffmann drawing of the interior of one of the stationary power houses on the Allegheny Portage Railroad.

**Top of Plane Number Six, 2397 feet above sea level, looking east. Lemon House, at the right, is today being used by the National Park Service as a Portage Railroad Museum. The locomotive is an early type, introduced on the portage in the 1830's. (Drawing by George W. Storm.)**

The valley of the Little Conemaugh is passed on a viaduct of the most beautiful construction. It is of one arch, a perfect semi-circle with a diameter of 80 feet.

"The fourteen miles of this second level are passed in one hour and the train arrived at the foot of the second plane, which has 1760 feet of length and 132 feet of perpendicular height. The third level has a length of one and five-eighth miles, a rise of 14½ feet and is passed by means of horses. The third plane has a length of 1480 feet and a perpendicular height of 130 feet. The fourth level is two miles long, rises 19 feet, and is passed by means of horses. The fourth plane has a length of 2196 feet and a perpendicular height of 188 feet. The fifth level is three miles long, rises 26 feet, and is passed by means of horses. The fifth plane has a length of 2629 feet and a perpendicular height of 202

feet and brings you to the top of the mountain 2397 feet above the level of the ocean, 1172 feet above Johnstown and 1399 feet above Hollidaysburg.

"Thus three short hours have brought you from the torrid plain to a refreshing and invigorating climate. The ascending apprehension has left you but it is succeeded by the fear of the steep decent which lies before you and as the car rolls along on this giddy height the thought trembled in your mind that it may slip over the head of the first descending plane, rush down the frightful steep and be dashed into a thousand pieces.

"The length of the road on the summit of the mountain is one and five-eighths miles and about the middle of it stands a spacious and handsome stone tavern. The eastern quarter of a mile, which is the highest part

Johnstown Inclined Plane, still is use for transporting passengers between upper and lower levels of the city. Built after the Johnstown Flood of 1889, as a device for rapid evacuation of the flood-prone areas along the Conemaugh River. (Photo by the author.)

of the entire route is a dead level; in the other part there is an ascent of 19 feet. The descent on the eastern side of the mountain is much more fearful than the ascent on the west for the planes are much longer and steeper, of which you are made aware by the increased thickness of the ropes, and you look down instead of up.

"There are also five planes on the eastern side of the mountain and five slightly descending levels, the last of which is nearly four miles long and leads to the basin at Hollidaysburg. This is traveled by cars, without steam or horse, merely by the force of gravity.

"In descending the mountain you meet several fine prospects and arrive at Hollidaysburg between 12 and 1 o'clock."

The figures quoted by Mr. Nicklin are not necessarily the same as those preserved by the Pennsylvania Railroad in its files of statistics on the Portage Railroad. However, they are reasonably close.

Separate tables of data on the planes are included for the benefit of those who wish to have an official record of elevations and distances on this unusual railroad.

| No. | Horizontal length in feet. | Length measured on plane. | Total rise in feet. | Rise per 100 feet. | Angle of inclination. |
|---|---|---|---|---|---|
| 1 | 1600.50 | 1607.74 | 150.00 | 10. | 5° 42′ 38″ |
| 2 | 1755.32 | 1760.43 | 132.40 | 8. | 4° 34′ 26″ |
| 3 | 1473.70 | 1480.25 | 130.50 | 9.50 | 5° 25′ 36″ |
| 4 | 2187.74 | 2195.94 | 187.86 | 9. | 5° 8′ 34″ |
| 5 | 2620.82 | 2628.60 | 201.64 | 8. | 4° 34′ 26″ |
| 6 | 2700.52 | 2713.85 | 266.50 | 10.25 | 5° 51′ 9″ |
| 7 | 2641.98 | 2655.01 | 260.50 | 10.25 | 5° 51′ 9″ |
| 8 | 3101.49 | 3116.92 | 307.60 | 10.25 | 5° 51′ 9″ |
| 9 | 2714.05 | 2720.80 | 189.50 | 7.25 | 4° 8′ 48″ |
| 10 | 2288.46 | 2295.61 | 180.52 | 8.25 | 4° 42′ 58″ |

From the Report of A.P.R.R. Chief Engineer Sylvester Welch, published November 1, 1832.

| PLANES AND GRADES OF THE PORTAGE RAILWAY | | |
|---|---|---|
| (As reported by Sylvester Welch, Engineer, on November 1, 1833) | | |
| From West to East - Johnstown to Hollidaysburg | | |
| Plane or Grade | Length in Miles | Elevation Overcome in feet |
| Johnstown to Plane 1 | 4.13 | 101.46 |
| Plane 1 | 0.30 | 150.00 |
| Plane 1 to Plane 2 | 13.06 | 189.58 |
| Plane 2 | 0.33 | 132.40 |
| Plane 2 to Plane 3 | 1.49 | 14.50 |
| Plane 3 | 0.28 | 130.50 |
| Plane 3 to Plane 4 | 1.90 | 18.80 |
| Plane 4 | 0.42 | 187.86 |
| Plane 4 to Plane 5 | 2.56 | 25.80 |
| Plane 5 | 0.49 | 201.64 |
| Plane 5 to Plane 6 (Summit) | 1.62 | 19.04 |
| Plane 6 | 0.51 | 266.50 |
| Plane 6 to Plane 7 | 0.15 | 0.00 |
| Plane 7 | 0.51 | 260.50 |
| Plane 7 to Plane 8 | 0.63 | 5.40 |
| Plane 8 | 0.58 | 308.00 |
| Plane 8 to Plane 9 | 1.25 | 12.00 |
| Plane 9 | 0.51 | 189.50 |
| Plane 9 to Plane 10 | 1.76 | 29.58 |
| Plane 10 | 0.43 | 180.52 |
| Plane 10 to Hollidaysburg | 3.74 | 146.71 |
| | 36.65 | 2570.29 |

From "The Pennsylvania Main Line Canal" by Robert McCullough and Walter Leuba.

Interior of Reading Railroad terminal at Philadelphia, about 1900. (Courtesy George R. Wills.)

# Chapter X

# STEAM RAILROADS IN PENNSYLVANIA

October, 1829 is the date considered by railroad historians to be the true beginning of our modern railway age. It was during this month that the famous Rainhill Trials of steam locomotives were held by the Liverpool and Manchester Railway of England, with a prize of 500 pounds offered to the winner. The Stevensons, father George and son Robert, who had been building and developing various types of steam locomotives in England since 1814, won the Rainhill contests handily with their "Rocket". This interesting machine, which had a top speed of 29 miles an hour, won the coveted first prize in the 1829 contests for speed, pulling power and endurance against stiff competition.

Tramways and railways had been built previously in both England and America, but rail power had always been the horse or other beast of burden. In 1829, it became obvious to the world that a new era in the history of transportation had begun. Within the next ten years, the steam railway had captured the imagination of people everywhere. Americans became just as excited about railroads as they had been about canals twenty years earlier. Highway building received another drastic set-back. Canal-building programs already underway were also adversely affected. Railroads could be built virtually anywhere but canals were limited to appropriate terrain, and locations close to adequate water sources.

Public interest and acceptance of the idea of steam locomotion applied to tramways, or railways, did not come about suddenly. The way had to be paved by foresighted individuals who foresaw the possibilities thirty years before it became an accomplished fact. In the United States, two such individuals were preaching steam-railroads from the turn of the Nineteenth Century.

One was John Stevens, an engineer of Hoboken, New Jersey, who had experimented with steamboats

The Stephenson's "Rocket," which won the Rainhill Trials in England in 1829. (Drawing by the author.)

prior to Fulton's success with the "Clermont". In 1811 Stevens applied to the New Jersey legislature for permission to build a railroad there, the first such application in America. Permission was granted in 1815, when he was authorized to build a railway between Trenton and New Brunswick. However, he failed to get the necessary financing to proceed with the project. In 1819, Stevens urged the Pennsylvania legislature to build a railroad from Philadelphia to Pittsburgh, but his suggestion received no encour-

Experiments were tried with other means of locomotion. Here a sail is applied to a rail car in America in the early 1800's.

agement. Exasperated, he returned to his estate in Hoboken and proceeded to build a miniature railway on his own property, powered by a small steam engine of his own design, on which he himself was the passenger. He demonstrated this device repeatedly to the complete amazement of all who visited his property. So far as is known this was the first railway locomotive to be built or to be run on tracks in America. (Rumor has it that John Fitch had possibly done something similar before his death in 1798.)

Stevens continued his attempt to convince the Pennsylvania legislature that a steam railroad was practical and in 1823 actually secured a charter from the State, empowering him to build a railway from Philadelphia to Columbia. When the plan was made public it produced a storm of public controversy – most of it opposed to the idea. As a result, Stevens was unable to raise the necessary money to proceed, and the project was temporarily abandoned.

## Oliver Evans

A native Pennsylvanian was the other of the two early American advocates of steam railways – Oliver Evans of Philadelphia. In 1804 he ran his steam-powered "Orukter Amphibolus", an amphibious digger, through the streets of Philadelphia. This machine was undoubtedly the first steam propelled land vehicle in America. In 1812 Evans, who was a persuasive writer, published an article in the Niles Register which truly reflects the public attitude of all times:

"When we reflect upon the obstinate opposition that has been made by a great majority to every step toward improvement; from bad roads to turnpikes, from turnpikes to canal, from canals to railways for horse carriages, it is too much to expect the monstrous leap from bad roads to railways for steam carriages, at once. One step in a generation is all we can hope for. If the present shall adopt canals, the next may try the railways with horses, and the third generation the steam carriage . . . I do verily believe that the time will come when carriages propelled by steam will be in general use, as well for the transportation of passengers, as of goods, traveling at the rate of fifteen miles an hour, or 300 miles per day."

Within a year, Evans' conviction of the possible speed of steam railways had been even further strengthened, and he wrote: "The time will come when people will travel in stages, moved by steam engines, from one city to another, almost as fast as the birds fly, fifteen or twenty miles an hour. A carriage will set out from Washington in the morning, the passengers will breakfast in Baltimore, dine at Philadelphia and sup at New York, the same day . . . (they will) travel at night as well as by day, and the passengers will sleep in these stages as comfortably as

Oliver Evans' "Orukter Amphibolus", first steam propelled land vehicle in America, 1804.

they do now in steam boats". This was in 1813!

As a result of such articles, and continual pressure by such individuals as John Stevens, Pennsylvanians at least began discussing the possibilities of steam railroads. Late in 1824 an organization was formed called the "Pennsylvania Society for the Promotion of Internal Improvements in the Commonwealth". The following year, with the backing of various wealthy businessmen in Philadelphia, Engineer William Strickland was retained by this Society, and sent to England, with express instructions to find out how railroads were being constructed there, and what success they were having with the development of a steam locomotive.

Strickland spent a year in England and returned with an excellent report, published by the Society in August of 1826, with many drawings of trackage and locomotives (even though yet inefficient) of the type in use in England. This published report created great interest in the United States and undoubtedly influenced the State Canal Commissioners to authorize construction of the Columbia-Philadelphia Railroad in 1827. No doubt it also influenced the promoters of the B. & O. Railroad to charter their project in 1827.

In August of 1829, at Honesdale, Pa., the "Stourbridge Lion" became the first full-size steam locomotive to run on tracks of an American railroad – the Gravity Railroad of the Delaware and Hudson Canal

Company. It was purchased from Foster, Rastrick and Company of England. Unfortunately, The "Lion" proved too heavy for the wooden rails of the D. & H., and it was abandoned and allowed to rust into the

An experimental rail car powered by a horse and treadmill.

93

Company, whose first short section of road opened in 1830 between Baltimore and Ellicott's Mills. On this section of the railway, the "Tom Thumb" ran a race against a horse-drawn car. While the horse won, (due to mechanical difficulties on the locomotive during the race), the little locomotive was faster, at 18 miles per hour. However it was not large enough to be of practical use in pulling heavily loaded cars.

## First Coal Burning Locomotive

The following year, January 4th, 1831, Baltimore and Ohio Railroad Company advertised publicly that they would pay $4000 for a practical, American-made steam locomotive, using coal or coke as fuel, which could attain a speed of 15 miles per hour. Phineas Davis of York, in partnership with Israel Gardner, was already at work on a steam locomotive in the same machine shop where he and John Elgar, a few years earlier, had constructed the "Codorus" steam boat.

Davis and his crew worked night and day, and by February 15th loaded their completed "York" locomotive into an ox cart and headed for Baltimore. So well had Davis done his work that "The York" engine not only won him the coveted $4000, but turned up an incredible maximum speed of 30 miles per hour – the fastest thing on wheels in the United States!

Davis was commissioned to build two additional B. & O. locomotives – the "Atlantic" and "The Travel-

The "Stourbridge Lion" – first full-scale locomotive to run on tracks in the United States, 1829.

ground, while horses were substituted on the levels of the Gravity Railroad.

The first commercial steam locomotive built in the United States was the "Tom Thumb" designed by Peter Cooper for the Baltimore and Ohio Railroad

The "York", first successful coal-burning locomotive built in the United States, 1831.

94

**Eastern terminus of the Columbia and Philadelphia Railroad at Stock Exchange corner in Philadelphia, about 1843. A sectional packet boat is leaving, via rail, for Columbia.**

er'' – and joined the regular B. & O. payroll in 1834. Unfortunately, he was killed in a rail accident the following year.

Thus, York, Pennsylvania, was the site for the building of the first successful, coal-fired steam locomotive in the United States.

## The Columbia and Philadelphia Railroad

We have previously referred to the ''Main Line'' Columbia and Philadelphia Railroad as one of the earliest commercially operated railroads in the country and the first to be constructed with government funds. Planned by the Pennsylvania Canal Commissioners in 1827, and completed in 1834, it became a testing ground for early steam locomotives built in Pennsylvania and was later made a part of the Pennsylvania Railroad system. We feel this line rates special attention in our railroad chapter.

The Columbia and Philadelphia Railroad was officially opened by Gov. George Wolf April 15th, 1834. While there were a number of horse-drawn vehicles

on the road initially, the first train over the line (in which the governor's party rode) was powered by an English-built locomotive, the ''Black Hawk.'' This train made the first run between Columbia and Philadelphia in two days, including a number of stops for ceremonies and celebrations along the line.

The railroad was at first considered a public thoroughfare, with the State's interest being limited merely to the collection of tolls. Anyone with a vehicle which would fit the track and had the means of propelling it (either horse or steam power) was permitted to

**Market Street Bridge in Philadelphia, rebuilt in 1850 to accommodate tracks of the Columbia and Philadelphia state-owned railroad.**

95

State-owned Columbia and Philadelphia Railroad passing through downtown Lancaster, 1842. (Drawing by Philip J. Hoffmann.)

use the line as long as he paid the proper toll. Particularly during the first six-month period, when only one track was available, the resulting confusion, brawling and ill will which resulted were completely indescribable.

The State realized that it would have to exercise some sort of scheduling and control over the entire line and finally bought its own locomotives and ran them at regular intervals to haul cars owned by individual shippers. They also attempted to separate the locomotive drawn traffic from horse drawn traffic on the road by publishing, on March 28, 1836, a ruling that all locomotives must leave the Belmont plane between 4 and 10 in the morning and between 5 and 8 in the evening. The last one out in each period was to carry a special signal to let everyone know that it was safe to start out with horse-drawn cars. Even with this separation of traffic by motive power there were many delays because of the absence of sidings to permit the fast trains to pass the slower ones moving in the same direction.

The earliest locomotives were wood burners, but anthracite coal was successfully introduced in 1838. The following year, bituminous coal from the western end of the state was tried and was found even better than anthracite. Horses were banned from the line entirely April 1st of 1844, when the state elected to provide motive power for all cars being moved between the Belmont plane and Columbia. The addition of a telegraph line along the right of way in 1850 considerably improved the efficiency of the entire operation.

For a description of travel on this interesting, early railroad, we turn again to the works of writer Philip Nicklin of Philadelphia. Nicklin writes of his trip from Philadelphia to Columbia August 1, 1835:

"Two cars filled with passengers and covered with baggage are drawn by four fine horses for about four miles to the foot of the inclined (Belmont) plane, which is on the western bank of the Schuylkill and is approached by the spacious viaduct (the Columbia Bridge) extending across the river, built of strong timber and covered with a roof. The cars had scarcely begun to move when it was discovered that they were on the wrong track in consequence of the switchmaster having left the switches open, and everybody wished them applied to his own back. This error being

rectified by a retrograde movement, at length the cars started on the right track at the rate of six miles an hour.

"The ride to the foot of the plane is very interesting, first passing through a deep cut made forty years ago for a canal that was never finished, and then by a number of beautiful islands in the foreground, and the banks on both sides occasionally rising into bold hills crowned with romantic villas.

"At the foot of the inclined plane the horses were loosed from the cars; several of which (the number being in inverse proportion of the weight) were tied to an endless rope, moved by a steam engine placed at the top of the plane, and presently began to mount the acclivity. When the cars had all arrived at the top of the plane, some twelve or fourteen were strung together, like beads, and fastened to the latter end of a steam tug, which was already wheezing, puffing, and smoking, as if anxious to be off. All these little ceremonies consumed much time, and the train did not leave the top of the inclined plane until ten o'clock.

"The inclined plane is more than nine hundred yards in length and has a perpendicular rise of about one hundred and seventy feet; it occasions much delay and should be dispensed with, if possible.

"After many stoppings to let out passengers and let in water, and after taking into our eyes many enchanting views and millions of little pestilent triangular cinders, we arrived at Lancaster at 3 P.M. without accident or adventure.

"The Columbia Rail Road is made of the best materials, and has cost the state a great sum; but it has some great faults. The curves are too numerous, and their radii generally too short, in consequence of which the journey to Columbia (eighty miles) consumes seven or eight hours, instead of four or five. The viaducts are built of wood instead of stone, and the engineer, doubting their ability to bear the weight of two trains at once, has brought the two tracks on them so close together as to prevent two trains passing at the same time. Accidents have occurred from the collision of cars upon these insufficient viaducts. Their roofs are so low as to prevent the locomotives from having chimneys of a sufficient height to keep the cinders out of the eyes of the passengers and to prevent the sparks from setting fire to the cars and baggage. The chimneys of the steam-tugs are jointed, and in passing a viaduct the upper part is turned down, which allows the smoke to rush out at so small a height as to envelop the whole train in a dense and noisome cloud of smoke and cinders.

"Notwithstanding these inconveniences, a fine day and a beautiful country made our day's ride very pleasant; as we soon found that the smoky ordeals could be passed without damage by shutting our mouths and eyes and holding our noses and tongues.

"We took up our quarters for the night at Mrs. Hubley's Hotel in Lancaster and found the accommo-

Hinged stacks permitted locomotives to pass through low-clearance covered bridges, much to the discomfort of passengers and crew. (Drawing by Philip J. Hoffmann.)

The "John Bull", an English locomotive, is shown in this model pulling typical early passenger cars on the Columbia and Philadelphia Railroad. Mathias William Baldwin built his first locomotive in 1832 – "Old Ironsides", which was almost identical to the "John Bull", but more efficient. (Courtesy Dr. Ernest H. Coleman.)

dations very comfortable.

"We left Lancaster at 5 A.M. next morning in a railroad car drawn by two horses, tandem; arrived at Columbia in an hour and a half, and stopped at Mr. Donley's Red Lion Hotel where we breakfasted and dined, and found the house comfortable and well kept.

"Columbia is twelve miles from Lancaster, and situated on the eastern bank of the noble river Susquehanna; it is a thriving and pretty town, and is rapidly increasing in business, population, and wealth. There is an immense bridge over the Susquehanna, the superstructure of which, composed of massy timber, rests upon stone piers. This bridge is new, having been built within three years.

"Here is the western termination of the Rail Road, and goods from the seaboard intended for the great west are here transshipped into canal boats.

"At 4 P.M. we went on board the canal boat of the Pioneer Line to ascend the canal, which follows the eastern bank of the Susquehanna."

## Locomotives on the State Railroads

The Pennsylvania Commonwealth, through the canal commissioners, tried out five English locomotives built by Robt. Stevenson (inventor of the 1829 "Rocket"), and imported in 1835 by Mr. A. G. Ralston. These were the "Albion", the "Atlantic", the "Firefly", the "John Bull" and the "Red Rover".

They were four-wheel units, inside connected, 17000 lb. in weight, with 12" x 18" cylinders, and boilers 40" diameter by 8 ft. long. Three of these units had two 42" wheels and two 42" drives. The other two had two 40" wheels and two 60" driving wheels.

None of them had trucks; all had difficulty in staying on the rails and all required frequent repairs.

A report of Oct. 30, 1835, stated that there were 17 locomotives in service on the Commonwealth railroads – 10 by Baldwin, 2 by Norris and 5 by Robert Stevenson. It was also reported that the English engines were not efficient and required frequent repairs.

Two of these were evidently shipped to the Portage R.R. because Mr. McHaffey, superintendent at the Portage, in his report of Nov. 1, 1836, stated that the English locomotives, the "John Bull" and the "Red

Model of a sectional canal freight boat of the type carried on flat cars of the Allegheny Portage Railroad and the Columbia and Philadelphia Railroad in the 1840's and 1850's. (Courtesy Dr. Ernest H. Coleman.)

Rover" had recently been sold and that "it would have been a saving to the Commonwealth if they had been given away."

Meanwhile the two American locomotive builders, Mathias Baldwin and William Norris, both of Philadelphia, had so improved their engines, that when, in 1857, the State-owned railroads were turned over to Pennsylvania Railroad Company, practically all of the 73 locomotives transferred had been made by these two builders.

In the early days of railroading no one felt that the steam locomotive served any useful purpose other than to transport passenger and freight cars along relatively level stretches of track. For steep grades, the inclined plane was thought to be the only practical device.

In 1836, young William Norris built the "George Washington" locomotive, and prepared to deliver it to his customer, the Columbia-Philadelphia Railroad. The new engine, on which he had made a number of improvements over previous models, behaved so well in its trial tests that Norris, on a dare, decided to try it out on the Belmont Plane. To his delight, the "George Washington" puffed its way to the top of the steep Belmont Plane, to the complete amazement of a number of witnesses.

Afterward, when Norris told various railway "experts" what he had done, no one believed him, in spite of the witnesses who had seen it happen.

A. G. Steer of the Erie Railroad sent a long communication to the "Rail Road Journal", March 11, 1837, proving by elaborate algebraic formulas that the Washington did not climb the Belmont Plane, simply because it could not and no other locomotive could climb a steep ascending grade under its own power. Although Mr. Steer was tolerant of Norris's violation

Baldwin Locomotive Works, Philadelphia, one of the largest producers of steam locomotives in the world.

William Norris' "George Washington", which astounded the experts by climbing the Belmont Plane in 1836, with a full train of cars.

of the laws of gravity, he also noted that the many witnesses were, as he said, "victims of hallucinations."

However, on July 9th, 1836, Mr. D. K. Minor of the "Rail Road Journal" made a trip to Philadelphia to ask William Norris for a full demonstration. With the permission of the Commonwealth, owners of the controversial locomotive, the trial was made with Mr. Minor and a full company of scientific men present.

A test train was made up of cars for the many passengers and an attempt was made to climb the plane only to find someone had blown down the boiler with the fire in it. This damage repaired, the "George Washington" got under way again but started to slip at the bottom of the plane. It was found later that some of the railway workmen had greased the rails, as there was much wagering among them about the outcome of the test.

A generous sprinkling of sand overcame this difficulty. Then, with a total load of 19,200 pounds, the trial was again started. This time, without further delay, the ascent was made in two minutes and one second amidst much cheering from the company. After this the train was backed down the incline part way and was started from a dead start. It did well on this trial also. Although the track was wet with dew, there was no noticeable slipping. From this point on

Harrisburg, from the west shore of the Susquehanna, circa 1855. The Cumberland Valley Railroad bridge in the foreground was built originally in 1839, destroyed by fire and rebuilt in 1846. It was wooden construction with a wagon road inside; rebuilt as an iron truss bridge in 1856. Note "Camelback Bridge" in the background. (Courtesy George R. Wills.)

William Norris did a rushing business, at home and abroad, replacing inclined planes with duplicates of the "George Washington".

As with the canal-building spree, it took the pressure of possible competition from a neighboring state to get Pennsylvania actively involved in railroad activities. Maryland, even while starting its Chesapeake and Ohio Canal along the Potomac in 1828, also began work the same year, on the Baltimore and Ohio Railroad Company. They gambled that efficient steam locomotives would be available in the near future. The B. & O. thus became the first, and oldest, railroad company for public transportation in America. As the name implied, their aim was to make a direct connection between Baltimore and the Ohio River, (with the blessing of the Pennsylvania legislature) at Pittsburgh.

Permission was initially granted the B. & O. to cross the Pennsylvania state line for this purpose.

## The Schlatter Survey of 1839-40

However, Pennsylvania merchants of the 1830's, watching with an uneasy eye the progress of the B. & O. Railroad to the south, and the Erie Railroad from New York to Lake Erie to the North, began to realize that Pennsylvania's cumbersome "Main Line" was not going to be able to compete for western trade against the new, high-speed rail lines in neighboring states. After considerable pressure by both merchants and manufacturers, the Pennsylvania legislature in 1839 appropriated $30,000 toward a survey "for a con-

tinuous railway from Harrisburg to Pittsburgh.''

The responsibility for the survey was placed in the hands of the Canal Commission, who in turn hired Colonel Charles H. Schlatter, C.E. One of the Colonel's survey teams was headed by John Augustus Roebling.

Over the next two years Col. Schlatter came up with three separate possibilities for a Harrisburg-Pittsburgh rail line. His "Northern Route" followed the Susquehanna River north from Harrisburg to Northumberland and then along the West Branch to Lock Haven, ascending Bald Eagle Valley and crossing Allegheny Mountain through Emigh's Gap, up Clearfield Creek and across another ridge for a connection with his Middle Route near Ebensburg. Highest point on this route would have been 2062 feet above sea level, with only 45 feet per mile grade maximum, but the overall length would have been 320.5 miles.

The "Middle Route" ran up along the Susquehanna and Juniata Rivers to Lewistown, cut into Kishacoquillas Valley, back to the Juniata at Huntingdon, up the Little Juniata to a crossing of the Allegheny Mountain at Sugar Run Gap and on to Ebensburg and Pittsburgh by a route north of the present Penn Central. Maximum grade per mile here, according to Schlatter, would have been 45 feet, with maximum elevation of 2200 feet, and a total length of 229.5 miles. With considerable modification, the Middle Route became the one later selected by the Pennsylvania Railroad Company.

Schlatter's "Southern Route" was 291.5 miles in length; with the highest summit 2677 feet above sea level and maximum grades of 60 feet per mile. This route ran west from Chambersburg, via Bedford and Laughlintown to Greensburg and Pittsburgh, more or less on the line of the Forbes Road and the present Lincoln Highway. Approximately the same route had been surveyed in 1838 by Hother Hage, presumably in the interest of the Cumberland Valley Railroad, and Schlatter was unable to improve materially on Hage's route. He did, however, recommend an alternate route for a McAdam Road, which a century later became the approximate route of the Pennsylvania Turnpike.

It was Schlatter's opinion that his Middle Route was superior to any of the lines then building toward the West in other states. In spite of the favorable expression of opinion on the part of the Canal Commissioners, upon receipt of the Schlatter report, no action was taken for the next six years.

While a number of smaller railroad companies were chartered and began construction in the state in the early 1830's, it was the Pennsylvania Railroad – a late starter – which ultimately dominated the cross-state steam transportation picture.

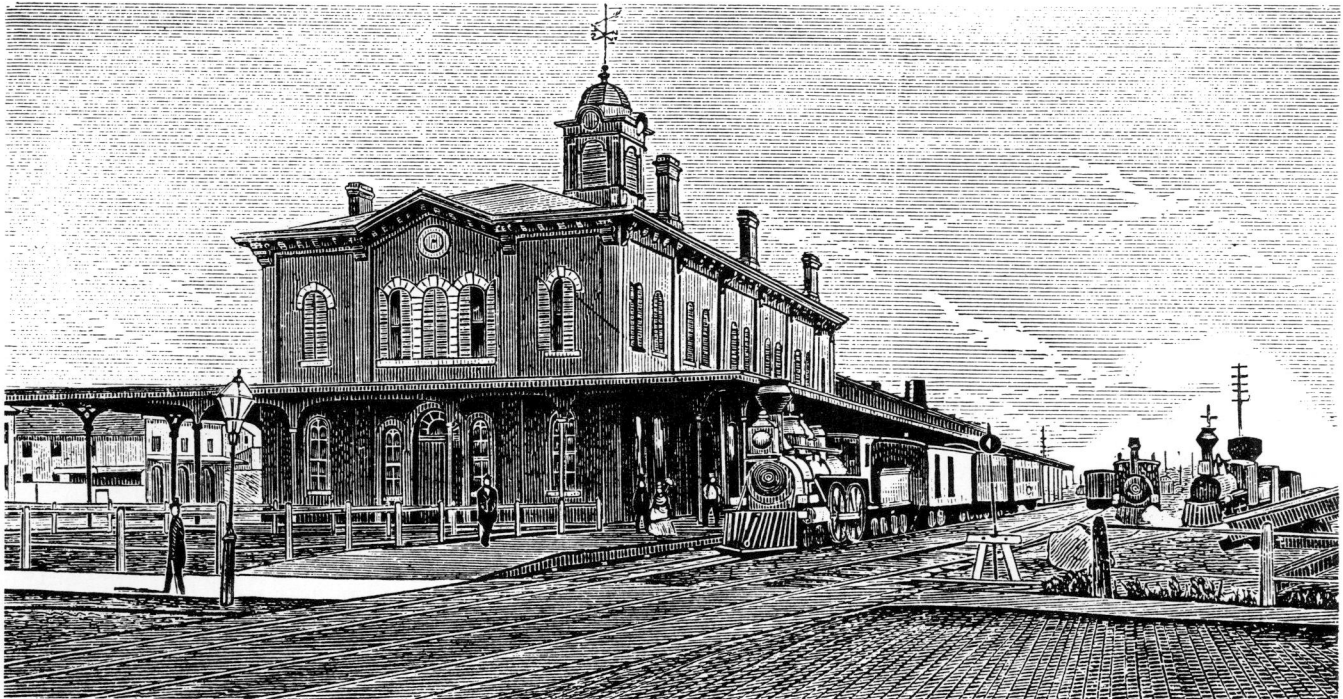

"Union Station", built in Erie in 1864, is typical of the grandiose construction of most railroad terminals of the mid-1800's. (Courtesy "Erie Story" magazine.)

Shortly after the Civil War, PRR sent out a photographic crew to take pictures of all major structures on the line from Philadelphia to Pittsburgh. Here the "Photo Special" pauses at a stream crossing – circa 1869.

## The Pennsylvania Railroad Company

The Pennsylvania Railroad was the lusty child of a political battle which raged for four months in the State legislature at Harrisburg in 1846, concerning the future course to be pursued in Pennsylvania's east-west transportation planning.

The political unheaval was brought about by the possible extension of the Baltimore and Ohio Railroad Company line into Pittsburgh. When the B. & O. was formed in 1827, the State of Pennsylvania had granted it permission "to construct a railroad through Pennsylvania in a direction from Baltimore to the Ohio River" provided that the line was completed in 1843. Having extended its lines to Cumberland, Md., in 1842, the B. & O. secured an extension from Pennsylvania, for the completion of its road, to February of 1847.

With the Main Line Canal route from Philadelphia to Pittsburgh failing to produce east-west trade comparable to that of the Erie Canal in New York State, the citizens of eastern Pennsylvania saw the B. & O. as a very real threat to their east-west commerce. This group favored a cross-state railroad to retain the Pittsburgh-Philadelphia western trade, which might otherwise slip away to Baltimore. The citizens in the western part of the state, particularly in the Pittsburgh area, favored a connection with the B. & O., which would permit them an immediate, less expensive sea-coast access route than that of the complicated Main Line canal system.

Numerous meetings were held throughout the State in support of either the B. & O. connection or a cross-state railroad. Public interest ran at fever height. At the meeting of the State legislature at Harrisburg

January 6, 1846, it was obvious that the railroad question transcended all other business. Two bills were introduced. The first was entitled: "An Act to authorize the Baltimore and Ohio Railroad Company to construct a railroad through Pennsylvania in a direction from Baltimore to the Ohio river, at the city of Pittsburgh." The second was "An Act to incorporate the Pennsylvania (Central) Railroad Company." Debate waxed hot and heavy for months, with opinion almost equally divided. Action on various amendments and re-readings of the two bills in the House and Senate was frequently decided by a majority of only two or three votes.

The B. & O. Bill was finally passed, but with a crippling amendment, which declared the whole Act null and void if the Pennsylvania Railroad could raise three million dollars in stock subscriptions and actually contract for at least thirty miles of road (15 of them at the Pittsburgh end) before July 30, 1847. The closeness of the struggle is indicated by the fact that the amendment passed by a vote of 50 to 48. The Act incorporating the Pennsylvania Railroad Company was signed by the Governor of Pennsylvania April 13, 1846. The Baltimore and Ohio Act (never to become effective) was signed on April 21st, 1846.

Thus was the Pennsylvania Railroad born. It had the solid financial backing of Philadelphians and Eastern Pennsylvanians, who quickly raised the required $3,000,000.

## John Edgar Thomson

The early history of the Pennsylvania Railroad revolved around the colorful John Edgar Thomson, first Chief Engineer of the company and in 1852 its third President. Thomson's first major task was to select the route for the connection between Harrisburg and Pittsburgh, and with all speed to let contracts for thirty miles of right-of-way to nullify the Baltimore and Ohio Act. After resurrecting and studying the Schlatter Report of 1839-40 carefully, and after conducting a number of surveys of his own, Thomson determined that Schlatter's Middle Route, with some modifications, was in fact the best. His decision made, he rushed through plans for the grading of fifteen miles of right-of-way at both ends of the proposed route, and let contracts for the work. As a result, the Governor of Pennsylvania on August 2, 1846 issued a proclamation declaring null and void the law which gave the Baltimore and Ohio Railroad Company a right-of-way through western Pennsylvania.

With this hurdle behind him, Thomson was able to take time for a detailed study of the difficult crossing of the Allegheny Mountain at the crest of the Middle Route. He thought it wise to make a temporary connection with the ends of the Allegheny Portage Rail-

"Indiana" Locomotive, purchased by PRR from the Baldwin Locomotive works in 1850 – the third such locomotive bought by the company – and one of many PRR locomotives by Baldwin. (Drawing by C. B. Chaney.)

road, (an inclined plane railroad operated by the State, as part of the "Main Line" between Johnstown and Hollidaysburg,) and use this as a connecting link until the Pennsylvania could complete its own road over the mountain.

He rejected Schlatter's 45-foot maximum grade line between Huntingdon and the Allegheny Summit, which would have thrown a considerable section of road further north into the mountains, with deeper cuts and fills, and more difficult grading throughout. Instead, he elected to go down the center of the Juniata Valley from Lewistown to Hollidaysburg at very low grade and take a steeper gradient (95 feet per mile) over the Allegheny in a much shorter rise, adding extra locomotive power at that point. This gave him the advantage of tying all of the valley towns into the route, as well as the eastern terminus of the Portage Railway at Hollidaysburg.

Thomson's final selection of his own route over Allegheny Mountain into Pittsburgh (including the famous Horseshoe Curve) has excited the admiration of the engineering profession for many years and remains virtually unchanged today. He took a number of short cuts on the Schlatter Middle Route which saved mileage. His greatest rise between Pittsburgh and the Allegheny crest was 53 feet per mile, by way of Turtle Creek, Greensburg, Blairsville and Johnstown. The Eastern Division was built west from Harrisburg, and was finally completed to the Portage at Hollidaysburg (137 miles) in 1850. Brisk passenger and freight service began at once.

After the difficult survey work was completed on the Western Division, this section was put under contract in 1850. Running 85 miles from Pittsburgh to a connection with the Portage at Stone Viaduct, just east of Johnstown, it was completed and opened to traffic in December of 1852. There was now, for the first time,

A last-ditch effort of the "Main Line" to meet the competition of PRR.

a continuous rail line from Philadelphia to Pittsburgh, (using the State-owned Portage Railroad).

The Mountain Division of PRR was next rushed to completion, and when the final section of line through the summit tunnel was opened to traffic on February 15, 1854, PRR was able to by-pass the cumbersome planes of the Portage Railroad for all time, and its own continuous line from Harrisburg to Pittsburgh was a reality.

## The Old "Main Line" Capitulates

Attention was now turned by President Thomson to the improvement of connecting service to Philadelphia from Harrisburg. PRR had entered into contract with the independent Harrisburg and Lancaster road in April of 1849, which permitted the Pennsylvania Railroad to conduct all operations over that line.

From Lancaster to Philadelphia the solution to the problem of coordinated schedules with the PRR was more difficult. The State-owned Philadelphia and Columbia Railroad, had never functioned with any great degree of efficiency, and its managers were particularly cool to advances by the PRR, which they now realized was rapidly putting their canal route out of business. As a matter of fact, the supporters of the Main Line System had written into the Pennsylvania Railroad Act a clause which forced PRR to pay the State a "tonnage tax" on freight moved over its lines between the months of March and December of each year, an obvious hedge against possible competition with the Main Line during the "open season" for canal commerce.

PRR, upon completion of its Mountain Division, began lobbying for repeal of the discriminatory tonnage tax and also for control of the Philadelphia and Columbia. The supporters of the Main Line of the Public Works, their position weakened by the high volume of passenger and freight traffic now handled by the PRR, not to mention the heavy indebtedness of their Main Line, finally capitulated and put the state

Northern Central Susquehanna Railroad Bridge, built in 1858 between Marysville and Dauphin – originally a wood-arch, Howe Truss structure. Abandoned in 1882, after PRR controlled its operation. Note the "Main Line" Canal in the foreground.

104

An 1869 PRR "Photo Train" pauses on the Granville Bridge, west of Lewistown, Pa. – a tubular cast iron bridge, with wrought-iron cross bracing.

system from Philadelphia to Pittsburgh up for sale. PRR bought the entire "Main Line" for $7,500,000, in 1857, and the tonnage tax was repealed in 1861.

PRR formed a subsidiary company, the Pennsylvania Canal Company in 1867, which continued to operate various sections of the canal system in the eastern half of the state until 1903. However, they abandoned the Portage Railroad and most of the western division of the Main Line Canal almost immediately. They, of course, maintained and greatly improved the Philadelphia and Columbia Railroad.

The phenomenal growth of the Pennsylvania Railroad during the 1800's, under the guidance of John Edgar Thomson, Thomas Alexander Scott, George Roberts, and their successors is a matter of recorded history. Dozens of railroads were chartered throughout the state, many of them chronologically ahead of PRR, but few of them survived as "independents". The Pennsylvania Railroad acquired many of these railroads by the simple expedient of purchasing a controlling interest in their stock, setting up subsidiary operating companies, and leasing them to PRR.

Among the better known "independents" thus added to the PRR family were the Cumberland Valley Railroad Company – (1859); the Northern Central Railway Company (1875); Philadelphia and Erie Railroad (1862); Pittsburgh, Fort Wayne and Chicago Railroad Company (1869); Philadelphia, Wilmington and Baltimore Railroad Company (1881); the Columbia and Port Deposit Railway (1877); the United Railroads of New Jersey (1871); Columbus, Chicago and Indiana Central (1869); the Lehigh Valley Railroad Company (1962) – the list goes on and on. Thus, Pennsylvania Railroad became one of the two great railroad "giants" of the East – the other, New York Central. Many finan-

cial and political battles were fought between these two companies over control of smaller railroads in the territories of both. Today, exhausted from competition with automobiles, trucks and planes, these two old adversaries have finally "buried the hatchet" and **merged into the Penn Central,** *(now Amtrak and Conrail.)*

Certainly worthy of mention in our chapter on railroads in the state are some of the railroad companies who were able to survive the pressures of competition with PRR or New York Central.

## The Reading Company

While it has undergone several periods of financial crisis in the past, the Reading railroad system emerged in the 1900's as one of the strong systems in Eastern Pennsylvania. With its close ties with Central Railroad of New Jersey (in which it owned a controlling interest until recently) it offered freight service in much of the anthracite region and passenger connections between many eastern Pennsylvania cities and Jersey City, as well as other points in New Jersey. As of December 1962, trackage in Pennsylvania totaled 1209 miles. Trackage of Central of New Jersey the same year stood at 576 miles, some of it in Pennsylvania.

Historically, the company was incorporated as the Philadelphia and Reading Railroad Company by act of the State legislature dated April 4, 1833, to haul coal from Schuylkill County to Philadelphia along the Schuylkill River. In this endeavor, it was in direct competition with the older Schuylkill Navigation Company, which it finally acquired in 1870, and continued to operate until 1931. By acquisition or leasing of other, short rail lines in eastern Pennsylvania it ex-

The famous Reading "Camelback" locomotive, circa 1890. Note the "P. & R." marking on the coal tender for "Philadelphia and Reading Railroad Company" – the old name before the Reading Company purchase of 1896.

tended its original operations to Allentown, Sunbury, Williamsport, Benton, Harrisburg, Columbia, Lancaster, Wilmington, and as far west as Shippensburg and Gettysburg. In 1871 it acquired its own coal mining areas, through a subsidiary, the Philadelphia and Reading Coal and Iron Company.

In the 1880's it went through several periods of receivership, and in 1891 attempted the organizing of a huge monopoly involving both coal mining and transportation in the Pennsylvania anthracite region and including a number of other railroad firms. The unwieldy operation failed in 1893, leaving the company in another period of financial disaster. It was sold at public auction in 1896, and bought by the Reading Company. The new management succeeded in bringing the company into the Twentieth Century in stable condition, but like all railroads it has suffered a considerable loss of business in recent years to competitive forms of transportation. A hedge against this competition has been the Reading Transportation Company, a subsidiary, which operates trucks and buses over much the same territory as that served by the railroad.

The principal railroad in Pennsylvania of Reading's Associate, the Central of New Jersey, was originally the old Lehigh and Susquehanna Railroad, built by Josiah White in 1841 across Penobscot Mountain in 1841, and extending along the Lehigh River to Easton. Complete with its "Ashley Planes" (which continued operations until after World War II) this old railroad was leased from the Lehigh Coal and Navigation Company in 1871 by Central RR of N.J. and the final purchase was consumated in 1962.

Unusual, double-deck bridge between Columbia and Wrightsville, built in 21 days, circa 1897, to replace a wooden bridge wrecked in a windstorm. It was intended that the PRR track would run at one level, local vehicular traffic at another, but all traffic was finally "bottlenecked" for years at the lower level. (Photo by G. Ross Bond – 1914.)

## The Baltimore and Ohio Railroad Company

Surprisingly, the B. & O. currently has about three times as much trackage in the western half of Pennsylvania as in its native state. Statistics compiled in December of 1962 indicated 976 miles of tracks in Pennsylvania; 318 in Maryland. The B. & O. at that time also had 1822 miles of track in Ohio; 1354 in West Virginia; 559 in Indiana; 517 in Illinois and 181 in New York State

First railroad opened in America for public use, the B. & O. was chartered in 1827, and operations began in June of 1830 over a short section of track west of Baltimore. As previously indicated, it was the intention of the B. & O. to run its line directly to the Ohio River at Pittsburgh, but they were thwarted in this plan by the promoters of the Pennsylvania Railroad, in 1846. It was not until 1871 that the B. & O. finally gained access to Pennsylvania, by the acquisition of the Pittsburgh and Connellsville line. Over the next fifty years, the B. & O. acquired many other lines in

western Pennsylvania (one of them extending as far north as Buffalo) serving a dozen counties, with a number of connecting lines to Ohio and West Virginia. In 1904 the B. & O., through its subsidiary, the Fulton Bedford and Somerset Railroad Company, acquired much of the right-of-way of the partially completed South Penn Railroad, which could have provided them with an east-west line in Pennsylvania competitive with the Pennsylvania Railroad. The line was never completed by the B. & O., however, and was finally sold to the Pennsylvania Turnpike Commission in 1938.

## The Erie-Lackawanna Railroad Company

The Erie-Lackawanna, formed in 1960, is a consolidation of a number of much older lines. One of them was the New York and Erie Railroad, chartered by New York State in 1832 to make a connection, above the northern Pennsylvania boundary, from the Hud-

Thought to be the interior of the Northern Central Railroad Bridge across the Susquehanna, this photo shows smoke-stack discoloring of the roof rafters – a reminder of the ever-present fire hazard with steam locomotives.

son River to Lake Erie. Another was the Liggett's Gap Railroad chartered in 1832, which later became the Lackawanna and Western (1851), which combined with the Delaware and Cobb's Gap Company in 1853 to form the Delaware, Lackawanna and Western. The New York and Erie in the meantime had gone into receivership, to emerge as the Erie Railroad in 1895. The Erie and D. L. & W. merged in 1960.

Through the years, these various companies have extended their lines deep into northern Pennsylvania, one line running through Scranton, as far south as Northumberland, another into Stroudsburg and Northampton County; others into Mt. Jewett, Dubois, Oil City, Meadville and New Castle. In 1962 Erie-Lackawanna trackage in Pennsylvania totaled 852 miles as compared with 1312 miles in New York, and lesser mileages in Ohio (460) and New Jersey (339). Twenty-two counties in Pennsylvania are served by this road.

## Other "Independents"

Space does not permit a review of all of them, but other important railroads such as the Bessemer and Lake Erie, the Delaware and Hudson, the Lehigh and

Hudson River, the Nickel Plate, the Pittsburgh and Lake Erie, the Pittsburgh and West Virginia, the Monongahela and the Western Maryland – all still serve various sections of Pennsylvania as independent railroad companies.

## Rails and Tracks

The evolution of railroad tracks began with wooden tracks, usually mounted on "sleepers" of stone, or wood blocks, set in the ground independently, under the rails on each side of the track. This permitted a smooth path for horses or mules down the center. Greater wearing properties, and a smoother ride developed by applying strap-iron to the tops of the wooden rails. Later entire rails were made of cast iron, in a "T" shape with wide wearing surface at the top, and narrow bottom edge which was supported in a cast-iron "chair" fastened to the sleeper. Winter frost in the ground, or just plain mud soon changed the spacing and position of the rails. This led to the development of the cross ties and stone ballasting to keep the track bed steady and the rail spacing constant. Ultimately the "I" shaped rail was developed, which was much simpler to fasten to the wooden cross ties. Rail metal changed from iron to steel.

Since there was originally no national "standard" for the width between rails, early rail companies developed their own track width, which varied from the narrow-gauge width of two feet, to the extra wide tracks with rails six feet apart. In the South for years five-foot track was the standard. The confusion when rail lines of different widths made connection was apparent. Rolling stock of one line was not usable on another. Passengers had to change cars and freight had to be laboriously transferred. It was not until 1886 that the difference in gauges was finally narrowed down to four feet, nine inches in the South, almost matching the North's "true-standard" of four feet, eight and a half inches. The latter was based on Pennsylvania trackage, where most of the freight cars originated. "Narrow gauge" tracks are still popular in many parts of the country, on mountain routes in particular.

(Facing page) The Kinzua Viaduct (near Mt. Jewett, Pa.), world's highest railroad bridge, was built for the New York, Lake Erie and Western Railway (now a part of the Erie-Lackawanna) in 1882. Height 301 feet; length 2052 feet. Built in 94 days, its use was discontinued about 1956, and it is now part of a State Park.

Starrucca Viaduct, built in 1848, was one of the first of the masonry railway bridges. Built for the New York and Erie Railroad (now a part of the Erie-Lackawanna), it spans Starrucca Creek, near Susquehanna, Pa. at an elevation of 110 feet. It is 1200 feet long. It still carries heavy rail traffic today.

# Railroad Bridges

Early railroad rolling stock was fairly light in weight, so the problem of conveying the new medium over streams was at first handled by the same type of wooden bridges which previously carried the old turnpike traffic. Major railroad bridges of wooden construction were built at Market Street, Philadelphia, for the "Main Line" into the downtown area, also the well-known "Columbia" bridge across the Schuylkill at the foot of the old Belmont Plane.

An existing wooden bridge (longest covered bridge in the world) across the Susquehanna, Columbia to Wrightsville, was adapted for the independent York and Wrightsville Railroad. The Cumberland Valley Railroad crossed the Susquehanna at Harrisburg on a wooden Town lattice-truss type bridge.

The Pennsylvania Railroad, chartered in 1846, built its first major bridge across the Susquehanna at Rockville, Pa., a combination of Burr arch and Howe truss wood construction. The Northern Central Railroad, later absorbed by PRR, built a similar wooden bridge just north of the Pennsylvania Railroad crossing at Dauphin.

Wood bridges carried early railroad traffic satisfactorily, in spite of the ever-present danger of fire from locomotive sparks, until about 1850. By this time railroad rolling stock was becoming more sophisticated, much heavier, and a need for a radical improvement in bridge design for railroad use was being felt.

Prior to this, bridge building had been primarily a matter of craftsmanship, wooden-model testing, and "trial and error" – mainly by skilled carpenter-designers.

However, a new breed of bridge designers were developing – Col. Ellet, John Roebling, Herman Haupt (of Gettysburg, Pa.) and Squire Whipple – who, for the first time, applied mathematical principles in computing stresses in bridges. Some basic guide-lines to the understanding of truss action were published, independently, by Whipple and Haupt in the 1840's and, happily, were in agreement.

## Iron Railroad Bridges

There now developed a trend toward the use of iron in bridges – cast iron for compression members and wrought iron for bridge members in tension. The first such bridge was designed by Squire Whipple in 1841. The movement toward iron bridges gained momentum until 1850, when a metal truss bridge on the New York and Erie Railroad at Lackawaxen, Pa., collapsed while a train was crossing it. Following this fiasco, the New York and Erie ordered the removal of all its metal bridges and re-conversion to wooden structures. For a few years metal bridges were in disrepute.

In spite of this the trend to metal railroad bridges picked up again, often using the Pratt and Howe truss types originally developed for wooden bridges. Vertical wooden members gave way to cast iron cylindrical or octagonal tubular pieces, with the diagonal members being converted to wrought iron "straps". Scientific calculations entered into the design, based on the compressive strength of cast iron and the much greater tensile strength of wrought iron.

Such confidence developed in metal bridges that unusually high-span viaducts and tressle-type structures began to appear around the State. Typical of these was the Kinzua Viaduct over Kinzua Creek in Hamlin Township on the Bradford branch of the New York, Lake Erie and Western (now the Erie-Lackawanna) Railroad in northwestern Pennsylvania.

This viaduct, at the time of its completion, in 1882, was the highest bridge in the world, towering 301 feet above Kinzua Creek. It carried a single-track on an 18-foot wide deck across a 2052 foot gulf, using 20 viaduct towers supporting Warren type trusses. Fifteen hundred tons of wrought iron were used in the construction.

The ordinary metal bridges which began to appear at railroad stream crossings throughout the State, however, were supplied by such firms as Keystone Bridge Company of Pittsburgh; Phoenix Bridge Company of Phoenixville, Pa., and other bridge building firms in neighboring States. Competition in keeping costs low also reduced what factors of safety may have been in use, and such things as "allowance for wind velocity" were unheard of. Bridge construction continued, using relatively light-weight tubular and rod construction while the weight of the locomotives, pas-

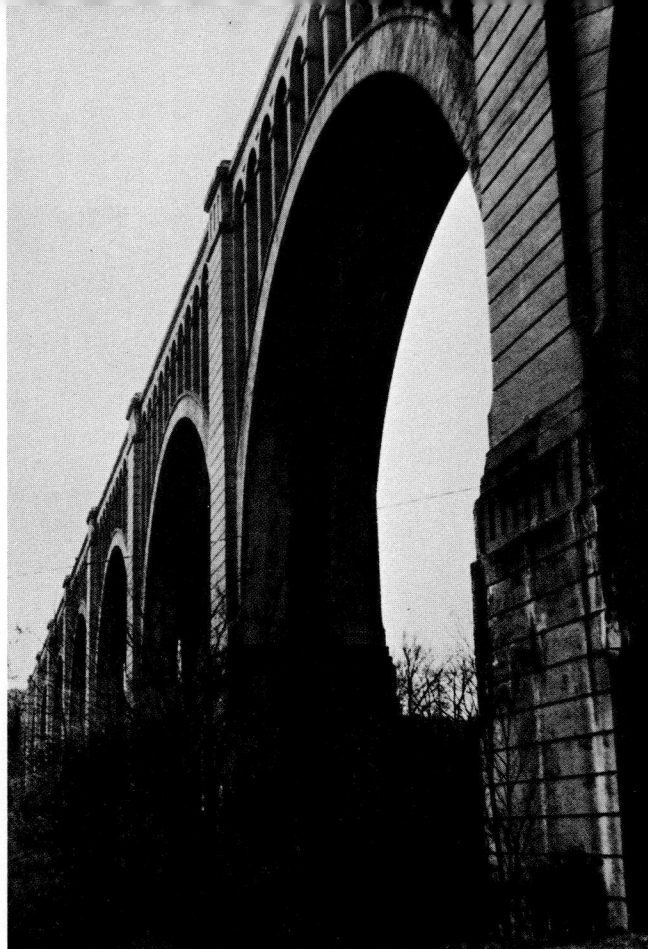

The Tunkhannock Viaduct, built in 1915 for the Delaware Lackawanna & Western (now the Erie-Lackawanna) at Nicholson, Pa., towers 240 feet above the valley below. A good example of the use of steel-reinforced concrete. (Photo by the author.)

senger cars and freight cars increased.

It was almost inevitable that trouble was in the making. Starting in 1877, a series of railroad bridge failures swept the country, with considerable loss of life. Public faith in metal bridges sank to a new low.

## Stone Arch Bridges

So alarmed was the Pennsylvania Railroad by the failure of existing metal bridges that they began converting all their bridges to stone-arch construction – a much more expensive, but certainly a more enduring type than the available cast iron-wrought iron structures. Out of this development evolved such famous structures as the "Stone Bridge" in Johnstown (1887), so strongly built that it withstood the Johnstown flood several years later – as well as the present Rockville Bridge across the Susquehanna – built in 1902 – the longest stone arch railroad bridge in the world. The Pennsylvania Railroad viaduct at Coatesville and the Delaware crossing opposite Trenton were also rebuilt in stone.

A fine example of an early 20th Century steel railroad bridge, built about 1907, is this 1780-foot-long, cantilever structure designed by A. R. Raymer for the Pittsburgh and Lake Erie Railroad, crossing the Ohio River at Beaver, Pa. (Courtesy of Dr. George Swetnam.)

There were some examples of stone arch railroad bridges in existence even before the metal bridge failures of the 1870's. One such "classic" is Starrucca Viaduct in northeastern Pennsylvania on the New York and Erie (now a part of the Erie) Railroad. This 110-foot high stone structure, built in 1847-48, originally carried a single track of the Erie over Starrucca Creek, at its junction with the Susquehanna River near Susquehanna, Pa. It has 17 flat arch spans, each 51-feet long, and the total length of the structure is 1200 feet. So well built was this viaduct that it is today still carrying Erie rail traffic, now two tracks wide, and live loads many times heavier than those which first passed over it in the 1800's.

Reinforced concrete was used in the famous Tunkhannock Viaduct on the Erie-Lackawanna Railroad at Nicholson, Pa. built 1912-15. 2,375 feet long and 34 feet wide, it carries double track traffic 240 feet above the creek below.

## Steel Bridges

The ultimate answer however was steel, a light yet strong metal with working strength 20% greater than wrought iron. Steel had previously been extremely expensive, but with the development of the Bessemer converter in 1856 and the open-hearth method of con-

version in 1867, commercial structural steel became practical and economical.

With the trend to steel bridge construction there also developed the realization that special engineering talent was necessary. Thus a new breed of professionally trained bridge engineers rapidly came into being, who set standards, who insisted upon destructive testing machines for bridge materials in the interest of public safety, and held the line against unsafe cost-cutting procedures.

Engineering colleges quickly incorporated courses in their curricula for investigation of all factors involving structural design. Materials testing machines were installed by bridge builders such as Pencoyd Iron Works, Pencoyd, Pa.; Phoenix Bridge and Iron Works, Phoenixville, Pa.; and American Bridge Company at Ambridge, Pa.

Bridge design, primarily as a result of the railroad boom of the 1850-1900 period, thus moved quickly from the wood craftsmanship stage; through the mathematically designed tubular, cast iron-wrought iron stage; to the professionally and scientifically engineered steel bridge stage, at the opening of the Twentieth Century.

It was a painful period in bridge development, but one during which many useful lessons were learned and during which much excellent literature on proper bridge standards was written.

In the mid-1800's, Plank Roads lifted the Pennsylvania farmers out of the mud for a few short decades.

# Chapter XI
# THE PLANK ROAD

By 1850, the inter-city highway and turnpike building era, so nobly begun in the early 1800's, had ground to a halt. First, canals and later, railroads had provided such severe competition for the existing highway system in Pennsylvania that most of the privately financed turnpike companies had gone into bankruptcy. What few public roads still existed had reverted to the counties and townships through which they passed, where the archaic system of "working out the tax on the roads" (a relic of the European feudal period) did little to improve them.

Except for a few turnpikes which made connection with the railroads or canals, most of the private roads had been unable to collect sufficient tolls to amortize their construction costs, maintain their right-of-way, or pay dividends to their stockholders. Hence, by 1850, most of the inter-city roads had reverted to nature. Pennsylvania farmers were particularly hard-hit by this breakdown of the rural road system. In dry weather, travel conditions in the farming sections varied from poor to fair; in wet weather they were virtually impossible. Some farmers attempted to maintain their own roads by dumping loads of dirt into the worst mud-holes, but even so travel conditions to the nearest town were indescribably bad.

The idea of surfacing roads with wood, rather than stone, was born in Russia and was first introduced into Canada, with the blessing of Sir Charles Edward, Governor-General. Darey Boulton built the first plank road in North America at Toronto, 1835-36, using eight-foot long planks, 8 inches wide and 3 inches thick, laid at right angles to travel on stringers resting on a "bed", with run-off ditches at each side. The plank road was just wide enough for one-way traffic. A parallel dirt track was provided for passing.

The first plank road in the United States was built between Syracuse, New York and Oneida Lake, in 1846, a distance of about fourteen miles. Other plank roads followed in New York. It was found that these roads could be constructed at a cost of about $1500 per mile, as opposed to the stone-surfaced National Road, for instance, which had cost about $10,000 per mile. Turnpike companies tottering at the point of bankruptcy became intensely interested in this new and apparently economical way of rejuvenating their properties.

Within the next few years, the "Plank Road Craze" hit Pennsylvania. An examination of State records discloses that between 1849 and 1854 some 290 private companies applied for charters to build plank roads throughout the State. One of the oldest (and most successful) of these was the "Alleghany and Butler Plank Road Company", incorporated in 1849. Other companies were formed, such as "The Altoona and Clearfield Plank Road Company" (1853); "The Bald Eagle Plank Road Company" (1850); "The Catfish, Brady's Bend and Butler Plank Road Company" (1851); "The Darby and Chester Turnpike or Plank Road Company" (1869); "The Erie to Meadville Plank Road Company" (1854); "The North Lebanon and Mount Hope Plank Road Company"; "The Shrewsbury, Hopewell and Chanceford Plank Road Company" (1851) – and many, many others, in all corners of the State.

Some of these companies were able to raise the necessary funds for initial construction of their plank-surfaced right of ways and survived to offer improved rural transportation, on a toll basis, to farmers and other inter-city travelers throughout the State.

One of these gained the reputation of being one of

A plank road in Lancaster County (Courtesy "Old Lancaster" 1964.)

the most profitable plank road operations in the United States. This was the so-called "Butler Plank Road", running 27 miles between Etna, on the north side of the Allegheny River at Pittsburgh, and Butler, Pa. It was originally incorporated as "The Alleghany and Butler Plank Road Company" in 1849. After raising $30,000, the company first installed flagstone paving, quarried locally. Difficulties developed within a few years, as the iron rimmed wheels of the heavy wagons cut into the soft flagstone, and the road was re-paved, about 1870, with planks. The latter were eight feet long, three inches thick and of varying widths. They were not sawed, but split directly from logs, hand-hewn on top for smoothness.

There were four toll gates on the Butler Road where farmers, hauling their goods to Pittsburgh, and stage coaches paid for the use of the road. Annual tolls collected in 1855 were $9,030; in 1856 – $13,070; and $10,800 in 1857. Like most plank roads, only one half of the graded surface was paved; the other half was for "turn-offs." The planks were offset at intervals, as shown in the accompanying drawing, to permit the heavy wagon wheels easy re-entry to the road surface. It is said that most of the horses on wagon teams using the plank road regularly didn't have to be guided back onto the planks after a "turn-off". They knew that the going was easier on the plank surface and got back onto it as quickly as possible.

It was a common sight in the 1890's to see twenty or thirty farm wagon loads of hay moving along the Butler Plank Road to be weighed on the wagon scales at the Etna General Store before delivery. In 1880 the road was completely rebuilt with sawed planks, which were kept in good repair until 1905, when the Alleghany and Butler Plank Road Company sold the lower half of the road to the Allegheny County Commissioners for $65,000. The company was unsuccessful in a similar attempt to sell the northern half to Butler County; hence, the road operated half-toll and half-free until 1913, when it was taken over by the State Highway Department, and was finally hard-surfaced in 1921.

Other plank roads around the State were not as financially productive as the Butler Plank Road. In York County for instance, the Shrewsbury and Hopewell Plank Road Company, formed in 1853, with Simon Klinefelter as President, reported tolls for the year 1856 of only $994.59, which was probably barely enough to keep up their maintenance of the road. However, there is evidence that they continued operations well into the 1900's.

In general the plank roads were unable to survive for more than several decades because of increasing competition with the railroads, as well as unexpected maintenance problems. With the poor wood preservatives then available, most of the wooden planks had to be completely replaced about every ten years due to rotting from the damp earth surface underneath, or from plank breakage due to the heavy loads of the farm wagons, their major source of revenue. After the first ten years, most of the plank road companies found maintenance and repair costs mounting much faster than toll income. Most of them failed long before the close of the nineteenth century.

This delightful, posed photo is simply captioned "Harrisburg Wheel Club – Aug. 27, 1887". No doubt it was made at some challenging distance from the State Capital – such as Devil's Den in Gettysburg. The aproned gentleman at the left center suggests that a sumptuous picnic, or other prepared meal, awaited the riders at their destination.

# Chapter XII
# THE BICYCLE CRAZE

The idea of a two-wheeled vehicle propelled by the foot power of the rider dates back to ancient times. Winged figures straddling a stick mounted between two wheels were illustrated on frescos in the ruins of Pompeii. A cherub mounted on a vehicle something like a child's "kiddie car" was the theme of a stained-glass church window manufactured in Italy about 1580.

Various versions of "celeriferes" or "velocipedes" appeared in France, Austria and Germany in the seventeenth and eighteenth centuries. In 1818 German Baron Karl von Drais developed a two-wheeled vehicle, foot propelled, with a pivoting front wheel. The following year Dennis Johnson of England patented a similar version called a "pedestrian curricle".

In United States a "velocipede" (swift foot) was patented by W. K. Clarkson June 26, 1819, which became known as the "Hobby Horse". It was manufactured for a few years by David Ball and Jason Burrill of Hoosick Falls, New York. However, it was costly and clumsy and was not accepted by the American public.

Kirkpatrick Mac Millan in England in 1839 developed a bicycle propelled with front wheel pedals attached to reciprocating bars and cranks on the rear wheel, which was a bit too complicated to be widely accepted.

In 1867 a crude bicycle was developed by Ernest Michaux in Paris with two wooden wheels with iron rims, driven by foot pedals attached to the front axle. It was introduced into the United States, where it was dubbed "The Boneshaker" because of its rough-riding qualities. Popular in France, it was not well received in America, but at least aroused interest in this type of vehicle.

The first bicycle to capture the full attention of the American public was the "Ordinary Bicycle" developed in England in 1872 and manufactured in quantity by Mssrs. Rudge Whitworth Limited under the trade name "Rudge" Ordinary Bicycle. This amaz-

ing vehicle had an enormous, solid-rubber-tired front wheel which sometimes reached a diameter of 65", with a small steering wheel to the rear. The motive power was provided by foot cranks to the front wheel from a precarious perch almost directly above the wheel. It was first introduced into the United States in 1876 at the Philadelphia Centennial Exposition and caught the popular fancy almost at once.

The "Ordinary Bicycle", while more comfortable and speedier than the old "Boneshaker", was difficult to mount and dangerous to ride. A sudden stop, or hole in the road, could catapult the operator over on his head! The hardy clan of riders who mastered these vehicles soon formed an organization known as the "League of American Wheelmen".

## The League of American Wheelmen

The influence of The League of American Wheelmen was so strong that in April of 1879 an act was passed by the Pennsylvania legislature which provided for the appointment of "Side Path Commissioners" to have general supervision over the "construction and maintenance of side paths along the highways of the townships of this Commonwealth for the use of bicycles and pedestrians – bicycle riders, however, to have the right of way thereon." Bicycle paths became much more practical for the general use of the public than the miserable existing dirt roads. "Old timers" who traveled these bicycle paths describe them as approximately three to four feet wide, often paved with hard cinders, which were quickly compacted by bike traffic into a smooth surface. Many private bicycle paths were built, with cyclists who used them being charged $1.00 for a small metal tag which they fastened to their vehicles to identify themselves. Bicycle paths are still popular in Europe, with their own traffic lights, bridges, etc., and are now making a come-back in various parts of the United States. Bicycling is once again taking hold in Pennsylvania.

Fortunately for the more conservative citizens, and the women cyclists, a bicycle was developed in 1884 in England called, appropriately, the "Safety Bicycle". The English trade name was the "Humber Safety Bicycle". It was introduced into the United States and was the forerunner of our modern bicycle. For the first time the motive power was applied to the rear wheel by means of foot cranks and chain drive, with the driver's seat suspended between the wheels. The rear driving wheel was, at first, considerably larger than the front, but this arrangement was later modified to make both wheels the same diameter. The introduction of pneumatic tires about 1892 and later, the coaster brakes, made the bicycle a truly useful and practical vehicle of rapid transportation.

The "Hobby Horse" of 1819

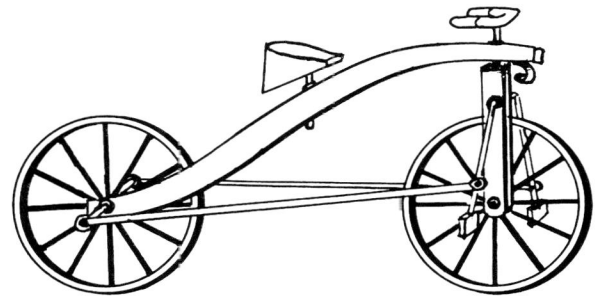

MacMillan's Bike of 1839

The "Boneshaker" of 1869

The "Ordinary Bicycle" of 1872

Special uniforms were often the identification of the hardy clan of young men who rode The Ordinary Bicycle. Here, a member of the Harrisburg Wheel Club poses proudly with his trusty vehicle for a studio photograph.

During the "Gay Nineties" in America, the entire country was "on wheels". Cycling was as popular with the women as with the men. The emancipation of women truly began with the bicycle; even their dress was affected – special pantaloons and special "low-cut" bicycles were developed for their exclusive use. For those who had difficulty balancing on a two-wheeled vehicle a special "tricycle" was developed, with one large wheel to the front, two smaller wheels spread aside to the rear. Also the favorite among young couples – the "Bicycle Built for Two" was developed, which was later extended to the in-line family bicycle, built for three or even four!

In 1894 one cycle manufacturer was turning out his product at the rate of a "cycle a minute", and the industry was grossing $60 million a year. Another $12 million was spent on accessories, such as lights, bells, baskets and padded seats. Bike races and marathons drew more attention than baseball. Numerous speed trial and "six-day bike races" were held throughout Pennsylvania and the rest of the country. One man became nationally famous by riding behind a railroad train to become the first human to cycle a measured mile in less than sixty seconds!

## The Motor Cycle

The advent of a small and efficient one or two-cylinder gasoline engine in the early 1900's soon had cyclists experimenting with a new medium known as the "Motor-cycle", which became one of the fastest (and most dangerous) land vehicles ever developed by American ingenuity. With its very light weight and tremendous acceleration powers, the Motorcycle quickly gave the intrepid user a superior advantage over motorists in the low-powered and sluggish early automobiles. Traffic policemen in the early decades of the twentieth century were all equipped with high-powered motorcycles to quickly overtake and arrest any speeding motorists. The sound of a motor cycle engine, and possibly a siren to the rear, became an unwelcome part of the life of the early auto enthusiast.

A "side car" became one of the accessories for the motorcycle, which permitted an additional passenger, usually a woman, to ride along in something approaching comfort. Goggles and dust masks were standard equipment. Early motorcycling, on the bad roads of the period, was not a sport for the timid or weak of heart. Casualties were many. Today, special rules and regulations govern motor-cyclists (including such devices as crash helmets) to take some of the danger out of the sport.

The League of American Wheelmen grew in size and influence at the turn of the century, and supported by the new automotive enthusiasts, put considerable pressure on local and state authorities to do something about the truly miserable inter-city roads in Pennsylvania, and elsewhere.

The "Safety Bicycle" of 1884 put American women on wheels.

"Pride of the Nation", built by the John Stephenson Company of New York City in 1875, was probably the largest Omnibus in the world. Drawn by ten horses, it was displayed at the Centennial Exposition in Philadelphia in 1876 and made a cross-country tour in 1918. Since then, its fate is unknown. (Smithsonian Institution.)

# Chapter XIII
# URBAN RAIL CARS

To this point we have talked primarily about intercity transportation but have said little about travel conditions within Pennsylvania cities themselves. While more concentrated than our wide-spread metropolitan areas today, the larger communities in Pennsylvania in the early 1800's were beginning to develop a certain "urban sprawl" as the rapidly expanding population pushed housing and commercial establishments further away from the central "hubs" of the cities.

The more well-to-do city residents maintained stables and carriages for personal transportation within their urban areas, but for the most part, people walked to work, to the stores, to church, to the schools, and in bad weather ventured no further from home base than absolutely necessary.

The need for vehicles for urban mass transit was felt in the European cities early in the nineteenth century. A large coach, for primary use within the city limits was developed in Paris, circa 1825, and was dubbed the "Omnibus". Freely translated, this indicated "transportation for all". It was introduced into downtown London – a rather clumsy vehicle, pulled by three horses, with compartmented sections and seats for 18 passengers at a shilling per fare. Despite opposition from the hackney coachmen, it caught on at

once and within short order there were a dozen of them running around London. The Omnibus was tried out in New York City in 1831. John Stephenson, a coachmaker, built the first American Omnibus, with seats running lengthwise and the entrance door at the rear; fare, twelve and a half cents. The idea was picked up in Philadelphia a few months later. The first omnibus in the Quaker City was announced December 18, 1831 via the following newspaper advertisement:

"Joseph Boxall, having been requested by several gentlemen to run an hourly stage-coach for the accommodation of the inhabitants of Chestnut Street, to run from the lower part of the city, begs to inform the citizens generally that he has provided a superior new coach, harness, and good horses for that purpose. Comfort, warmth and neatness have in every respect been carefully studied. This conveyance will start from Schuylkill, Seventh and Chestnut Streets every morning (Sundays excepted) at 8:30 o'clock and every hour until 4:30 in the afternoon down Chestnut Street to the Merchant's Coffee House in Second Street and return from the Coffee House at 9:00 and every hour until 5:00 in the evening. This accommodation will be conducted and driven solely by the proprietor who hopes to merit patronage and support. Fare each way 10c, or tickets may be had of the proprietor at 12 for $1.00."

# J. G. BRILL COMPANY,
## PHILADELPHIA.

The cuts "Harlem & Manhattanville" represent a novel form of tow cars, being convertible from Winter Car to Summer

Car by removing panels and sash and substituting for panels the wire screens shown.

**Cars taken apart carefully and boxed for export.**

**Cane Cars, Hand Cars, Small Merchandise Cars.**

The operation proved profitable and on July 1, 1833 an additional omnibus line was added between the Navy Yard and Kensington. This line also flourished and within the next few years regular omnibus service began running on most of the principal Philadelphia Streets. Over the next several decades omnibuses provided the only means of mass transit within the Quaker City.

## The Horse Car

Taking their cue from the inter-city railroads then being built, it was not long before the promoters of mass urban transit came up with the idea of an omnibus running on tracks in the cities. New York City pioneered the horse-drawn street car with its "John Mason" compartmented street-rail car of 1832 on the "New York and Harlem Railroad Company" but it was not until several decades later that Philadelphians were ready to accept a rail-operated streetcar, and then only as a "spin-off" from what had started as a steam railway line. A charter had been granted to the "Philadelphia and Delaware Railroad Company" in 1854 to build a steam-railroad line from Kensington to Easton. When the promoters were unable to carry out this project in its entirety they conceiving the idea of utilizing the Philadelphia end of the line as a horse-railway for local transport. On January 21, 1858 this street car company began operations with fifteen horse cars.

Not to be outdone by Philadelphia, Pittsburgh followed suit August 5, 1859 by opening the "Citizens Passenger Railway Company" the first horse-drawn street car line in that city, which was later extended to Lawrenceville. Other horse car lines followed

Horse cars in the square at Harrisburg, circa 1880. (Dauphin County Historical Society.)

throughout the larger cities in Pennsylvania. Inspite of its early experiment with the horse car, New York City was slow to convert its public omnibus lines. In the 1850's the proponents of horse cars had made some inroads into the northern half of the city, but lower Manhattan stubbornly resisted the conversion. The last horse-drawn omnibus continued to operate on Fifth Avenue until the introduction of motor-buses in 1905.

In Philadelphia there was at first considerable opposition to the horse car. Some citizens claimed it was cruel to the horses, hard-worked in pulling omnibuses over the cobblestone streets, to expect them to pull the heavier rail cars loaded with many more people. To this objection the advocates of the railway replied that the new horse cars would have iron wheels running

Passengers assist the conductors in turning the San Francisco cable cars around for their return trip uphill.

on smooth iron rails, which would not only make the work of the horses easier, but would give passengers a smoother, more comfortable ride. Other objectors tried to prevent street car construction on the grounds that it would be a public nuisance. The Philadelphia "Sunday Dispatch", while generally opposed to horse cars, seems to have recognized them as an inevitable step in progress. The Dispatch Editor wrote: "It is perhaps scarcely worthwhile to allude to the fact that in New York City they kill one person each week on city railroads and mangle three or four on an average in the same space of time. Human life is really of little value nowadays". However, once a street rail line began service, public opinion usually changed. In 1859, cities like Chicago and Cincinnati followed the lead of New York, Philadelphia and Pittsburgh, and other cities throughout the country soon joined the conversion. Manufacturers of horse cars, and rails, did a rushing business.

During the next thirty years, the horse drawn street car invaded most of the Pennsylvania urban communities. Every town of any size developed its own "street car" line, usually as a private venture. Good horses were in great demand at a price of $125 to $200 per animal. It required about five to seven horses for each street car being operated, since each horse worked only about four to five hours a day. The small,

early cars used one horse per car, but in some of the larger cities larger cars with two horse teams were necessary. Each transit company required large stables to maintain their "horse-power", which had to be fed and tended twenty-four hours a day. Disposition of manure alone was a major operation. The horse car industry faced its worst crisis during the "Great Epizootic" of 1872, when a severe horse epidemic invaded the northeastern states, jumping from city to city, stable to stable, killing horses by the thousands. Horse cars throughout Pennsylvania virtually ceased operations, or were pulled by mules or even manpower. All this pointed up the need for a mechanical means of locomotion as a substitute for horse-power.

The proponents of steam had early tried to introduce small steam locomotives on the street car lines, but were howled down by the urban citizenry who contended, with some justification, that the place for the smoke and fire-belching steam locomotives was the open countryside. In spite of this opposition there were a few steam-powered street cars developed in the 1870's and 1880's. The Baldwin Locomotive Works, for instance, manufactured a passenger-carrying steam car, with the boiler partitioned off at one end, and the power plant so disguised that the whole unit looked like a regular horse car. This car, tried in limited quantities for a few years, was nick-

named the "Dummy" since its appearance generally was designed to fool horses into thinking it was a regular horse car and not scare them. The "Dummy" would sometimes draw several regular horse cars behind it. In 1876 steamcars puffed along Market Street in Philadelphia carrying visitors to the Centennial Exposition.

Other means of locomotion were tried, with modest success, by various inventors. The big objection to steam cars being the smoke nuisance, other media were used in a steam type engine, such as compressed air, and even ammonia. Large compressed air tanks were installed in a few experimental street cars, which operated over short distances, but required frequent returns to their source of power. Ammonia gas, with higher expansive powers than air, was also tried, but finally ruled out as too dangerous. A "naptha car" was developed in 1887 using an internal combustion engine powered with naptha, a little-known petroleum derivative, which behaved something like gasoline. A spring-loaded street car was developed by the "Automatic Spring Motor and Carriage Company" of Philadelphia which derived its power from a series of very large, clock-like springs, wound tight at the beginning of the run, and controlled by special governors. The company reported some "operational difficulties" in February of 1885, and after that nothing further was heard from them.

# The Cable Car

Although we are all familiar with San Francisco's famous cable-cars, it may come as a surprise to learn that at one time cable-car systems were operative in many of the larger cities of the United States. It all began, as one would expect, in San Francisco, whose extremely steep hills made horse-car operation in certain parts of the city almost an impossibility. A gentlemen named Andrew S. Hallidie first conceived of the idea of towing a rail car up the steep streets by a moving, remotely-powered cable beneath the car. He was granted permission by the city to try his idea on Clay Street, a half-mile route with a 20% grade in spots, and gambled his entire fortune – $20,000 – on the first "grip-car" rail line in the country. Raising additional capital from friends, he finally completed the construction of his unique system at a cost of about $100,000. It was successfully tried out on April 1, 1873, attracted wide attention, and was almost immediately duplicated in other parts of the city.

While the initial costs of such a cable system were high, the operating costs were about half that of the horse cars. The principle was simple. Each "grip car" (which sometimes provided the motive power for two or three additional trailer cars) had a strong gripping element which passed down through a slot in the center of the tracks to a moving steel cable in a small

Market Square, looking east, in Williamsport, Pa. circa 1900. By this time the old horse cars had been replaced by the "Trolleys", three of which are in evidence here. (Courtesy C. L. Siebert, Jr.)

**Adults and children alike enjoyed the open street cars on a hot summer day. Here is a Pittsburgh Railways Company car about 1905. (From the collection of the late Hugh Saraff.)**

tunnel beneath the street. The operator, or "gripman", had a lever in the car by which he could control the pressure on two, grooved, horizontal bars beneath the car to alternately grab and release the cable. Hill stops were accomplished by releasing the cable and simultaneously applying strong braking pressure to keep the car stationary. Sharp curves were found to be hard on the steel cables and large horizontal sheaves were installed underground at most corners, which the cable car could not follow. This meant that the operator, with precise timing, had to release his cable, coast around the corner and pick up the cable again after it had come back beneath the car. Needless to say this created some problems with the slower wagon and pedestrian traffic. If a grip car was forced to come to a halt on a curve, the embarrassed gripman had to ask the passengers to get out and push, until he could once again engage the cable. All this led to some rather reckless driving of the grip cars operators and frequent accidents.

The central power plant for these cable-car systems grew more complex with the length of the cable. The average cable length on each system was three to four miles, although one cable in Denver was almost seven miles long. Steam was generally the motive power for the cable, which wound in and out of the power house at the rate of about seven to nine miles per hour. Huge power sheaves, and take-up pulleys fastened to heavy counterweights in floor wells, kept the long close-circuited cables moving and taut. The cables were stopped and inspected for wear every night. Trouble sometimes developed when the gripper mechanism on individual cars jammed closed, or when small boys discovered they could "fish" a wire into the cable-car slots to tow their own wagons. But in general cable lines were reasonably efficient, and were immediately accepted by the public as a great improvement over the smelly, noisy and slower horse cars.

After its initial success in San Francisco the cable car was soon introduced into other cities, even those where no steep grades were involved. The cable car invaded Chicago in 1882, where the biggest and fanciest multi-cable-car system in the world was built. Philadelphia joined the cable-car movement in early 1883. Other cities followed the lead of Philadelphia and Chicago – among them New York City, St. Louis,

Oakland, Denver, Washington, Kansas City, Cleveland, Providence, Seattle and Baltimore. In Pittsburgh, the city's first cable car ran along Penn Avenue in February of 1888, and September 12, 1889 is noted as the date when the Pittsburgh Traction Company began operations of its cable car line over Fifth and Shady Avenues.

By 1890 there were approximately five hundred miles of cable-railway track in the United States and some 5,000 cars, carrying about four hundred million passengers annually. While the initial installation expense was great, cable-car systems soon proved their money-earning ability at an operating cost far less than the now out-moded horse-cars. Wherever even a rumor developed that a cable-car system was about to be installed, real estate in the vicinity immediately shot up in value.

## The Trolley Car

The "Trolley Car" is remembered with great affection by Pennsylvanians throughout the state even though its present operations are limited to a few dozen miles of trackage in Pittsburgh and Philadelphia. The name derives from the small, four-wheeled "troller" which was first used to pick up power from two overhead electric power lines, later changed to "trolley".

Ever since the mid-1800's various inventors had been experimenting with the use of electricity as the motive power for a street railcar. Battery-operated railcars were in use on a limited scale in a few areas. Charles G. Page ran a battery-powered railcar along the B. & O. railroad track near Washington in 1851 at the amazing speed of nineteen miles an hour, but he wore out his batteries on the trial run. Dr. Werner Siemens demonstrated a small electrical train on a short section of track at the Berlin, Germany Industrial Exposition of 1879. Thomas Edison was one of the first Americans to develop a high-speed electrical locomotive. His experimental model, built at Menlo Park, N. J. in 1880, ran so fast it scared his passengers half to death. However, Edison was more interested in power generation for city illumination purposes and did not pursue this invention. He did, however, inspire others to continue experimenting with the use of remote electrical power for rail cars, including a young naval officer named Frank J. Sprague.

Leo Daft built the first regularly-operated electric street car line in America in Baltimore in 1885 – a three-mile line using a third rail as a power source. It operated with moderate success, even though the company received many complaints in wet weather from citizens whose cats, dogs and chickens were electrocuted by contact with the 120-volt third rail.

In 1885, also, Charles J. Van Depoele, a Belgian sculptor who had been experimenting with electrical devices in the United States for years, displayed an overhead wire-powered rail car at the Toronto Agricultural Fair. This display caught the attention of James Gaboury, a street railway engineer of Montgomery, Alabama, who immediately invited Depoele to Montgomery to electrify the Capital City Railway in

Fifteen hundred trolley cars like this one were purchased by the Philadelphia Rapid Transit Company in 1912. (Courtesy C. L. Siebert, Jr.)

"End of the line" for one of the summer cars of the York, Pennsylvania trolley system. Hundreds of passengers disembark for a day of fun at Elm Beach Park on the Conewago Creek, north of Manchester.

that city. The following year, with fifteen miles of track, over-head wires and eighteen cars, Montgomery became the first community in the world to offer a city-wide system of electric transportation.

Van Depoele subsequently opened a similar system in Scranton, Pa., using the over-head troller, or "traveler" as Van Depoele called it. Operational difficulties with this device in Scranton called for the posting of a sign which read: "Engineers must oil their travelers every three hours". This sign caused the "Scranton Republican" to comment: "To set minds at rest, it may be well to state that 'travelers' has no reference to passengers riding in the cars, but only to the little arrangement which runs on the wire above." However, the trolley car movement received its greatest impetus when Frank J. Sprague, a young technical assistant to Thomas Edison, formed his own company – the Sprague Electric Railway and Motor

A wintry day on the Harrisburg and Mechanicsburg Electric Street Railway at Boiling Springs, circa 1898. (Courtesy R. H. Steinmetz.)

Company, and was invited to Richmond, Virginia in 1887 to set up a twelve-mile electric rail system, with forty cars, a 375-horsepower central power plant, and one hill! The hill almost proved Sprague's undoing. One of his early demonstrations was a test run of one of his cars up the steep Franklin Hill, which he pulled off to the amazement of hundreds of admiring witnesses, burning out his motor just after clearing the top. The latter detail was not made known to the enthusiastic visitors who swarmed over the car at the conclusion of the "hill climb". Sprague later had the car hauled away under cover of darkness by a good team of strong mules.

Sprague's Richmond system underwent its most severe test, in the summer of 1888 when Henry Whitney, owner of a large horse-car system in Boston, asked to see a demonstration of a number of cars being started at once on the same section of track. Whitney simply saw "no way" that the slim overhead wire could supply starting power for more than one or two cars simultaneously. Sprague told his power plant operator (in advance) to tie down the safety valve on the steam generator and "give it everything". At midnight he lined up twenty-two cars on a section of track which normally handled only three or four, and got Whitney out of bed. The cars moved out, one by one, until all were in motion. At first the car lights dimmed, but then they brightened again, and off they went, out of sight. Whitney was "sold". Sprague's system was hailed as the best in the country.

Word of the Richmond system got around, and by the 1890's horse car systems throughout the country began converting to electrical power. The big initial cost was the central power plant. Many of the old horse cars could be converted with minor alterations, by adding electric motors, geared directly to the wheels. The over-head "trolley" was improved by

making it a spring-loaded, single-wheel contact from underneath the overhead power wire.

One of the pioneers in Pennsylvania – Pittsburgh – on August 7, 1888 ran its first electric street cars on a route from South 13th and Carson Streets to Knoxville, ironically just six months after the opening of the first cable car system on Penn Avenue. The following year both the "Federal Street and Pleasant Valley Railway Company" and "Second Avenue Passenger Railway Company" began operations in the Iron City. That same year found nearly 200 electric street car lines forming in other parts of United States. Philadelphia's J. G. Brill horse car manufacturing company began offering four-wheel electric cars in the early 1890's and was swamped with orders. As the demand grew for electric cars of greater capacity, the Brill company became the first manufacturer in the country to produce a double-truck electric car.

By the turn of the Twentieth Century there were 15,000 miles of electric car trackage and some 30,000 trolleys operating in the United States. Cable cars were on the way out. Philadelphia abandoned its cable car system in 1895. Chicago converted its vast cable car network to electric drive in 1906. Only a handful of horse car lines were still in operation; most of them had converted to the much-cheaper electric operation. The "Trolley Car" had captured the hearts of Americans everywhere, just as the automobile was to do, a generation later.

Amusement parks, built by the trolley companies "at the end of the line" in some cool grove near a swimming hole, became an American institution. So-called "open cars" were added to all trolley companies' rolling stock primarily for week-end use to get the crowds to the amusement parks in the summertime. Waldemere Park in Erie, Carsonia Park in Reading, Willow Grove Park in Philadelphia, Maple Grove Park at Lancaster, Sanatoga Park at Pottstown, Highland Park in York, and dozens of other parks operated by the trolley companies were swamped with pleasure seeking citizens on summer weekends, at a "nickle a ride". Needless to say the transit companies also made

"Chick" Siebert, who has won national recognition for the unbelievable perfection of his model trolley layout in Camp Hill, Pa. is responsible for much of the material in this chapter.

money on the roller-coasters, fun houses, swimming pools and all the other concessions in the parks of the early 1900's. Some of these parks are still around, even though the rail companies that built them have long since been forgotten.

## The "Inter-Urbans"

So prosperous and extensive did the trolley car systems become in the early half of the century that they soon reached out to challenge inter-city connections of the steam rail lines. Luxurious and heavy rolling stock was developed by some of the electric lines, which followed their singing wires and tracks through the countryside, radiating out from the metropolitan areas in Pennsylvania to reach countless nearby communities. Both Pittsburgh and Philadelphia developed a vast network of such inter-urban electric lines, some of which remain in operation today. The Butler Short Line, the Liberty Bell, the Harmony Route, The Lehigh Valley Transit, The Northwestern Pennsylvania Railway, the Hershey Transit Company, the Valley Railways, the Lancaster Ephrata and Lebanon Street Railway, the Conestoga Transportation Company, and scores of other electric lines, provided rapid transportation between boroughs, and even between cities, never equalled by any other mass transportation medium before or since. It was possible for a Pennsylvania traveler (with proper guide book) to travel by trolley across the entire state, and many miles beyond its borders, without ever setting foot on a steam rail car.

A three-unit train of the Philadelphia and Western "Bullet" cars pose for the camera during a special excursion November, 1971. These cars, built in the 1930's, are noted for their quick acceleration and high speed.

Elevated tracks of the Southern New Jersey Rapid Transit System which daily brings commuters into Philadelphia from across the Delaware. (Courtesy Gannett Fleming Corddry and Carpenter, Inc.)

## "Overhead and Underground"

Jammed with traffic of all sorts on its main streets, New York City took the lead in building the world's first elevated railroad system in 1876. The first lines were powered by small steam locomotives. Chicago got into the act in 1892, also with steam to start, but by the time it built its famous "Loop" in 1897, Chicago had electrified its overhead lines, using the principle proposed by Frank Sprague of providing a separate driving motor for each car, with a single multi-car control in the lead car, an arrangement still in use today.

Boston had the distinction of building the first real subway in America in 1897, even though the Beach Pneumatic Railroad Company had operated a short section of air-blown "tube cars" under Broadway in

Typical low-floor "yellow car" used by the Pittsburgh Railways Company 1914 to 1954. In the background, cars of the type still in use in Pittsburgh. (Courtesy Arden Trolley Museum.)

Station of the S.N.J.R.T. System – a 1970 innovation of modern mass transit. (Courtesy Gannett Fleming Corddry & Carpenter, Inc.)

New York for a few months in 1870.

Philadelphia followed the lead of New York and Boston in the early decades of the 1900's with its combined Market Street Subway and elevated system connecting Sixty Ninth Street and Frankford, and later, the Broad Street Subway.

These rail systems are still with us, and the need for a rejuvenation of additional high-speed electric rail lines in Pennsylvania is manifested by such modern lines as the 1970 Southern New Jersey Rapid Transit System which brings thousands of cross-Delaware rural commuters into downtown Philadelphia daily, literally in minutes. This elevated system, which travels across the Benjamin Franklin Bridge, has been described as the most technologically sophisticated in the World.

This amazing six-wheel "Pullman" was built experimentally in 1903. A two-cylinder, "pan-cake" engine provided power to the center wheels. The steering wheels, both front and rear, were linked together to turn in opposite directions, when the operator moved the "tiller". A difficult car to drive, it was soon converted to a conventional four-wheel auto, with four cylinder engine. (Built in York, Pa.)

## Chapter XIV

# THE AUTO ERA OPENS

The beginning of the Twentieth Century also marked the beginning of the wide use of the power-driven "horseless carriage" for individual transportation. Charles E. Duryea of Springfield, Massachusetts was the first inventor in America to come up (in 1893) with a practical application of a small single-cylinder gasoline engine to a four-wheeled vehicle. Duryea, who later moved his automobile manufacturing operation to Reading, Pennsylvania probably had no idea, in 1893, of the tremendous impact which his invention would have on the entire American way of life.

The basic idea of the "Automobile" (a word coined by the French to mean a self-propelled vehicle) was not new. Inventors in all parts of the world had been experimenting with various types of power-units, applied to wheeled vehicles. Here are a few milestones of

motor history which preceded our modern automobile:

1767 – Nicholas Joseph Gugnot constructed in Paris a 3-wheel steam car, which carried passengers.

1829 – Sir Goldsworthy Gurney, a surgeon in London, developed a steam carriage which led to the extensive use of steam driven motor buses in England during the mid-19th century.

1860 – Etienne Lenoir, a Frenchman, patented the first gas engine. Hitherto all power units had been steam driven.

1876 – Dr. N. A. Otto, a German, brought out the "Otto Silent Gas Engine," which was the first to operate on the new 4-stroke cycle.

1879 – George B. Seldon, of Rochester, New York, applied for patents to an explosion type engine driven

1893 Duryea was driven with a one-cylinder engine and steered with a "tiller", which also served as a gear-shift lever. It is obvious why these early cars were called "horseless carriages".

motor car. Although Seldon never actually built a car till 1908, this patent was approved in 1895 and enabled him to claim royalties on most American manufactured automobiles until 1911, when Henry Ford successfully contested Seldon's patent.

1882 – Copeland, of Philadelphia, put on the market and sold some 200 steam tricycles.

1884 – Gottlieb Daimler, a German, patented a gasoline driven motor cycle and shortly afterward developed the first commercially successful motor car.

1892 – Dr. Rudolph Diesel applied for the first patent on an oil powered explosion type engine, now used extensively on trucks.

1893 – Charles E. Duryea built a single cylinder "Buggyaut" in Springfield, Massachusetts, the first gasoline-engine-driven motor vehicle made in America.

1894 – Henry Ford built his first motor vehicle.

1895 – The first automobile race in United States was held, between Chicago and Evanston, Illinois. The winner was J. Frank Duryea (brother of Charles E.) in a Duryea, which averaged 7½ miles per hour.

1897 – Twin brothers, Francis Edgar Stanley and Freelan O. Stanley of Kingfield, Maine, built the first successful American steam car and subsequently (1902) organized the Stanley Motor Company.

1900 – The first national automobile show in America was held in Madison Square Garden, New York City.

1902 – The American Automobile Association was formed to supervise racing. It subsequently formed local clubs throughout the country to provide travel information and emergency road service to motorists. Highway improvement, motor legislation and safety education are also part of the modern AAA program.

1903 – Dr. H. Nelson Jackson of Burlington, Vermont, became the first person to make a transcontinental automobile trip. On the road for 63 days in a 20-H. P. Winton touring car, his actual travel time was 44 days.

1906 – A Stanley Steamer set a world speed record of 127.66 miles per hour; and, unofficially, 197 miles per hour in 1907.

## "Steamers" & "Electrics"

At first it appeared that the "Steamer" was the speediest and probably the most economical automobile made. Both the "Stanley" and "White" Steamers became popular in the early 1900's and the "Stanley" was manufactured in quantity until 1925. However, the advocates of internal combustion, not to mention the gasoline producers, continued to make improvements to their engines as well as the quality of their fuel, to the point that they were able to compete with the "Steamer" in performance. Auto folklore early discredited the Stanley as a "dangerous" vehicle, although its boiler was actually constructed in such a way that it was impossible to blow up.

Another type of automobile, popular with women because of its simplicity, quietness and ease of operation, was the battery-powered electric car. However, it was slow, and its range was only about 40 or 50 miles without recharging, so its use was limited primarily to short trips in the cities. Most of the "Electrics" disappeared from general usage by about 1925, although

This "Stanley Steamer" was owned by John Hartley, of York, Pa. who sits at the wheel. Photo made in Gettysburg circa 1909. Note 'blow-out patch' on left front tire.

127

Jimmy Kline at the wheel of his "Kline Kar" Racer about 1910. The Kline Kar was manufactured in York, Pa. originally – moved to Richmond, Virginia about 1911, where Jimmy Kline continued to produce quality automobiles until 1922. (Courtesy Wm. W. Thompson II.)

there is currently a movement to get them back on the streets and highways of the nation to alleviate our ever-increasing air pollution, not to mention our gasoline shortage.

Many of the old carriage or wagon-building shops (like Studebaker, founded in Adams County, Pennsylvania in 1830) converted their operation to motor-driven vehicles. Corner machine shops began turning

A model "C" Pullman built in York, Pa. in 1906, now on permanent display in the Historical Society of York County. (Photo by the Sunday News.)

out automotive parts, or even entire automobiles. Almost every manufacturer in the metal-working trade became involved, either directly or indirectly, in the manufacture of automobiles or parts for them. Within the next twenty years there were a total of nearly 2500 different automobiles placed on the market in the U.S.A. Such names as the "Apperson", the "Chalmers", the "Kissell", the "Metz", the "Durant", the "Franklin", the "Mercer", the "Paige", the "Cleveland", the "Moon", the "Stutz", the "Chandler", the "Flint", the "Locomobile", became popular for a while and then faded from the scene as their manufacturers failed or sold out to larger automotive interests. Some of these were purely hand-tailored assembly operations, with the assembler's name on the end product, but others were bona-fide production cars, with engines and other major parts being fabricated in the same plant in which the cars were assembled.

By the year 1900, the automobile had captured the popular American fancy as had the canal boat, the steam locomotive, the trolley car and the bicycle of the Nineteenth Century.

The more conservative citizens tended to look down their noses at the noisy, dust-raising "horseless carriage," and considered it a new fad which would soon die out. These people continued to ride the trolley cars, drive their own horse carriages and occasionally shout "get a horse" to a broken-down automobile team stranded along the road, or stuck in the mud.

The last word in mass transit in 1915 – this open-air motor bus is loaded with a crowd of Pennsylvanians on a tour of Toronto, Canada.

The pioneers of the automobile era, however, would not be denied. Manufacturers and auto enthusiasts tested the capabilities of their cars against competition by regulated racing contests, or by endurance races between cities over the unbelievably bad roads of the early 1900's. Most of the early drivers were hardy individuals with lungs impervious to dust in summer, with hipboots to dig their way out of the mud in winter, with natural mechanical ability, lots of tools, tire chains, tow ropes, extra tires, blow-out patches, and with an unfailing spirit of optimism and adventure inbred in their souls. They delighted in joining with other equally hardy enthusiasts in taking long group tours across country to show the public what could be done, (the Glidden Tours, for instance). Had it not been for the unquenchable spirit of these early automotive pioneers, the movement to "put America on wheels" would have ended at the first highway mud hole.

## Auto Manufacturing in Pennsylvania

In the first two decades of the Twentieth Century there were a number of manufacturers in the Eastern Pennsylvania area producing both passenger cars and trucks. Much of the activity centered around Reading, where, in addition to the famous Duryea – the Acme, the Bertolet, Boss, Daniels, Dile, Meteor, Middlebury, Reber, Riviera, Snader, and S.G.V. were made – all presumably gasoline-driven – not to mention the "Reading Steamer".

This sporty Pullman "Speedster" of 1913 sold for $1675. With electric self starter and electric lights – $1875.

In Allentown, the emphasis was on truck manufacture, with the (still existing) Mack Truck operation, the Bethlehem Truck, the Maccar Truck, the Penn Unit Truck and the Starbux Truck. In nearby Easton, the Wilson Steam Truck was produced. Wilkes Barre had its Mathewson automobile (and truck) and the Owen Magnetic – a forerunner of Chrysler's push-button-gear-shift car. In the Pottstown-Phoenixville area were produced the Chadwick, Champion and Phoenix, as well as the Autocar Truck (the latter operation now located at Exton, Pa.)

Lancaster County had its "Conestoga" Truck Company in the city of Lancaster, the "Carrol" Motor Car Company at Strasburg, and the "Light" Commercial Car Company at Marietta – all producing gas-driven vehicles in the early 1900's.

The above list is by no means all-inclusive. There were many other manufacturing operations of short duration, such as the "Imperial" Electric Car in Williamsport, the "Chester" auto and the "Rowe" Truck at Coatesville, the "Hahn" Wagon Works in Hamburg, the "Randall" at Newtown, the "Vim" Motor Truck Company production plant in Philadelphia, the "Morton" Truck at Harrisburg, the "Storm Queen" and "Kearns" at Deavertown, and the "Bangor" Truck at Bangor. A number of "Electrics" were manufactured in Philadelphia.

There were a variety of self-propelled vehicles manufactured in York and York County in the early 1900's:

One of the last Pullman production models was this 1916 deluxe coupe, with push-button gear shift, designed especially for women drivers. It sold for $990.

the "Mayflower" Truck, 1905; the "Hart-Kraft" Truck, about 1908; the "Martin" Truck and "Kline-Kar", 1909; the "Atlas" Truck in 1912; the "Sphinx" Motor Car, 1914; the "Bell" in 1915; and the "Hanover" in 1917. A car named the "Pritz" was also said to be built in York at one time. But by far the most significant automobile manufacturing operation ever undertaken in York, or perhaps in this part of the United States, was that of the "Pullman" Motor Car.

Fresh out of Lehigh University, the author sits proudly on the running board of his 1930 Studebaker "Dictator" business coupe, for which he paid $200 in 1937.

Some of the finest cars ever built in America were produced, paradoxically, in the depression years of the 1930's. The Auburn-Cord-Dusenberg Company of Auburn, Indiana produced this front-wheel drive "Cord", with super-charged engine in 1937. Recently a plant in Tulsa, Oklahoma was producing a scaled down model of the famous Cord classic, shown here.

## The "Pullman" Motor Car

Including the amazing six-wheel "Pullman" of 1903, and various other models, such as the "York", "York-Pullman" and "Pullman Junior" – the Pullman Motor Car Company of York, Pennsylvania, at the peak of its operations (about 1915) was producing a car every fifteen minutes. Its factory, at North George and North Streets in York, employed some 900 people and was fully equipped with the same sub-assembly and production lines which made Henry Ford famous. Its early cars were large, well made and fully competitive with such luxury cars of the day as Buick, Locomobile, La Salle, Cadillac, and Pierce Arrow. Spurred by the "Model T Ford" low-price, mass-assembled car, Pullman converted about 1914 to a full production-line operation making various models of the "Pullman Junior", competitive with other small cars such as Ford, Maxwell, Willys Overland, Briscoe, Chevrolet and Saxon, at a selling price of $740.

Final models of the "Pullman", produced in 1916 and 1917, included such innovations as the "Pullman Delux Coupe", designed especially for women drivers, with a "Magnetic" Push-Button Gear Shift. Mis-management by "experts" imported from out of state, plus the national conversion to war-time economy in 1917, forced the company into receivership. Otherwise the Pullman Motor Car Company might have continued to challenge its Detroit competition for many more years.

The experience of Pullman was typical of many other large auto manufacturers of the early 1900's, starting with large and expensive, almost custom-built cars, which only the well-to-do Americans could afford, but being forced by Henry Ford to convert to mass-production methods, from which only a handful of car-builders ultimately survived.

This Reeves 1911 "Octoauto", made in Columbus, Indiana, was one of the last attempts at a multi-wheeled passenger car.

131

This Pullman racing team encountered some slight delays on their inter-city endurance run, circa 1909. (Courtesy Wm. W. Thompson II.)

# Chapter XV
# PENNSYLVANIA HIGHWAYS IN THE 20TH CENTURY

The advent of the horseless carriage, plus the pressure already being exerted by the League of American Wheelmen, put teeth in the movement for good roads. The "Office of Road Inquiry" was authorized as part of the U.S. Department of Agriculture by Act of Congress, approved by President Benjamin Harrison March 3, 1893. This organization was charged with the responsibility of conducting tests and experiments on road building materials and dissemination of information on road improvement. In 1897, the O.R.I. built a short experimental stone road in New Brunswick, N.J. using the best methods and materials then available as an "object lesson" road. The movement for better roads had at last begun.

## Turnpikes Rejuvenated

By the year 1900, with automobiles increasing in number and range of travel, there was also an attempt by the surviving turnpike companies to rejuvenate their long-neglected right-of-ways. Some of them re-macadamized their roads and re-opened their toll houses to collect maintenance funds. By 1903, approx-

imately 1100 miles of toll roads were again in use in Pennsylvania. However, it was obvious that the problem was too great to be solved solely by private turnpike companies, many of which had long since gone into bankruptcy.

While the rural roads were still in the hands of the townships and counties, the taxpayers were now ready for substantial government aid on their inter-city highway improvement programs.

Travel conditions were considered fairly good on this section of the York-Gettysburg Pike in Adams County, June 11, 1910. (Courtesy PHMC State Archives.)

The Lincoln Highway winds across the George Westinghouse Bridge in East Pittsburgh, 235 ft. above Turtle Creek Valley. The bridge, with the largest reinforced concrete arches in America, was built in 1930 – required 73,350 cubic yards of concrete plus 3,500,000 pounds of reinforcing steel. (Courtesy Carnegie Library of Pittsburgh.)

The State of Pennsylvania was one of the first to form its own highway department. With the backing of Governor Pennypacker, on May 31, 1903, an Act was passed organizing the Pennsylvania Department of Highways. Under the provisions of the Act, the townships and counties were to receive state assistance up to two-thirds of the cost of reconstruction of township roads, with the balance paid by the county and/or township, according to the agreement. The townships and counties were slow to realize the potential benefits being offered them and at first only a few hundred miles of roads were paved.

By Act of 1905, state aid on Pennsylvania roads was increased to three-quarters of the cost of construction, and an Act dated May 31, 1911 increased the state's responsibility to a system of 8835 miles of roads to be constructed and maintained solely at the expense of the Commonwealth. A report (issued in 1967) indicated that the Pennsylvania Departments of Highways had extended its responsibility to 43,481 miles of public thoroughfares, with the townships controlling 48,801 miles of roads and streets; the boroughs, 7,151 miles; and the cities, 6,033 miles.

## Federal Aid

The federal government in 1916 also instituted a system of grants to the states for highway construction, which is still being continued today, and comprises a key element in determining the size of the state road-building program.

The automobile brought with it the need for new techniques in road building. The fine stone surface in use on the "macadamized" roads did not lie quietly in place with the automobile as it did for the horse and buggy. The pneumatic tires of the automobile, traveling over these roads at high speed, kicked the fine, loose surface material aside, exposing the coarser material beneath to water penetration, and further kicking up of the sub-surface. Not only that, it created a serious dust problem, making breathing and visibility difficult for all drivers on the road, as well as the inhabitants of houses along the highways.

Beginning in 1905 the Office of Public Roads (U. S. Department of Agriculture) conducted a series of experiments in the application of various crude oil and coal tar products to both macadamized and earth roads. The heavier the oil, the better it worked in laying the dust and improving the road surface. Tar worked best. The following year the State Board of Public Roads of Rhode Island also experimented with a tar-macadam road, covered with a stone dust after the final tar application, and recommended this treatment for all future macadam roads.

Other road-building materials were also tried. The first brick-surfaced rural road was laid between Cleveland and Wooster, Ohio, in 1893, and was found satisfactory but expensive. Concrete was tried in 1909 on a rural road in Wayne County, Michigan and was received with great enthusiasm by the local motorists. The first concrete test road in Pennsylvania is said to have been built about 1919 in Union County, between Mifflinburg and Hartleton.

## Lincoln Highway

One of the most ambitious projects of early automotive highways was the Lincoln Highway, which involved a continuously improved route, over existing roads, from New York to San Francisco. Plans to pave this road were started in 1913 with the forming of the Lincoln Highway Association in Detroit, Michigan. The Federal Aid Road Act of July 11, 1916 made U. S. road building funds available and improvements along sections of the Lincoln Highway were then made by the highway departments of the states through which it passed, utilizing federal funds. By 1925, much of the original route had become "U. S. Route 30", but in Pennsylvania it is still referred to as the "Lincoln Highway", essentially following the route of the old Pennsylvania Road. Its mountain crossings, while steep, afford some breath-taking views of the surrounding country-side. In inclement winter weather, these mountain sections of the road are still somewhat difficult to travel.

The Lincoln Highway crosses the new Ray's Hill By-Pass of the Pennsylvania Turnpike, east of Breezewood. (Courtesy Buchart-Horn.)

The South Penn Bridge Piers in the Susquehanna at Harrisburg were ready for steel in 1885, when the project was abandoned. (Photo by the author.)

This old photo, circa 1885, shows the nearly completed Ray's Hill Tunnel of the South Penn Railroad, which lay abandoned for the next fifty years. In the foreground are Andrew Carnegie and Henry Oliver – both of whom invested heavily in the South Penn.

Under the two administrations of Pennsylvania's Governor Gifford Pinchot, the Keystone State led a movement to "get the farmer out of the mud". In 1931, the state took over 20,167 miles of small rural dirt roads, and began paving them with a bituminous macadam surface. The Rossville-Lewisberry road, in York County, was the first such road to be paved. When completed, these small arteries were dubbed the "Pinchot Roads" by a grateful rural population.

## Pennsylvania Turnpike

An important development in world highway history occurred in Pennsylvania on May 21, 1937, when Governor George H. Earle signed an Act creating the Pennsylvania Turnpike Commission. Its objective: to build the first modern four-lane turnpike in the United States.

The history of the Pennsylvania Turnpike actually begins May 5, 1854 when an act of the General Assembly of Pennsylvania authorized the incorporation of the "Ducannon, Landisburg and Broad Top Railroad", which later became known as the South Pennsylvania Railroad Company. It was the intention of this firm to develop Col. Charles Schlatter's "Southern Route" across the State, as surveyed in 1839, into a new cross-state railroad – more direct and with a lower grade than that of the existing Pennsylvania Railroad route along the Juniata River. The "South Penn" struggled along for years with insufficient funds to lay more than a few miles of track between Harrisburg and a point west of Carlisle. Its significance was recognized by Frank Gowen, president of the Philadelphia and Reading Railroad in the 1870's, as a possible extension of the Reading lines to Pittsburgh.

Financial difficulties prevented Gowen from pursu-

ing the matter as a company project, but he succeeded in getting the interest and support of William H. Vanderbilt, owner of the New York Central Railroad, in forming a syndicate for completion of the South Penn to Port Perry, on the Monongahela River, near Braddock, Pa. The syndicate, formed in the early 1880's, included such colorful personalities as Andrew Carnegie, Henry Frick, Henry Oliver, Donald Cameron, and John D. and William Rockefeller.

The proposed new railroad constituted a serious threat to Pennsylvania Railroad's existing cross-state route, offering a saving of some thirty to fifty miles of travel across the state, with a much lower grade line. Needless to say, George Roberts, president of Pennsylvania Railroad, was not happy about the proposed South Penn, and while certain overtures were made to him by the Syndicate promoters, he rejected them and announced publicly that he "would smash the South Penn like a bubble!"

For the next few years it was open warfare between Roberts and Vanderbilt. The latter pushed hard for completion of the South Penn and by the summer of 1885 had nine tunnels through the Allegheny Mountains virtually finished, about 90% of the two-track right-of-way between Harrisburg and Pittsburgh fully graded, and piers of a new bridge across the Susquehanna River at Harrisburg ready for steel.

Double tunnels were constructed on the Pennsylvania Turnpike, 1965-68. In this photo, a track-mounted drilling "Jumbo" is shown at the working face at the west portal of Kittatinny Mountain. (Courtesy Pa. Turnpike Commission.)

At this point a new personality entered the picture – J. Pierpont Morgan, who had been handicapped in his sales of American railroad stocks in England by just such cut-throat competition as that engaged in by Roberts and Vanderbilt. U. S. Railroad stock values, and dividends, had hit a new low. Morgan returned to the United States to act as peacemaker, and finally persuaded Roberts and Vanderbilt to bury the hatchet, and trade railroads in Pennsylvania and New York to their mutual advantage. Pennsylvania Railroad was to acquire the nearly completed South Penn in exchange for their bonded interest in the New York, West Shore and Buffalo Railroad – a line competitive with Vanderbilt's New York Central.

However, the other members of Vanderbilt's Syndicate violently objected to what they considered a "sell out" of their interests and got an injunction in Harrisburg to prevent the transfer of the South Penn to PRR. All work ceased on the South Penn in September of 1885, and the abandoned tunnels and right-of-way became known locally as "Vanderbilt's Folly". After years of litigation the South Penn right-of-way was sold at public auction. The Baltimore and Ohio Railroad Company bought most of it. The B. & O. did

The author (left), and two friends, explore the interior of the original Blue Mountain Tunnel in 1937. Note the excellent condition of the Vanderbilt portal masonry overhead.

Allegheny Mountain was the first to be double-tunneled, 1965-66.

nothing to push the line through to completion, and finally sold their interest to the Pennsylvania Turnpike Commission October 21, 1938.

The Pennsylvania Turnpike Commission "holed through" six of the old South Penn tunnels, regraded the 2% slopes of the South Penn route to 3% – an easy climb for the autos of the 1930's, and proceeded to create America's first "super-highway". The only other highway in the world approaching it was Hitler's "Autobahn" in Germany, built several years earlier. Known originally as the "all-weather" road between Harrisburg and Pittsburgh (actually Middlesex to Irwin), it provided the best, low-grade crossing of the Allegheny Mountains yet built, and also ushered in the present era of high-speed, limited-access highways in this country.

The first 164-mile section through the mountains was opened to traffic October 1, 1940, and it was immediately obvious that extensions were necessary. Laws were passed directing that extensions be built west to the Ohio line and east to the New Jersey line, and construction of these extensions was consummated in 1950 and 1951. In 1957 the Northeast Extension from Philadelphia to Scranton was also opened to traffic, completing a total of 470 miles of toll road.

When the first mountain section of the Turnpike was opened in 1940, traffic averaged about 26,000 vehicles daily. On the east-west section of the Turnpike today traffic averages more than 100,000 passenger cars, buses and trucks daily. The seven two-lane tunnels of the original road became bottle-necks, particular on weekends and holidays. In 1960, the Turnpike Commission began a series of studies to either double-tunnel, or "by pass" the old tunnels.

As a result of these studies, the Laurel Hill tunnel, at the west end of the mountain section of the Turnpike, was by-passed by a 145-foot deep cut through the crest of Laurel Hill mountain. A second and much longer mountain ridge by-pass was constructed east of Breezewood to eliminate both the Rays Hill and Sideling Hill tunnels. The remaining tunnels at Allegheny, Tuscarora, Kittatiny and Blue Mountains were supplemented by new two-lane tunnels paralleling the old ones. A third lane for trucks was added on the steeper up-grades of the by-pass routes.

These improvements, plus continuous barriers separating opposing lanes of traffic, were completed in October of 1968. For the first time there was now uninterrupted four-lane traffic on the east-west section of the Pennsylvania Turnpike from the Ohio line to New Jersey.

137

Of the sixteen major toll-roads of the nation, many of them patterned after this "Grandaddy" of all modern high-speed roads, the Pennsylvania Turnpike today stands in third place as a revenue producer. Only the New York Thruway and the New Jersey Turnpike have greater gross annual incomes. Turnpike Commissioners are happy to point out that construction and maintenance work on their toll-road has cost the taxpayers not a penny. The "all-weather highway" through the Allegheny Mountains, conceived during the depths of the great depression of the thirties, has been a complete success.

## The Keystone Shortway

Another important milestone in American highway development occurred on June 29, 1956, when federal legislation created the National System of Interstate and Defense Highways. While many miles of existing four-lane high-speed highways, such as the Pennsylvania Turnpike, were included in the new system, the Act also authorized the federal government to pay 90% of the cost of constructing a system of 41,000 miles of multi-lane, controlled-access super-highways joining most of the nation's cities with over 50,000 population, with the States assuming the remaining 10% and supervising construction.

The Keystone Shortway in Pennsylvania, which became part of this interstate highway system in 1957, had originally been conceived as a second Pennsylvania toll highway. Groundwork was laid in 1939 by Charles E. Noyes, manager of the Community Trade Association in Williamsport, who pictured a major highway east to west near Williamsport as virtually a straight-line route between New York City and Cleveland. The idea was revived by the Williamsport Chamber of Commerce in 1952. State Senator Z. H.

Improved tiling and lighting are features of the new turnpike tunnels. (Courtesy Pa. Turnpike Commission.)

Confair was made chairman of a "Keystone Shortway Association," with Charles Noyes as executive director. With the cooperation of Governor Leader and the Pennsylvania Department of Highways, Confair and Noyes were instrumental in arranging hearings before the Bureau of Public Roads in Washington. The result was the incorporation of the Keystone Shortway as a toll-free road into the Interstate Highways System, May 23, 1957.

The 312.9-mile route of the "Shortway" was selected by a team of consultants working with the Pennsylvania Department of Highways and the national Bureau of Public Roads, with the active participation of the Keystone Shortway Association in Williamsport and other citizens groups along the proposed route through north central Pennsylvania. It starts at Sharon, on the Ohio line, and travels almost due east through some of the most beautiful virgin territory of the State to Stroudsburg on the Delaware River.

The entire Interstate 80 route, of which the Keystone Shortway is a part, runs 2870 miles from New York City to San Francisco almost "as the crow flies." When fully completed it will be the shortest transcontinental east-west highway in the United States. The Pennsylvania section was under construction in the early 1960's and its full 312.9 miles were completed and opened to traffic in the summer of 1970. A connection across New Jersey has now been made directly into New York City. The western end of the Shortway already ties into the Ohio Turnpike near Youngstown.

Eastern section of the Keystone Shortway, approaching the Susquehanna River, north branch. (Photo by the author.)

The Keystone Shortway passes through some of Pennsylvania's most scenic sections. It is shown here crossing the Clarion River on a 1635-foot long deck-truss bridge. (Courtesy Modjeski and Masters.)

Travelers taking this route between New York and Cleveland save more than 75 miles as opposed to old route via Philadelphia and the Pennsylvania Turnpike. When the Shortway was officially opened in 1970, a lightening of east-west traffic on the Pennsylvania Turnpike was noted almost immediately.

The economic impact of the Shortway on the towns along its route began to be felt as the new highway neared completion in the 1960's. Real estate prices near every proposed interchange began doubling and tripling in value. A dozen new industrial parks have moved into areas close to the right-of-way. Over 100 service stations have been built, and many new motels have appeared. Tourism promotion along the route began in earnest in 1970. The Shortway is literally "opening up" sections in northern Pennsylvania which had previously been considered depressed areas.

Looking at Pennsylvania's Interstate Highways in general, as of this writing, only a few miles of Pennsylvania's 1574 miles of Interstate Highway remain to be completed. These few remaining miles are located in the Pittsburgh, Scranton and Philadelphia metropolitan areas and should be finished in the next few years.

The state's highest bridge, where the Keystone Shortway crosses the Allegheny River at Emlenton, towers 271 feet above the river bed. (Courtesy Buchart Horn.)

139

# Chapter XVI
# AIR TRAVEL IN PENNSYLVANIA

Re-enactment of an air battle between an allied "Sopwith Pup" biplane and a German Fokker triplane during World War I. (Courtesy "Modern Maturity.")

For centuries mankind had dreamed of traveling through the air like a bird. Inventors since medieval times have developed all sorts of weird contraptions and harnesses to give men wings, none of which ever "got off the ground". The first successful man-made device to become air-borne was a large, hot-air, paper balloon made by the brothers Montgolfier at Annonay, France in 1783, which rose 1,000 feet into the air. The same year, Jean Pilatre de Rozier of France became the first human being to go aloft in a captive balloon with his own fire pan to maintain the hot-air supply. In the next few years balloonists ("aeronauts") blossomed forth in other countries, and

free ballooning became a popular sport. Captive ballons were used by observers in the Civil War in the United States – and in later European wars. The first successful, power-driven, "lighter-than-air" device was the German "Zeppelin" of 1900.

The first "heavier-than-air" machines were gliders. Captain Le Bris of France made the first glider flight in 1855. Otto Lilienthal of Germany made many glider flights between 1891 and 1896, when he was killed in a glider crash. In the United States, Octave Chanute, a railroad engineer of Chicago, was the first American to make a flight in a glider, at the age of 64 years (1896).

Professor Samuel Pierpont Langley, of the Smithsonian Institution, built two pilotless "airdromes" as he called them, which looked like huge dragonflies, approximately 12 feet wide and 15 feet long, driven by 1½ horsepower steam engines. One of these planes was flown from the southern slope of Observatory Hill in Pittsburgh in 1896, stayed in the air for one minute and 49 seconds, and traveled approximately 4300 feet. Later he developed a larger, gasoline-engine plane, which was flown by Glenn Curtis. However, to the Wright Brothers of Dayton, Ohio went the honors for the first successful, manned flight of a heavier-than-air machine at Kitty Hawk, N.C., December 17, 1903. The era of airplane travel thus began just ten years after the invention of the first successful automobile. Development of the airplane thus lagged the enthusiastic attention given the automobile by at least a decade. The Germans, however, developed Count Ferdinand von Zeppelin's "flying cigar" to the point that by 1910, the Zeppelin Company was operating the world's first commercial airship service between cities hundreds of miles apart in Europe. During their first three years of operation they safely transported a total of 14,000 passengers a distance of 100,000 miles.

It was the First World War which gave the new "flying machines" their most rapid impetus. At first, German Zeppelins (or "dirigibles", as they were later called) ranged over England, giving the British their first taste of aerial bombing, however, these airships soon proved to be easy targets for the rapidly developing new British fighter planes. Airplanes at first were used in France primarily for observation purposes, but when it was discovered they could be adapted for machine guns, firing bullets between the rotating blades of their propellers, they became instruments of war.

After World War I, there was much interest in the development of dirigibles for long-distance air travel. However, an un-ending string of disasters with these unwieldy airships finally put a period to the dirigible era. The "Blimp" survived to become an important

The Helicopter has become a "work horse" for all sorts of unusual transporting and lifting operations. Here, a heavy drilling rig is being lowered into a very unstable talus bed on the side of Shade Mountain near Lewistown, Pa. Object: to determine sub-soil conditions for a possible highway along the mountain side. (Photo by the author.)

During the Agnes flood of 1972, the helicopter saved lives and brought aid to isolated flood victims. Governor Milton Shapp is shown checking a rescue operation. (PennDot photo.)

tool of anti-submarine warfare in World War II. The further development of the airplane languished during the 1920's and, except for the warnings of such individuals as Billy Mitchell of the important role of airplanes in future warfare, very little was done to improve them. They were, however, used for mail service. Pennsylvanians made important contributions to early airplane travel. In 1911, Calbraith Perry Rodgers, of Pittsburgh, flew from Long Island, New York to Long Beach, California, completing the first successful transcontinental flight. The first naval flying boat was built in 1917 in an aircraft plant adjacent to the Philadelphia Navy Yard. In 1918, the Bellefonte "Air Mail Field" was built, as the initial re-fueling stop on the first transcontinental airmail route.

In 1925, the City of Philadelphia built its first airfield, on the site of its present international airport, as a training facility for the Pennsylvania National Guard. In 1926 the City leased what was then called "the municipal aviation landing field" to the Ludington Exhibition Company, which later became Ludington Airlines, a fore-runner of Eastern Airlines.

In 1926, during the Sesqui-Centennial, the Philadelphia Rapid Transit Company began operations of the first scheduled commercial airline in the eastern part of the United States. With a fleet of three, eight-passenger, tri-motored, Fokker airplanes, the company flew passengers and mail between Mustin Field (Philadelphia Navy Yards) and Hoover Field at Washington, D.C., covering the 125 mile distance in 90 minutes.

In 1927, Clifford Ball, of Pittsburgh secured a contract for air-mail service between Pittsburgh and Cleveland, and later carried passengers. By 1930 he had extended his scheduled flights to Washington, D.C. and changed his company name to Pennsylvania Airlines.

By 1929, a group of Greensburg residents had organized the "Central Airways" to provide air service between Greensburg, Pittsburgh and Cincinnati. They merged with Pennsylvania Airlines to become Pennsylvania Central Airlines, later Capital Airlines (offering service over a large portion of Eastern United States) and finally combined with United Airlines, one of the largest airlines in the country.

Harold F. Pitcairn of Philadelphia, already a successful builder of a superior mail plane, in 1928 became the pioneer of the rotary wing industry in America, with the building of the first Autogyro in the United States under licensing arrangements with Autogyro inventor Juan de la Cierva of Spain. Pitcairn and his Philadelphia associates, including Kellett and Le Page, improved upon the Autogyro principle, working with La Cierva to tilt the rotor axis, for control as well as lift. However, Igor Sikorski, of Bridgeport, Connecticut succeeded in building and flying the first successful

One of the smaller commercial planes manufactured by Piper Aircraft Corporation, Lock Haven, Pa. Piper "Cubs" are known world-wide. The company has built more than 100,000 planes to date. (Piper Aircraft Photo.)

Model of the Piasecki "Heli-Stat", combination of blimp and multi-helicopter unit for extremely heavy lifting operations, with complete maneuverability. (Piasecki Aircraft Photo.)

Helicopter in America in 1939, a development which partly out-moded the Autogyro.

A significant event in aviation history occurred in 1938 when W. T. Piper assisted the financially troubled Taylor Brothers Aircraft Corporation in relocating their burned-out Bradford plant at Lock Haven, Pennsylvania and began building the inexpensive, Taylor-designed, small, high-wing, two-place monoplane called the "Cub". This plane was to become the "Model-T Ford" of the aviation industry in the United States. With the rumblings of war in Europe, the (re-named) Piper Aircraft Corporation became virtually the only company in America with the capacity for building a small, trainer-type airplane. Four out of five pilots in World War II got their original instruction in Piper "Cubs". The L-4 "Cub" was extensively used as an observation, or "spotter" plane in combat areas.

After the War, Piper Aircraft successfully converted its operation to civilian small-plane applications, such as agricultural dusting, pipe-line patrol, mapping and natural resources prospecting, ambulance airlift, taxi and commuter operations, and the increasingly important use of company planes by business firms. Piper Aircraft Corporation of Lock Haven today employs five thousand people in five plants, has sales outlets in 92 countries, and has recently manufactured its 100,000th airplane. (1975).

In 1939, Lytle S. Adams, a physician of Irwin, Pa., obtained an experimental contract to provide in-flight "grab" pick-up and dropping of mail bags (his own idea) for 52 of the smaller towns of Pennsylvania, Ohio and West Virginia. By 1948 his service had become so successful (he had missed only 8% of thousands of scheduled "pick-ups") that he had extended his mail service to two hundred towns. The company was then known as All American Aviation, whose service was later enlarged to include passenger pick-up for the major airline terminals. The operation became known as Allegheny Airlines, making connections with a number of airports in eastern United States.

Frank N. Piasecki of Philadelphia in 1943 again focused the attention of rotary wing enthusiasts on the Quaker City when he developed and flew his "PV-2", the second successful Helicopter to fly in America. Subsequently (1945) he designed and flew the World's first successful Tandem Rotor Helicopter for the U.S. Navy; and in 1953 the World's largest Helicopter for the U. S. Air Force. The Piasecki Helicopter Corporation was sold in 1955 to become the Vertol Division of the Boeing Aircraft Company. Piasecki has been the leader in the design of large transport-size Helicopters and, through Vertol, has supplied the majority of large Helicopters to the U. S. armed forces.

Mr. Piasecki has continued his activities, with the Piasecki Aircraft Corporation, formed in 1955, developing various rotary wing vehicles for civilian and commercial users. He has also continued to retain an

Frank Piasecki at the controls of his "AirGeep" during an early test, in 1958. (Piasecki Aircraft Photo.)

"Navajo Chieftan", one of Piper's larger, two-motored planes – pressurized and turbo-charged. (Piper Aircraft Photo.)

interest in military usage with such innovations as the "Sea Bat" (1958), the "AirGeep" (1958) and the "Sea-Geep" (1961) for the Army and Navy. For the civilian trade he has also developed the World's first shaft-driven Compound Helicopter (1964) with high-speed horizontal travel capabilities. A more recent innovation of the Piasecki firm (still in the design stage) is the "Heli-Stat", a combination helium-filled envelope and four Helicopter units, capable of lifting and positioning the unprecedented load of 140 tons. It is felt that this device would have wide usage in lifting major components of power plants, bridges, towers, pipelines, pre-fab buildings, and other heavy units, directly from their manufacturing plants to the erection sites.

In 1945, Philadelphia's city air field was re-named the "Philadelphia International Airport", thus becoming the first airport in the state to gain this status. The Greater Pittsburgh Airport added the word "International" to its title in 1971; Harrisburg Airport did the same in 1971; Erie Airport became "International", as

The Piasecki "Pathfinder" combines helicopter vertical-lift features with greatly increased forward speeds. (Piasecki Aircraft Photo.)

a port of entry, in the early 1970's. This meant that in each airport a division of the United States Customs department was installed, so that direct flights to and from Europe, Canada and South America could be properly processed at any of them.

In recent years the Pennsylvania Air National Guard has become a strong auxiliary force to support the national Air Force in time of war, or other emergencies involving the well-being of Pennsylvania citizens. Its state headquarters are at Fort Indiantown Gap, with supporting Flights, Groups or Squadrons at the Harrisburg International Airport, at the Philadelphia and Pittsburgh International Airports, and at Willow Grove and State College. Including both full-time and volunteer Officers and Airmen, its present

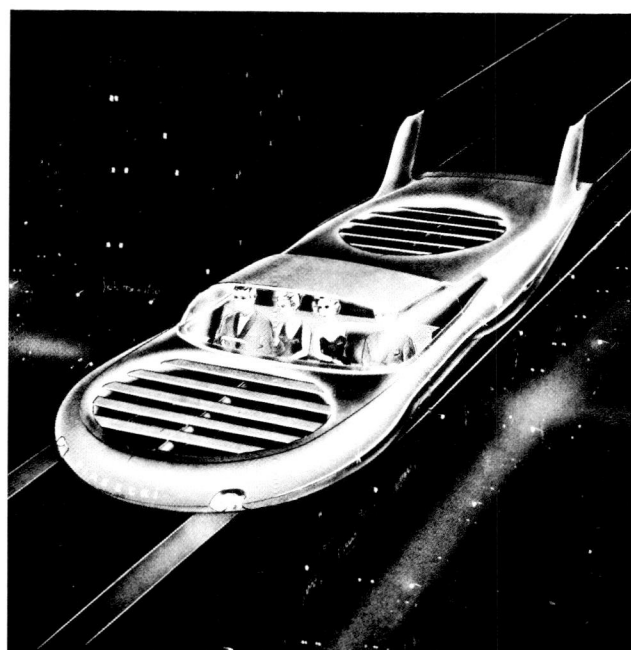

Sky car of the future – an advanced version of the AirGeep. (Piasecki Aircraft Photo.)

strength is close to 5,000, and its total assets are on the order of $140 million dollars. This organization was ordered to active duty during the Korean War, and augmented the activities of the Military Air Transport Service to bring wounded personnel home from Vietnam. In the latter connection they flew approximately 1,000 missions.

Currently, there are over 470 licensed airports in Pennsylvania, including jet terminals at Philadelphia and Pittsburgh, and approximately 475 smaller airfields for various commercial, municipal, military and private aircraft usage. Sixteen scheduled airlines, three aerial cargo carriers, and a number of charter lines, serve airports in Pennsylvania, from all parts of the United States and overseas. (Data collected in 1976.)

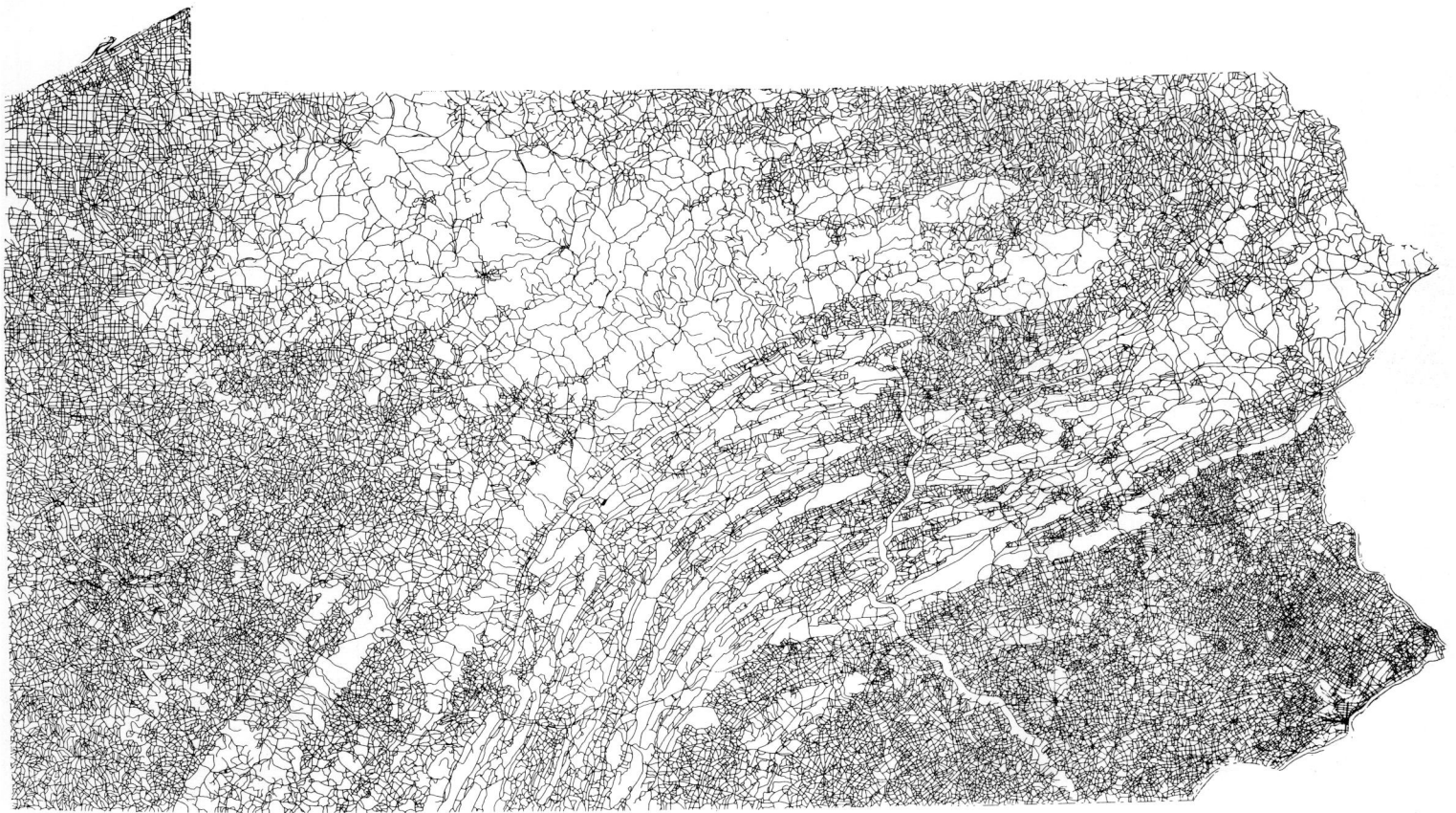

This unique map, developed by Penn-Dot, shows all roads maintained by the Commonwealth, without emphasis on relative importance. Many of these roads have evolved from the old Indian paths in Pennsylvania of 300 years ago.

# Chapter XVII

# THE PENNSYLVANIA TRAVELER - TODAY AND TOMORROW

When one considers the advancement made in travel, just since the beginning of the Twentieth Century, it is completely unbelievable! As a young boy I well remember riding around town, and into the country in a horse and buggy, and in a horse-drawn "bob sled" in winter. What few autos were in use in the summer, disappeared into barns and garages in the winter, where they were "blocked up" on bricks or logs to get the tires off the ground for their long winter hibernation. I still remember the excitement we all experienced when Dad got his first "self starter" for his old "Model T" and we didn't have to crank it anymore! The fastest thing on wheels, in those days, was the steam locomotive, which on good track could travel at sixty to eighty miles per hour. Today, we think of travel in the new 1450-mile-per hour "Concorde" as pretty much a routine development. After all, haven't we been hearing about space travel at 18,000 miles per hour and upwards, to the Moon and to Mars, as a commonplace kind of thing?

As we look around Pennsylvania in the year of 1976, we still see remnants of earlier forms of transportation, which at one time handled virtually all passenger and freight service around the State. Canal ruins, for instance, can still be found in many places, and their historical significance is being brought to our attention by such organizations as the Pennsylvania Canal Society, with field trips to seek out old lift-lock masonry and weed-filled channels, and to ride the canal boats still operating on the Delaware Canal at New Hope, the Main Line Canal at Lewistown and the D. & H. Canal at White Mills.

Railroad buffs schedule special rides "back of steam" on sections of the state's once vast network of rail lines which haven't been abandoned. They delight in such operations as the East Broadtop Railroad, the Strasburg Railroad (just across from the new state-operated railroad museum), or the New Hope and Ivyland Railroad, or the Inclined Planes at Johnstown and Pittsburgh. Much of the remaining rail trackage in

145

Pennsylvania is now being operated by the government-subsidized Amtrak (for passenger service) or Conrail for freight. There are still some independent rail lines which have been able to survive the tremendous competition of the automobile, the motor-freight truck, and the airplane, in eroding away their business. We saw a great revival of the use of the railways during World War II, when most of our gasoline was being shipped to our fighting forces overseas, and we may see it again, if the Arabs clamp a tighter rein on their oil supplies, but the Alaskan Pipeline has helped. We would be wise to maintain and improve the rail lines still remaining.

The beloved "trolley car" may still be seen in Philadelphia and Pittsburgh, on what few lines have not been abandoned to the city motor buses or "trackless trolleys" – and of course in such trolley havens as the Arden Museum near Washington, Pa. Even the city bus companies are finding it tough going in some communities, where people still insist on using their own cars to get back and forth to work instead of using available bus lines. Such lack of patronage has already forced many of the bus companies to abandon their suburban routes.

One mass-transit medium which is flourishing is the motor-trucking business. They have the advantage over the railroads, in that they can usually deliver from "door-to-door" and they do not have to maintain their own right-of-way. The latter is kept up for them by the taxpayers at large. The result is that during the past thirty years railroads in Pennsylvania have lost at least half of their freight business and are losing more each year.

Mass passenger travel between cities seems to have been taken over by the airlines, at the expense of the railroads, and even in competition with the newer inter-city bus lines. The latter have been able to recoup some of their losses by offering special excursion rates,

The "Comuta" developed by Ford Motor Company a few years ago, is a battery-powered, two-passenger car for short trips and local shopping. (Courtesy White Rose Motorist.)

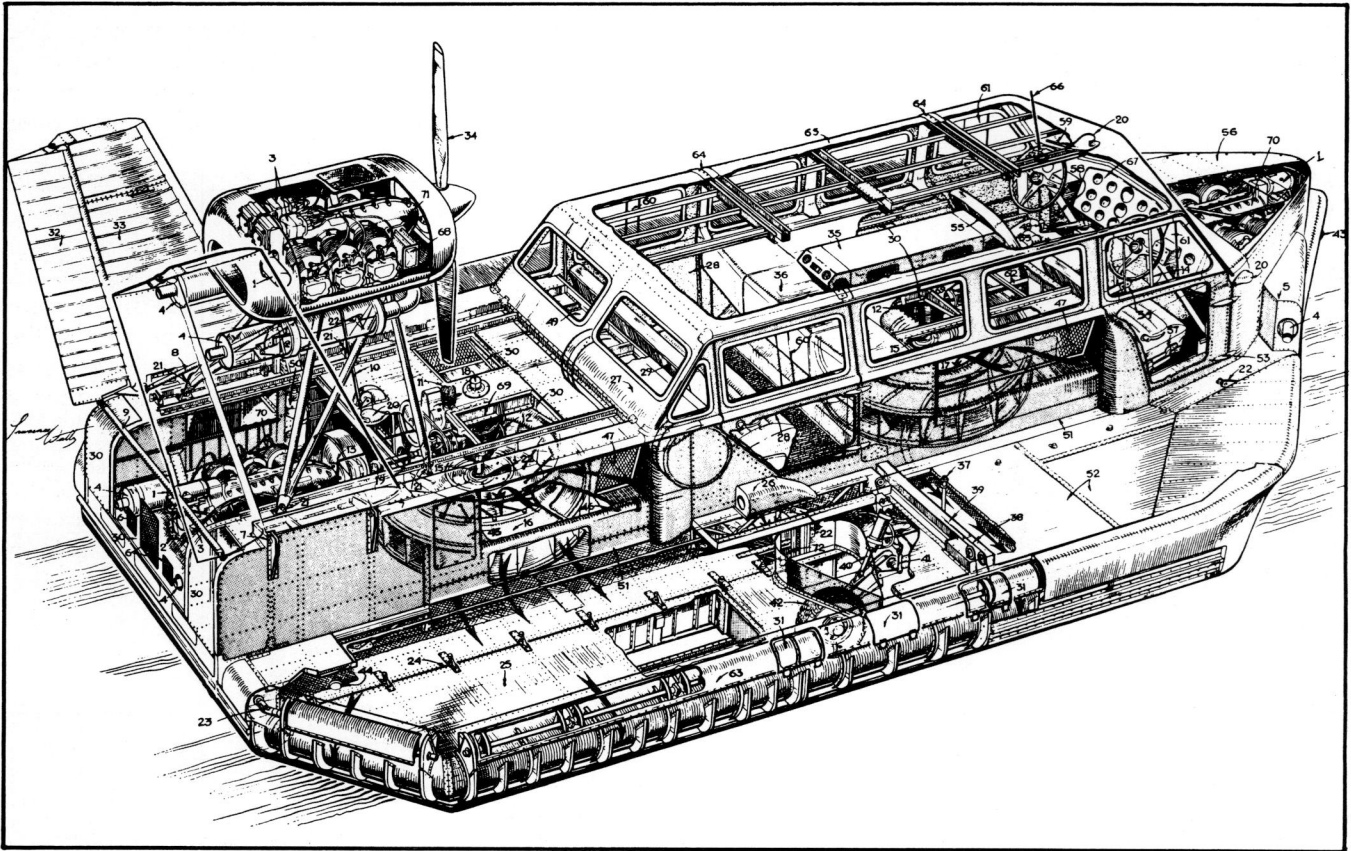

One of the smaller models of the "Hovercraft" currently in use in Europe, which operates over relatively level surfaces, either land or water.

monthly travel tickets good for unlimited mileage, and "charter" group travel for organizations on sightseeing trips. Passenger travel on the trains picks up only when the airports are "socked in" by bad weather.

The automobile still reigns supreme as the medium for transporting more Pennsylvanians to more places than any other form of transportation available – for work, for vacations, for *anything!* The family car (and usually there are *two* of them) is depended upon for just about every need that takes us out of the house. We will jump in the car just to run around the corner to the nearest grocery store or shopping center – would never *think* of walking! Takes too much time! Bicycling maybe, for exercise; or jogging if recommended by our doctors to take off weight, but where do we go that we don't first think of "jumping in the car"? Heavily populated metropolitan areas are the exception, of course, and here mass-transit media are frequently in great need, but not always available.

All this may change with the "Energy Crunch", and the fight against air pollution. Already we are seeing a reversal of the trend toward bigger and more powerful cars to the smaller, economical, European-

style "compacts." Bicycling is once again becoming popular. "Car-pooling" and group travel on buses is gaining ground rapidly.

In the next few years we are going to see many innovations in fuel-powered wheeled vehicles. The old "Electrics," popular for city travel in the early 1900's, are going to make a come-back in the form of small, clean operating, electric fuel cell powered cars. As a matter of fact, the Battronic Truck Corporation of Boyertown, Pa. has now developed electric vans and buses with a top speed of 60 miles per hour. The smaller, electric cars are not able to travel this fast – as yet. Car manufacturers and amateurs alike are experimenting with a modern version of the old "Steamers," discredited by gasoline producers sixty years ago. Sooner or later an atomic-powered land vehicle will also become practical.

In the next few years also, we are going to witness new developments in high-speed, mass-transit media – for inter-city as well as metropolitan areas – in the form of electric (and possibly even atomic) powered rail lines. The hey-day of the "Trolley Car" may not yet be over!

With a predicted population of 300 million people in the United States by the year 2000 A.D. it is doubtful

whether our present highway system would have been adequate if the previous automobile travel pattern had continued unabated for another few years. The bright side of the Energy Crisis is that the taxpayers probably will not be asked to expend excessive funds on new automotive highways, but will merely be taxed to maintain the facilities we already have.

There is always the possibility that the automobile may be replaced by some other type of land-based vehicle which does not need roads to operate. The "Hovercraft," being used on a small scale in England and Germany, is such a vehicle. It rides on an air cushion rather than wheels, and can travel equally well over land or water, as long as the surface is relatively smooth. Its use is presently limited to well cleared areas and flat terrain. Other non-wheeled vehicles, such as the Piasecki "Airgeep," will be forthcoming with even greater versatility than the "Hovercraft," for overland, water or air travel.

One thing is certain about future travel in the United States. We will have to get used to the idea that we are not going to be able to "go places" in the same careless, reckless manner that we have in the past. We are going to plan what traveling we do more carefully, and it will usually involve other people. Certainly we are not going to rule out the individual use of the "family car", in whatever form it may take, for errands and local travel. But future long-distance travel, by whatever means we elect, is going to involve close group association. Who knows, we might even enjoy it!

One of General Motors' answers to the Petroleum Pinch is this XEP research model, powered by a combination of long-range cruising batteries and a special bank of batteries designed for acceleration.

Another General Motors innovation is this steam-powered SE-101, in a Pontiac body.

Fisheye view of the Walt Whitman bridge across the Delaware at South Philadelphia, Twentieth Century bridge-building at its finest. (Courtesy Modjeski and Masters.)

# SUPPLEMENT

## The Author

The family of William H. Shank has been associated with the development of transportation and communications in Pennsylvania for six generations. Michael Shank, a German ship's carpenter, settled in the town of Liverpool, Pa. in 1820 and built some of the first canal boats on the old Susquehanna Division Canal. His son, John Shank, was an innkeeper in the same town. John's son, Wilson W. Shank, was Chief of Disbursements for the Philadelphia and Erie Railroad at the turn of the century in Williamsport, Pa. Clyde U. Shank, Wilson's son, was Inter-city Plant Engineer for the Bell Telephone Company at Harrisburg, Pa. Clyde's son, William H. Shank, is currently concerned with the history of transportation in Pennsylvania. J. William Shank, son of William H., is the artist who produced many of the drawings in this book, as well as the cover.

William H. Shank is a 1937 mechanical engineering graduate of Lehigh University, who worked in the air conditioning and mining machinery fields for a number of years, and more recently turned to civil engineering private practice. His military experience included a tour of duty with a special engineering detachment assigned to develop the Atomic Bomb at Oak Ridge Tennessee. For the past few years he has been acting as promotional consultant for a number of engineering firms in central Pennsylvania. In 1972, he assisted in establishing the American Canal Society and, soon after, the publishing venture known as the American Canal and Transportation Center.

In addition to "Three Hundred Years with the Pennsylvania Traveler," Mr. Shank has written "The Amazing Pennsylvania Canals," "Historic Bridges of Pennsylvania," "Indian Trails to Superhighways," "Great Floods of Pennsylvania," "Vanderbilt's Folly," "The History of the York-Pullman Motor Car" and "Historic Tour Guide to York County." He has lectured before historical, educational and service groups throughout Pennsylvania and neighboring states.

Mr. Shank has served as President of the Lincoln Chapter of the Pennsylvania Society of Professional Engineers, President of the York Torch Club, President of the York-Lancaster Lehigh Club, Superintendent of the Luther Memorial Church School, Vice President of the Pennsylvania State Society of Professional Engineers, Vice President of the Pennsylvania Canal Society, Vice President of the American Canal Society and a Director of the York Chapter S.P.E.B.S.Q.S.A.

The author, seated on the running board of his fully-restored, prize-winning 1931 "Model A" Ford Roadster. The usual complement of rumbleseat riders are shown, including son, J. William, on the extreme left. Circa 1960.

## Acknowledgements

The author is fully aware that no work of the sort published here could possibly have been put together without assistance from others who are far more knowledgeable in their respective fields than the writer. I wish to give special recognition to my life-long friend, "Chick" Siebert, for his pictorial and editorial contribution to the Urban Railway Chapter; to Julius Murphy for his excellent information on the Butler Plank Road and Harmony Trolley Line; to Dr. George Swetnam for his railroad and bridge photos; to Frank Piasecki for his generous help with the Air Travel Chapter; to Donald Sayenga for setting me straight on the relationship between John Roebling and Charles Ellet; to Dr. Ernest Coleman and George Wills for the many fine photos and drawings which they have supplied for this book; to "Dutch" Huber for his information on historic transportation sites and ferries; to the late Phil Hoffmann, whose canal and railroad drawings are used extensively in this book; to Glen Reichard for his fine drawings of Indian life and early road travel conditions; to my son, J. William, for his original sketches and drawings which appear on the cover, the chapter title pages, and as major illustrations throughout this book; to Bob Mayo for information on Robert Fulton's little-known canal projects; also to the various engineering firms who have supplied photographs, as indicated.

W. H. S.

# REFERENCES

Allen, Richard Sanders – "Covered Bridges of the Middle Atlantic States" 1959 (Stephen Greene Press, Brattleboro, Vt.)

Armstrong, Ellis L. – "History of Public Works in the United States, 1776-1976" – 1976 (American Public Works Assn., Chicago)

Beaver, Roy C. – "The Bessemer and Lake Erie Railroad" – 1969 (Golden West Books, San Marino, Calif.)

Burgess, George H. and Kennedy, Miles C. – "Centennial History of the Pennsylvania Railroad Company" – 1946 (Penna. R. R. Co., Philadelphia)

Compton, F. E. & Company – "Pictured Encyclopedia and Fact Index" – 1954 (F. E. Compton & Co., Chicago)

Dunbar, Seymour – "A History of Travel in America" – 1937 (Tudor Publishing Co., New York)

Edwards, Llewellyn N. – "A Record of History and Evolution of Early American Bridges" – 1959 (University Press, Orono, Maine)

Emmers, Robert H. – "A Stagecoach Tour of Old Centre County" – (T. & G., Sept. 1975, State College, Pa.)

Huber, Harold H. – "Pennsylvania's Nominations to the Bicentennial Transportation Catalog" – 1976 (PennDot, Harrisburg)

Jensen, Oliver – "The American Heritage History of Railroads in America" – 1975 (American Heritage – McGraw-Hill, New York)

Kulp, Randolph L. – "Short Trolley Routes in the Lehigh River Valley" – 1967 (Lehigh Valley Chapter N.R.H.S.)

Kulp, Randolph L. – "Railroads in the Lehigh River Valley" – 1962 (Lehigh Valley Chapter N.R.H.S.)

Kulp, Randolph L. – "History of the Lehigh Valley Transit Company" – 1966 (Lehigh Valley Chapter N.R.H.S.)

Kulp, Randolph L. – "The Liberty Bell Route's 1000 Series Interurban Cars" – 1964 (Lehigh Valley Chapter N.R.H.S.)

Livingood, James Weston – "The Philadelphia-Baltimore Trade Rivalry 1780-1860" – 1947 (Pa. Hist. & Mus. Comm., Harrisburg)

McCullough, Robert and Leuba, Walter – "The Pennsylvania Main Line Canal" 1976 (American Canal & Trans. Center, York, Pa.)

Miller, John Anderson – "Fares, Please" – 1960 (Dover Publications, New York)

Mitchell & Hinman – "Mitchell's Compendium of Canals and Railroads – 1835" – 1972 reprint (American Canal & Trans. Center, York, Pa.)

Moedinger, William M. – "The Trolley, Triumph of Transport" – 1972 (Applied Arts Publishers, Lebanon Pa.)

Morton, Eleanor – "Josiah White, Prince of Pioneers" – 1946 (Stephen Daye Press, New York)

Nicklin, Philip – "Journey Through Pennsylvania – 1835" – 1975 Reprint (American Canal & Trans. Center, York, Pa.)

Posey, R. B., Brig. Gen. – "Pennsylvania Air National Guard Fact Sheet" – (Pa. Dept. Military Affairs, Annville, Pa.)

Reese, Robert E. – "The Stage Tavern" (Vol. 71, 1967, Jrnl. Lancaster Co. Hist. Soc., Lancaster, Pa.)

Rose, Albert C. – "Historic American Highways" – 1953 (Amer. Assoc. of State Highway Officials, Washington, D.C.)

Rowsome, Frank Jr. – "Trolley Car Treasury" – 1956 (McGraw-Hill Book Co., Inc., New York)

Saylor, Roger B. – "The Railroads of Pennsylvania" – 1964 (Penn State University, University Park, Pa.)

Shank, William H. – "Indian Trails to Superhighways" – 1975 (American Canal & Trans. Center, York, Pa.)

Shank, William H. – "The Amazing Pa. Canals" – 1975 (American Canal & Trans. Center, York, Pa.)

Shank, William H. – "Vanderbilt's Folly" – 1975 (American Canal & Trans. Center, York, Pa.)

Shank, William H. – "History of the York Pullman Automobile" – 1970 (Hist. Soc. of York County, York, Pa.)

Shank, William H. – "Historic Bridges of Pennsylvania" – 1974 (American Canal & Trans. Center, York, Pa.)

Shank, William H. – "York County Historic Sites and Tour Guide" – 1973 (Colonial York County Visitors and Tourist Bureau, York, Pa.)

Siebert, C. L., Jr. – "Northwestern Pennsylvania Railway" – 1976 (Published by the Author, Camp Hill, Pa.)

Swetnam, George – Pennsylvania Transportation" – 1968 (Pa. Hist. Assoc., Gettysburg, Pa.)

Tanner, Henry S. – "Canals and Railroads of the United States, 1840" – 1970 Reprint (Augustus M. Kelley, New York)

Tyrrell, Henry G. – "History of Bridge Engineering" – 1911 (Published by the Author, Chicago)

Wakefield, Manville B. – "Coal Boats to Tidewater" – 1965 (Wakefair Press, Grahamsville, N.Y.)

Wallace, Paul A. W. – "Indians in Pennsylvania" – 1964 (Pa. Hist. & Museum Comm., Harrisburg)

White, John H., Jr. – "Horsecars, Cable Cars and Omnibuses" – 1974 (Dover Publications, New York)

White, Josiah – "Josiah White's History, Given by Himself" – C-1950 (Lehigh Coal & Navigation Co., Bethlehem, Pa.)

William Penn Tercentenary Committee – "Remember William Penn" – 1945 (Commonwealth of Pa., Harrisburg)

Wisom, Charles W. – "ARBA Pictorial History of Roadbuilding" – 1975 (Amer. Road Builder's Assn., Washington, D. C.)

# INDEX

**Shocks Mill Bridge of the Penn Central, connecting York and Lancaster Counties. Knocked out by the 1972 flood, this important bridge was quickly rebuilt to restore service on the "low-grade" freight route between Enola and Philadelphia. (Photo by the author.)** 151

**Rockville Bridge of the Penn Central is the longest stone-arch railroad bridge in the world. (Photo by the author.)**

The Duquesne Incline, built in 1877, still provides transportation for Pittsburgh visitors and pedestrians who get a marvelous view of the city from its two cars. (Drawing reproduced by special permission of the artist – J. Howard Miller of Glenshaw, Pa.)

# Other Productions Of The American Canal And Transportation Center

THE CANALS OF NEW YORK STATE (1995) — A Publication of the American Canal Society. The canals of the Empire State, past and present, are covered in whole or in part. 8 1/2" x 11" paperback, 48 pages, 85 illustrations.

THE AMAZING PENNSYLVANIA CANALS — 166th Anniversary Edition - By William H. Shank (1997). A much expanded variation of many previous printings. 125 illustrations, and tables of locks and mileages on most of the principal canals in the State, never previously gathered together in one volume. Four-color cover; two-color interior; 128 pages; a definitive work.

HISTORIC BRIDGES OF PENNSYLVANIA — By William H. Shank (1997 Edition). Traces the development of the bridge-building arts from the time of the first covered bridge in America, to modern bridges of the 20th Century. Biographies of such famous bridge builders as John Roebling, Theodore Burr, Charles Ellet and Ralph Modjeski included. Profusely illustrated.

PENNSYLVANIA TRANSPORTATION HISTORY — A Supplement — By William H. Shank (1990). In this book, Mr. Shank has discussed media and devices not covered in his other books. Early river craft, rope ferries, steam boats, inclined planes, gravity railroads, early steam locomotives, horse cars, cable cars, trolley cars, elevated rail and subway systems, and air-travel devices are included. An 8 1/2 x 11 book with 72 pages and approximately 100 old photos, drawings and tables. Four-color cover.

GREAT FLOODS OF PENNSYLVANIA — A TWO-HUNDRED YEAR HISTORY — W.H. Shank, (Seventh printing, 1993). Data, photos and non-technical text on all major floods in the Keystone State since records have been kept. Full chapters on the Johnstown Flood and the disastrous floods of 1936, 1955 and 1972 are included. A definitive work.

INDIAN TRAILS TO SUPERHIGHWAYS — By William H. Shank (1996 Edition). History of the development of Pennsylvania's historic roads and the many interesting vehicles used on them. Descriptions of Braddock's Road, Forbes' Road, National Highway, Lancaster Turnpike, Plank roads, Corduroy Roads, William Penn Highway, Lincoln Highway, Pennsylvania Turnpike and Keystone Shortway. Recent PennDOT plans for completion of Pennsylvania's Interstate Highway System.

THE BEST FROM AMERICAN CANALS — Number 5 (1989-1991). A publication of the American Canal Society (1991) including a complete history of the Panama Canal, update on the Rhine-Main-Danube Canal, description of several Chinese canals, and navigation tips on the Black River, the Hennepin, the Alabama and the Florida waterways. 8 1/2 x 11 paperback, 88 pages.

THE BEST FROM AMERICAN CANALS — Number 6 (1991-1993). A publication of the American Canal Society (1993) featuring many canals in the U.S.A.; international canal meets; cruises on the Mississippi, Lake Michigan, Louisiana, Canada, Japan, Portugal, Ireland and the Corinth Canal.

THE BEST FROM AMERICAN CANALS — Number 7 (1993-1996). A publication of the American Canal Society (1996) featuring the Columbia-Snake River Navigation; canal packets on the O & E; cruises on the USA Inland Waterways. ACS Canal meets at home and abroad. Robert Fulton, James Brindley, cruises abroad.

THE BEST FROM AMERICAN CANALS — Number 8 (1995-1998). Features a Panama Canal Tour and also covers outstanding articles published in our Quarterly. Journeys of the Canal Society of New York along the Erie Canal. The opening of the National Canal Museum in Easton, Pa. The World Canals Conference in England. The "Venice of America." Alvin Harlow's "When Horses Pulled Boats." Important changes in the leadership of ACS. An 88-page book, plus four-color cover, in the same format as its predecessors.

VANDERBILT'S FOLLY — A HISTORY OF THE PENNSYLVANIA TURNPIKE — W.H. Shank, (Tenth Printing, 1993). The railroad war of 1880-85 which created the tunnels and roadbed for the present turnpike. History of the Turnpike, 1940-1993, included.

HISTORY OF THE YORK-PULLMAN AUTOMOBILE, 1903-1917 — By William H. Shank, (1970). History of the "Six-Wheeler" Pullman, and its successors, which almost made York, PA the automotive capital of the United States. History of the early automotive industry in Eastern Pennsylvania also included. Profusely illustrated.

TOWPATHS TO TUGBOATS — A History of American Canal Engineering. By Shank, Mayo, Hahn and Hobbs (Fifth Printing, 1995). The works of such famous Canal Engineers as Benjamin Wright, Canvass White, Charles Ellet, William Hamilton Merritt, George Washington Goethals are detailed — with the canals they built. The Erie, the Welland, the "Soo", the Panama, the St. Lawrence Seaway and the Tenn-Tom are among the many waterways described in detail. A 72 page, 8 1/2 x 11 book, the publication contains more than 130 drawings, maps and photographs in the USA, Canada and overseas.

THE COLUMBIA-PHILADELPHIA RAILROAD AND ITS SUCCESSOR — William Hasell Wilson, 1896. This book is an on-the-spot account of the building of one of the oldest railroads in America by its chief engineer, later resident Engineer for the Pennsylvania Railroad, who purchased it from the Pennsylvania Canal Commissioners. This 1992 reprint is fully illustrated with 45 old photos, maps and drawings. (Second printing.)

PICTURE-JOURNEY ALONG THE PENNSYLVANIA MAIN LINE CANAL, 1826 - 1857 — By Philip J. Hoffmann, P.E. (1993). Edited by William H. Shank, P.E. Full-color drawings of entire state-owned route, Philadelphia to Pittsburgh. 8 1/2 x 11 paperback. 80 pages. Full Hoffmann Biography included.